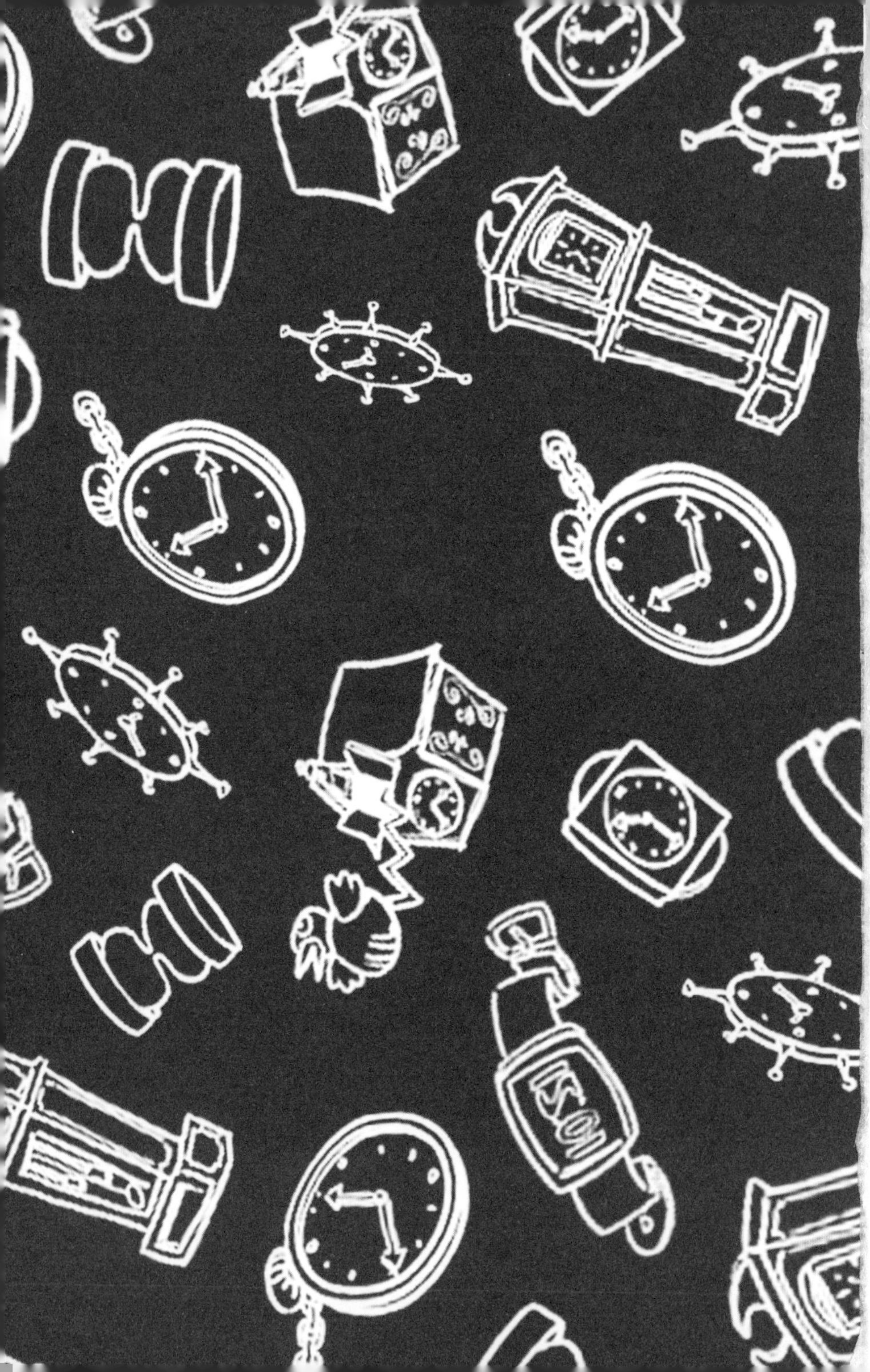

BIG IDEAS
THAT CHANGED THE WORLD

IT'S ABOUT TIME!

DON BROWN

ABRAMS FANFARE • NEW YORK

The artwork for this book was created digitally.

Cataloging-in-Publication Data has been applied for and may
be obtained from the Library of Congress.

ISBN 978-1-4197-7331-0
eISBN 979-8-88707-263-0

Text and illustrations © 2025 Don Brown
Edited by Howard W. Reeves
Book design by Melissa Nelson Greenberg

Printed and bound in China

10 9 8 7 6 5 4 3 2 1

Abrams Fanfare books are available at special discounts when
purchased in quantity for premiums and promotions as well as fundraising or
educational use. Special editions can also be created to specification.
For details, contact specialsales@abramsbooks.com or the address below.

Abrams Fanfare™ and the Abrams Fanfare logo are trademarks
of Harry N. Abrams, Inc.

ABRAMS The Art of Books
195 Broadway, New York, NY 10007
abramsbooks.com

Dedicated to Jan and Rich

Note to Reader: Unless otherwise noted, quotation marks signal actual quotes.

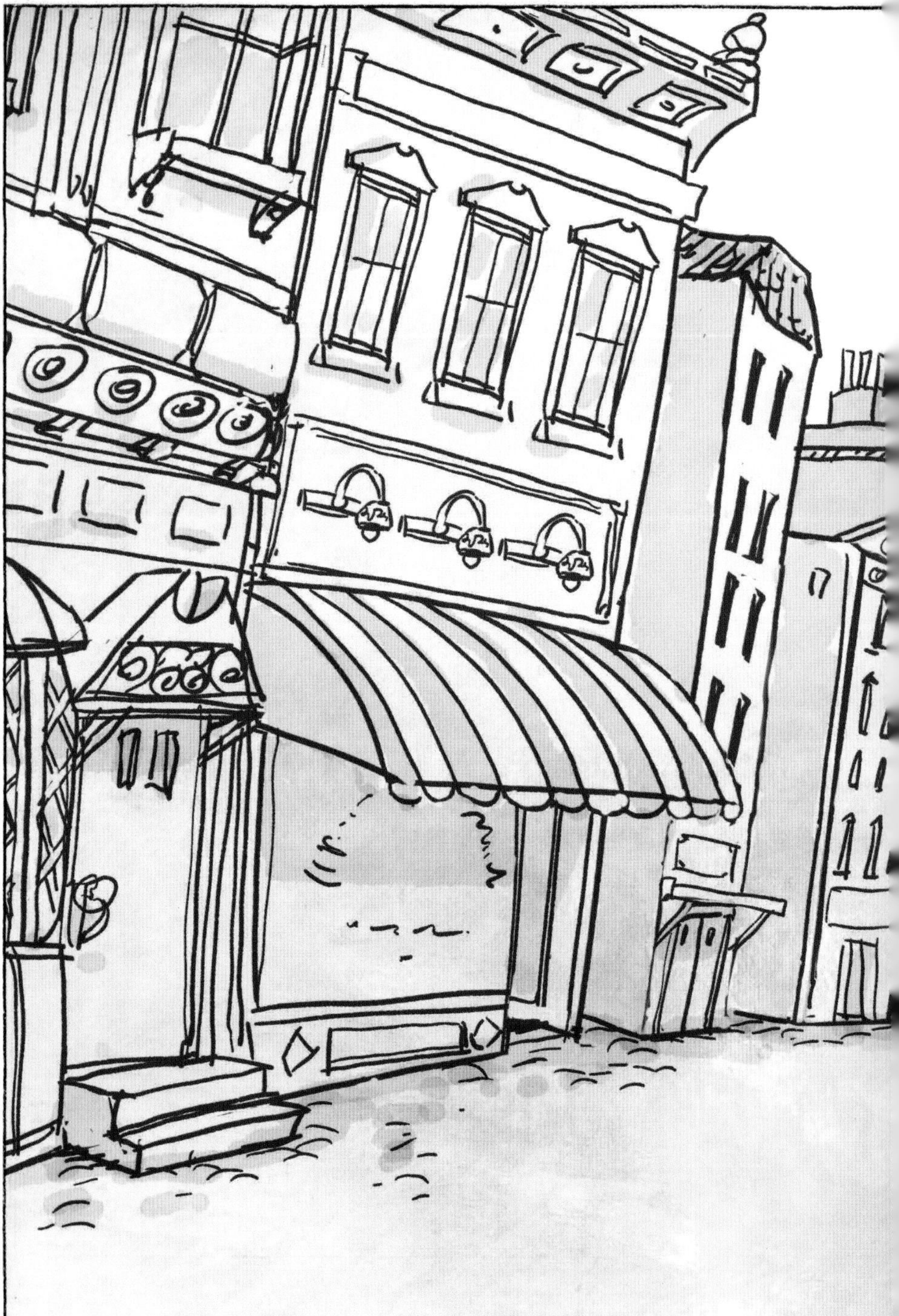

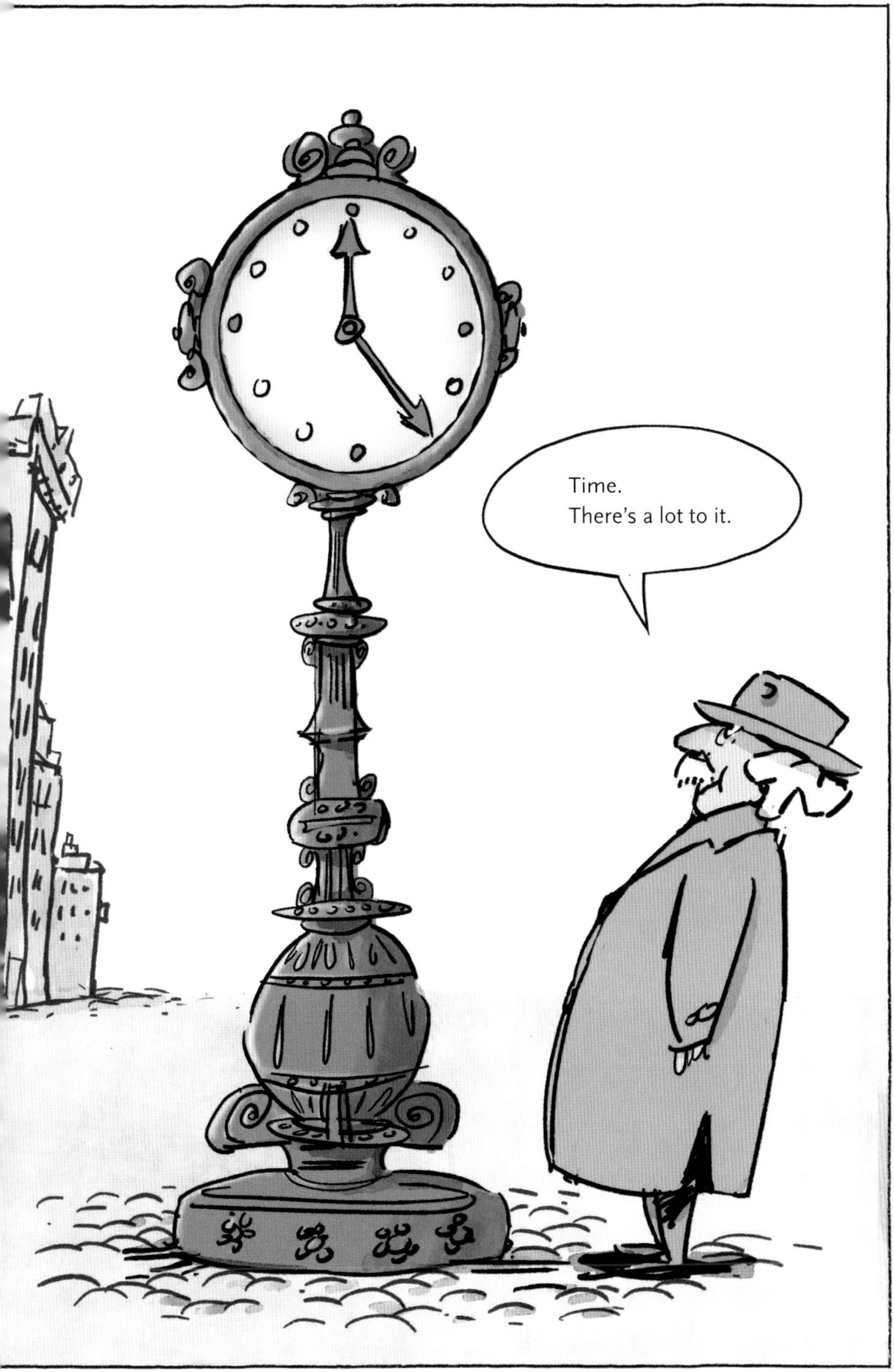
Time.
There's a lot to it.

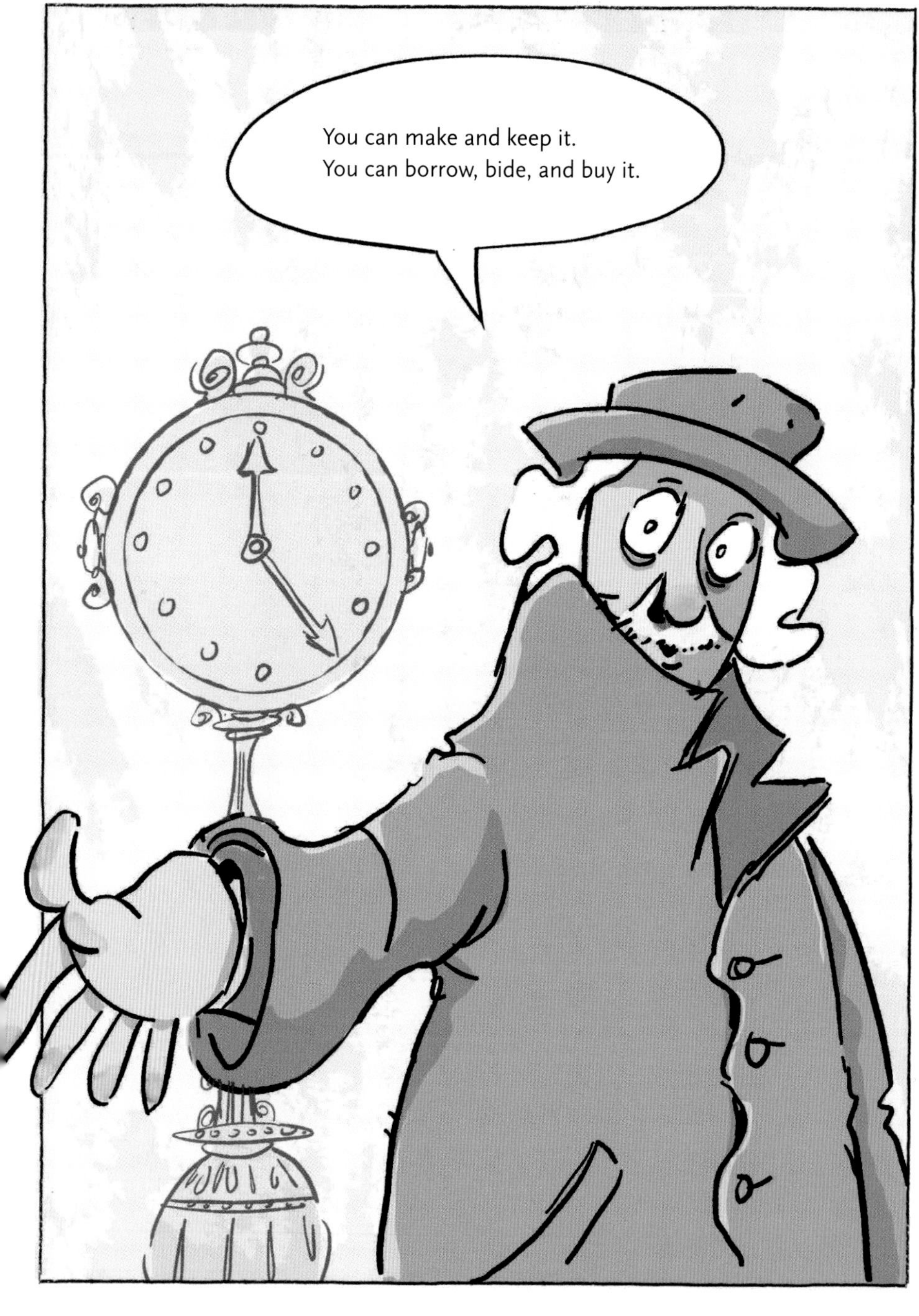
You can make and keep it.
You can borrow, bide, and buy it.

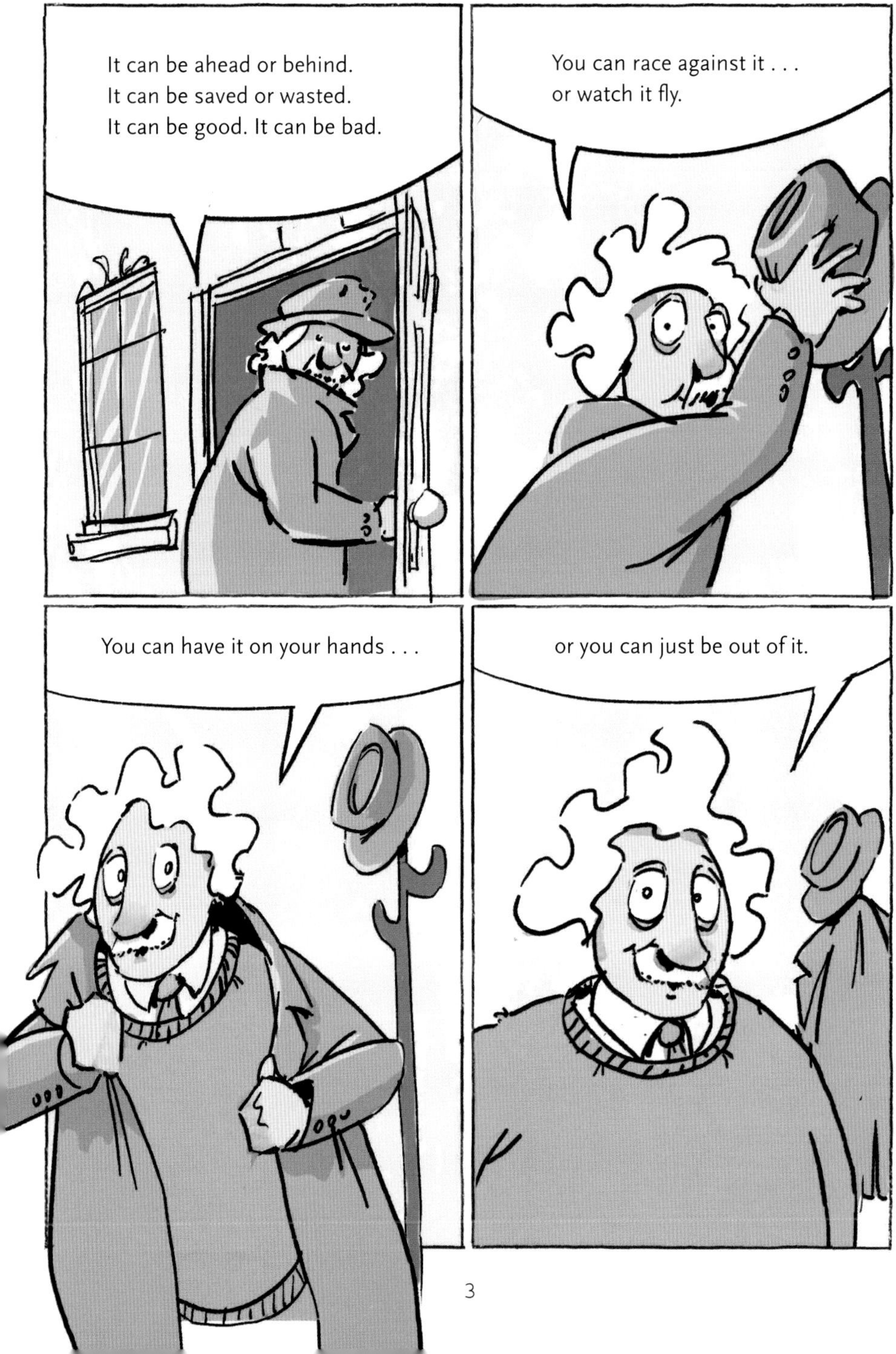
It can be ahead or behind.
It can be saved or wasted.
It can be good. It can be bad.
You can race against it . . .
or watch it fly.
You can have it on your hands . . .
or you can just be out of it.

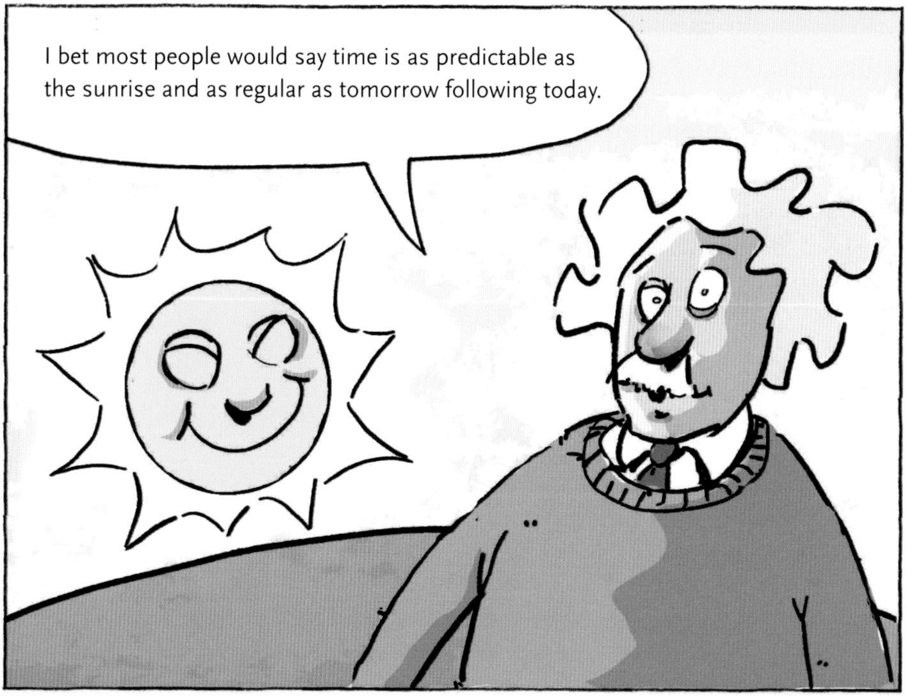
I bet most people would say time is as predictable as the sunrise and as regular as tomorrow following today.

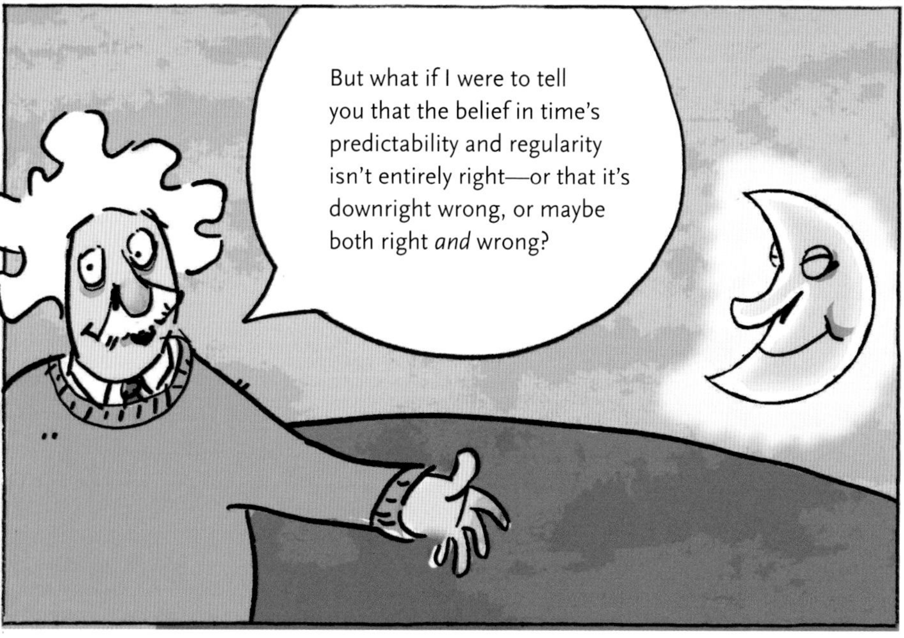
But what if I were to tell you that the belief in time's predictability and regularity isn't entirely right—or that it's downright wrong, or maybe both right *and* wrong?

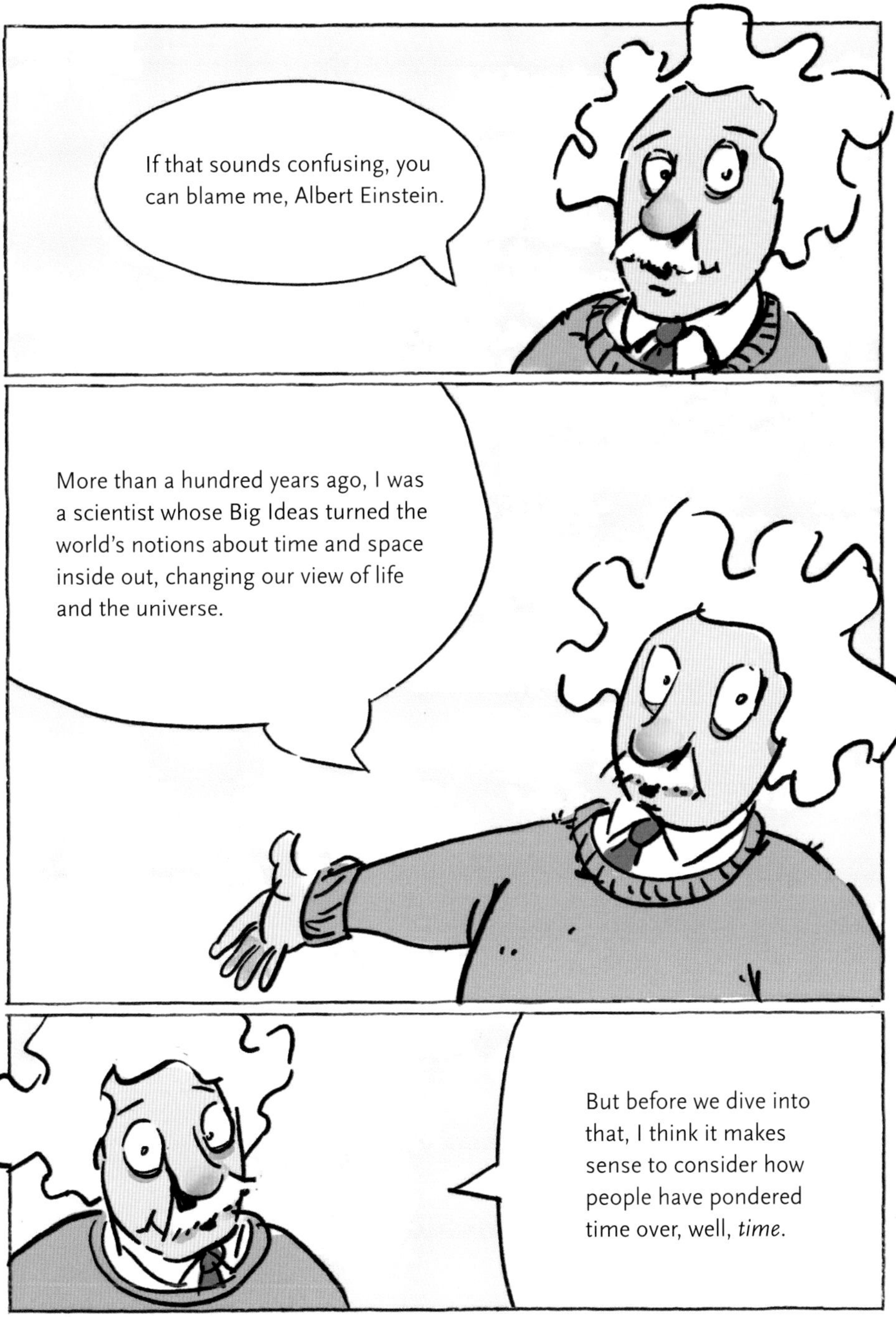
If that sounds confusing, you can blame me, Albert Einstein.
More than a hundred years ago, I was a scientist whose Big Ideas turned the world's notions about time and space inside out, changing our view of life and the universe.
But before we dive into that, I think it makes sense to consider how people have pondered time over, well, *time*.

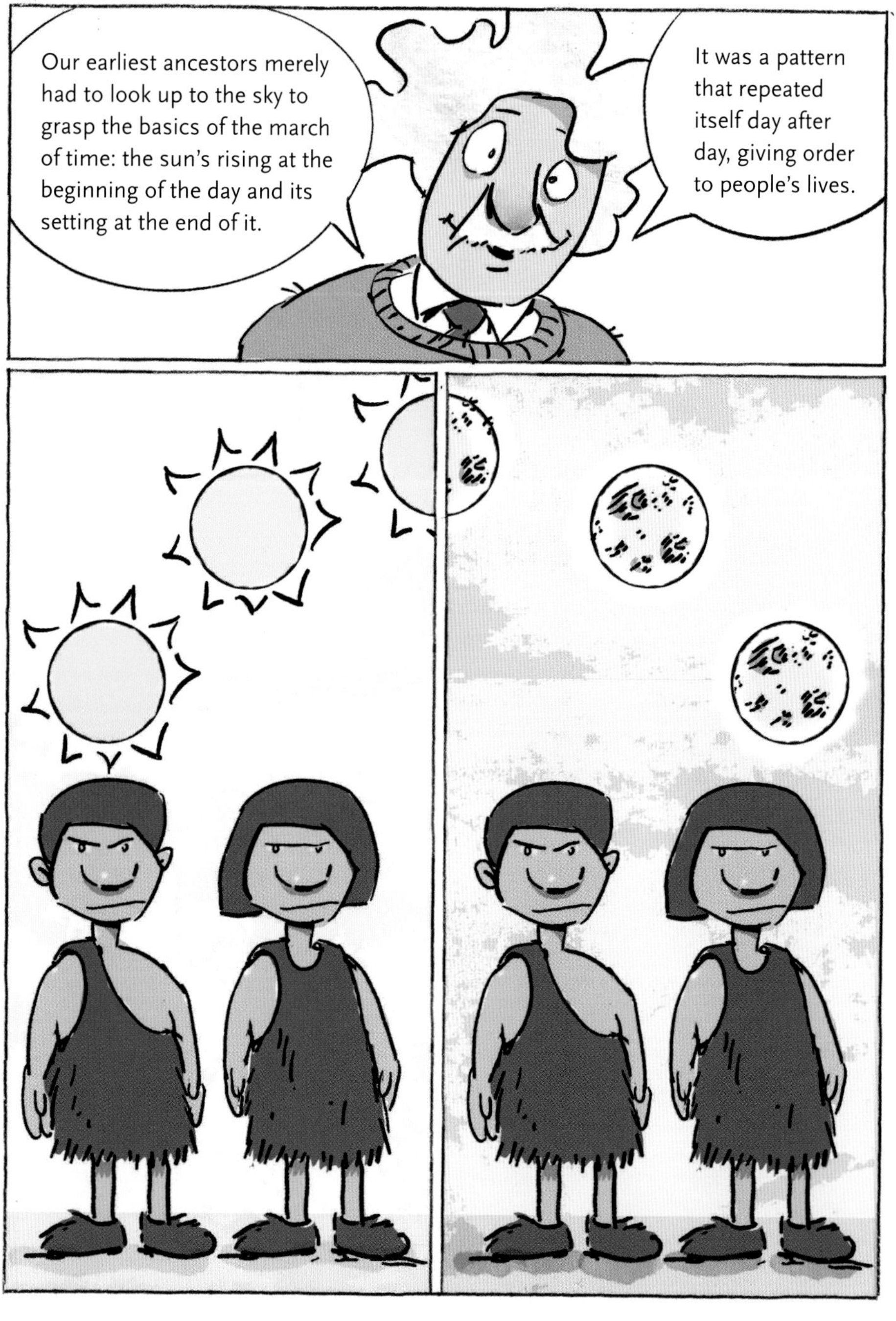
Our earliest ancestors merely had to look up to the sky to grasp the basics of the march of time: the sun's rising at the beginning of the day and its setting at the end of it.
It was a pattern that repeated itself day after day, giving order to people's lives.

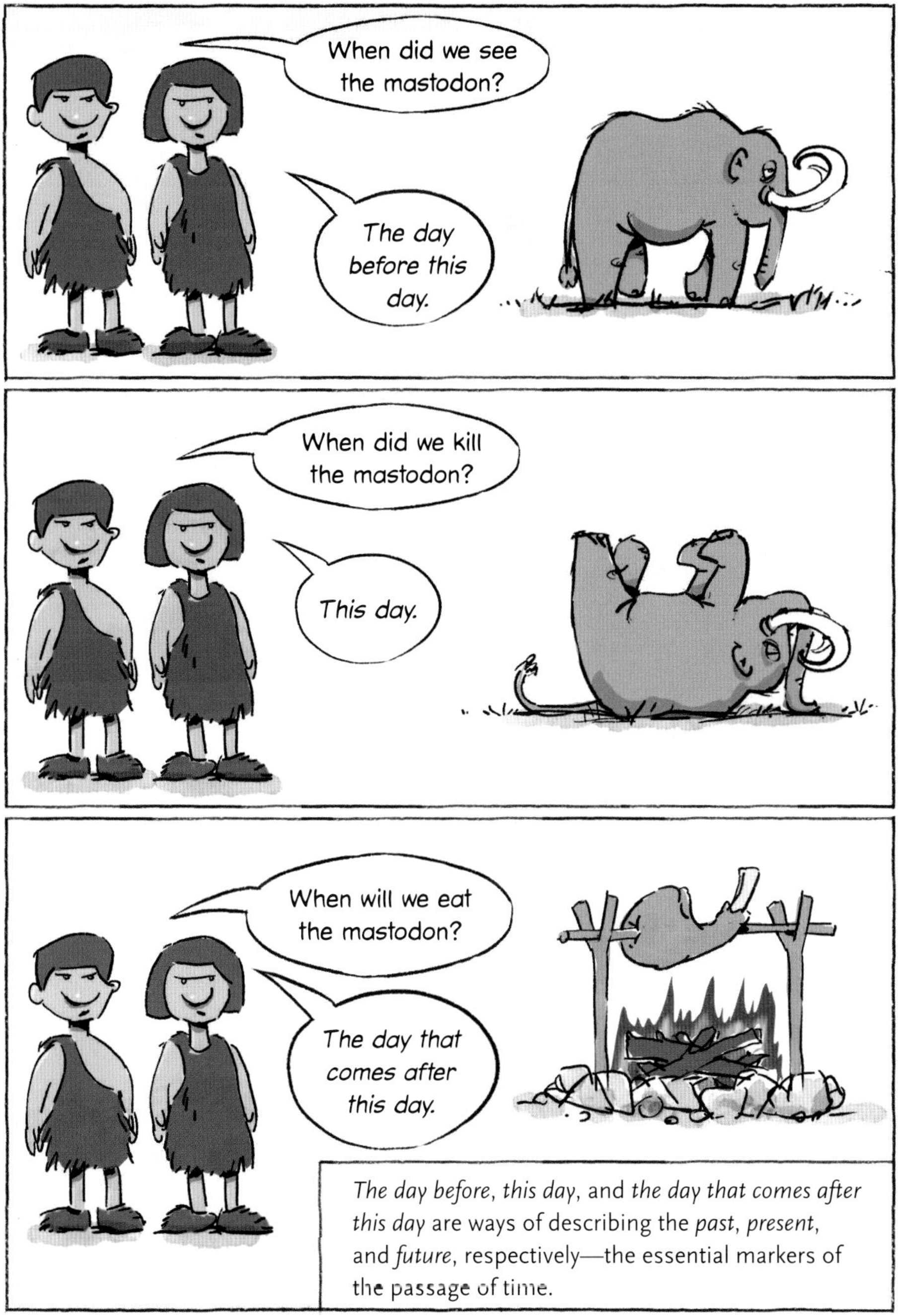
When did we see the mastodon?
The day before this day.
When did we kill the mastodon?
This day.
When will we eat the mastodon?
The day that comes after this day.
The day before, *this day*, and *the day that comes after this day* are ways of describing the *past*, *present*, and *future*, respectively—the essential markers of the passage of time.

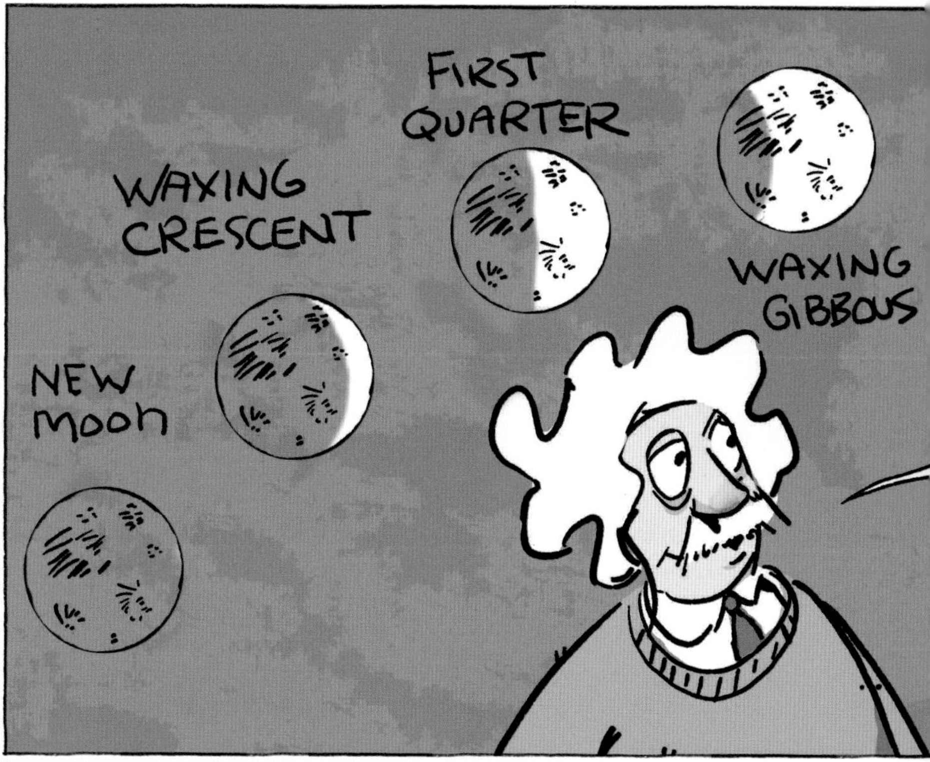
FIRST
QUARTER
WAXING
CRESCENT
WAXING
GIBBOUS
NEW
moon

There is evidence that thirty thousand years ago, people kept track of phases of the moon by marking animal bones and cave walls.

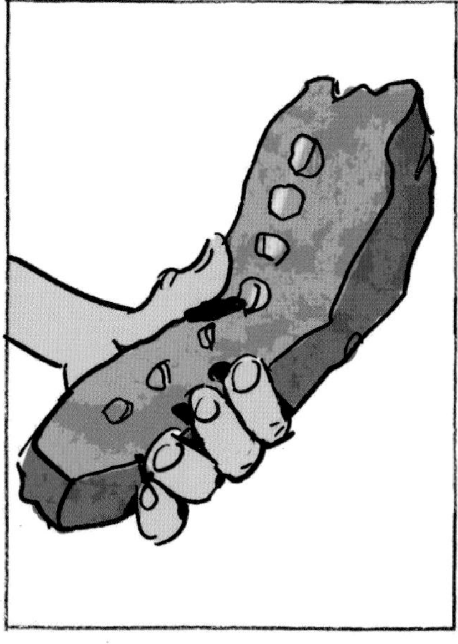

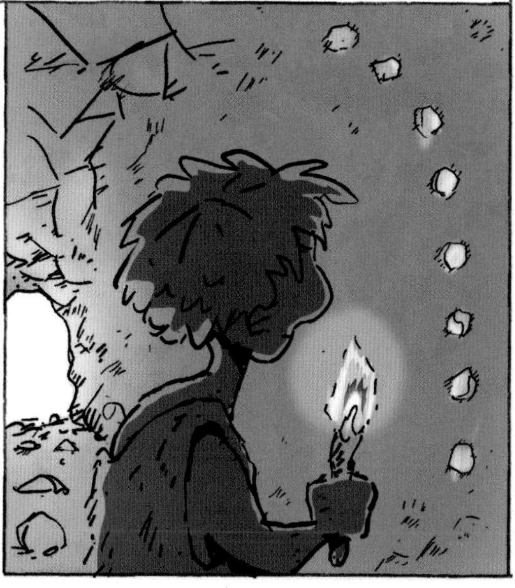

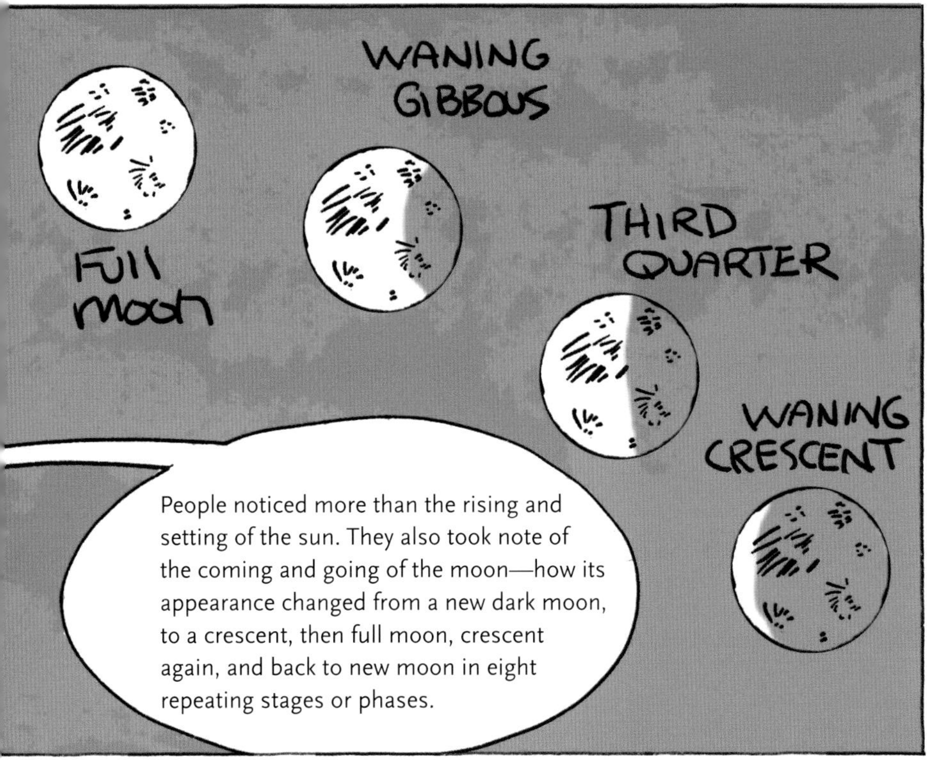
WANING GIBBOUS
FULL MOON
THIRD QUARTER
WANING CRESCENT
People noticed more than the rising and setting of the sun. They also took note of the coming and going of the moon—how its appearance changed from a new dark moon, to a crescent, then full moon, crescent again, and back to new moon in eight repeating stages or phases.

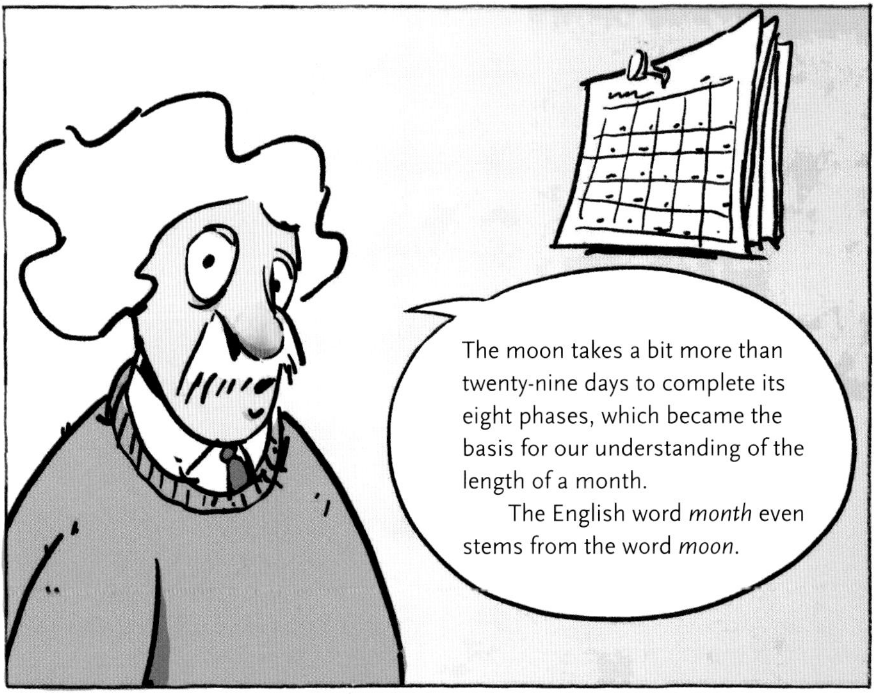
The moon takes a bit more than twenty-nine days to complete its eight phases, which became the basis for our understanding of the length of a month.
The English word *month* even stems from the word *moon*.

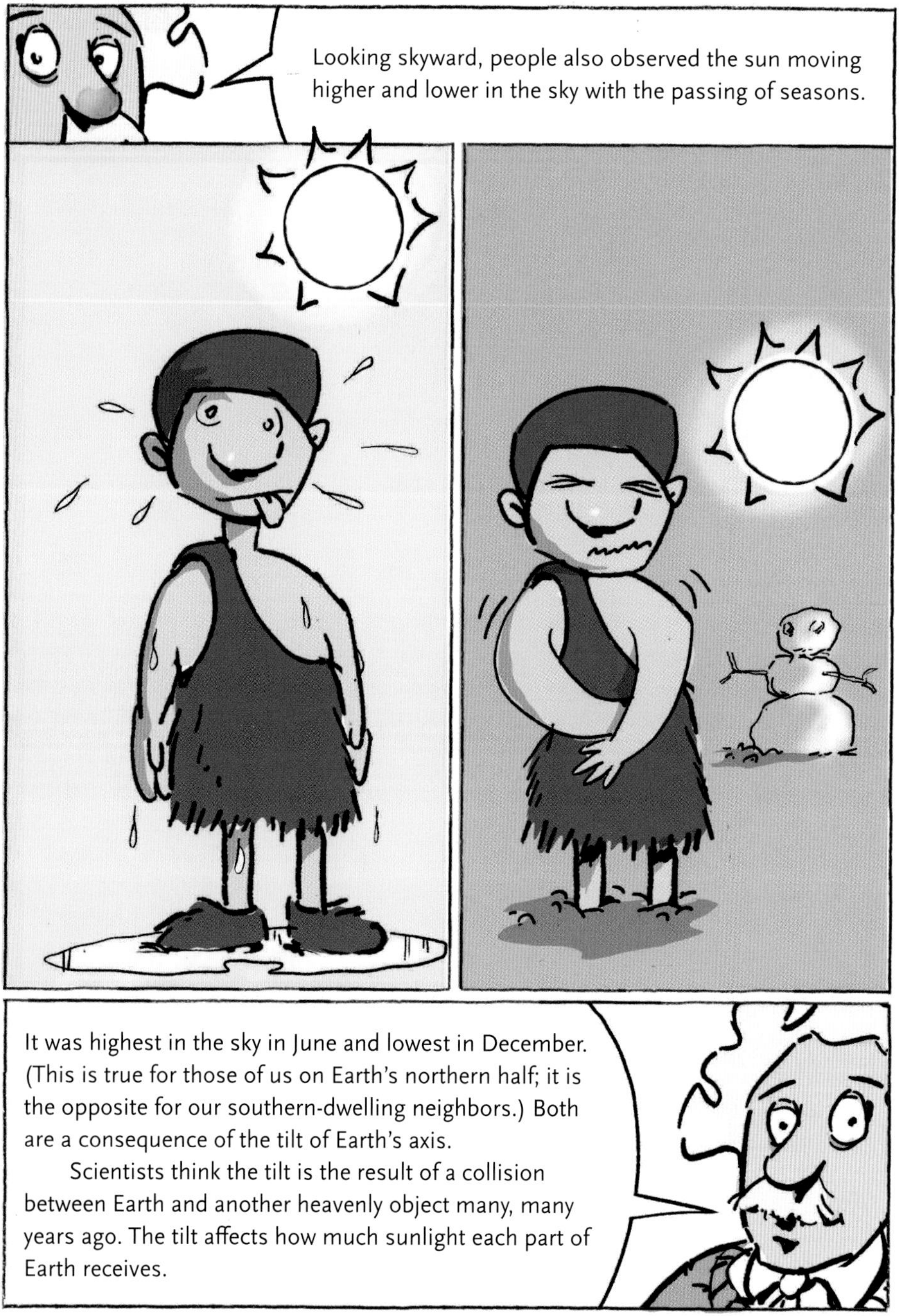
Looking skyward, people also observed the sun moving higher and lower in the sky with the passing of seasons.
It was highest in the sky in June and lowest in December. (This is true for those of us on Earth's northern half; it is the opposite for our southern-dwelling neighbors.) Both are a consequence of the tilt of Earth's axis.
Scientists think the tilt is the result of a collision between Earth and another heavenly object many, many years ago. The tilt affects how much sunlight each part of Earth receives.

The sun's highest position in the sky—the longest day of light—is called the summer solstice. Its lowest position—the shortest day with the least amount of light—is the winter solstice. *Solstice* comes from the Latin words for "sun stands still," which describes the pause before the sun changes direction.

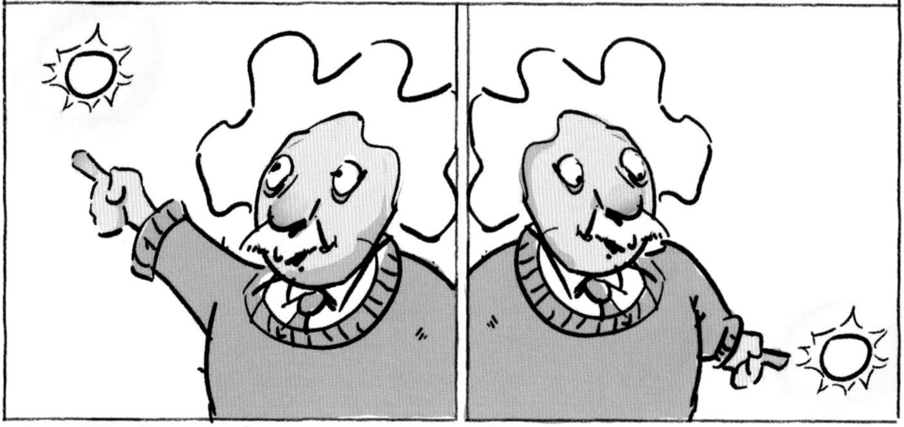

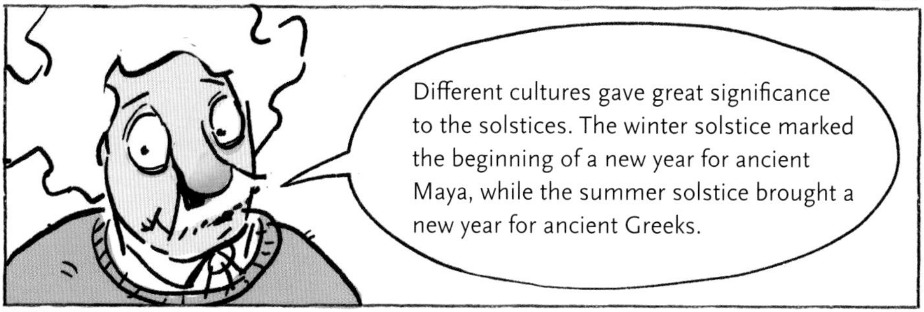
Different cultures gave great significance to the solstices. The winter solstice marked the beginning of a new year for ancient Maya, while the summer solstice brought a new year for ancient Greeks.

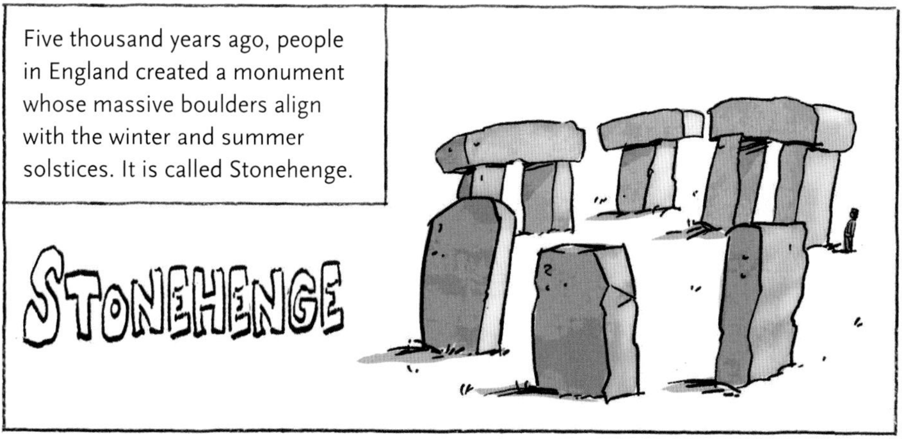
Five thousand years ago, people in England created a monument whose massive boulders align with the winter and summer solstices. It is called Stonehenge.
STONEHENGE

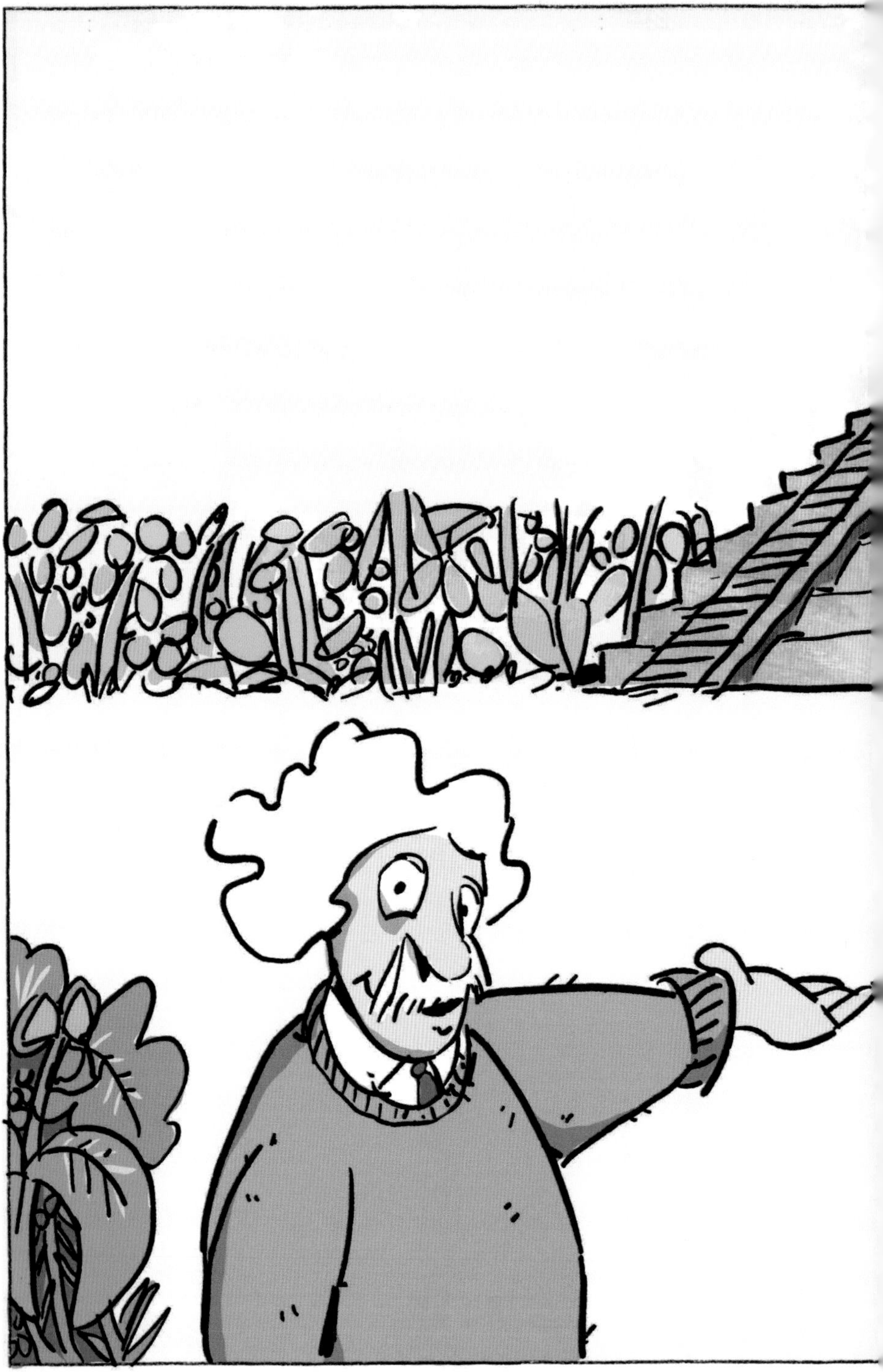

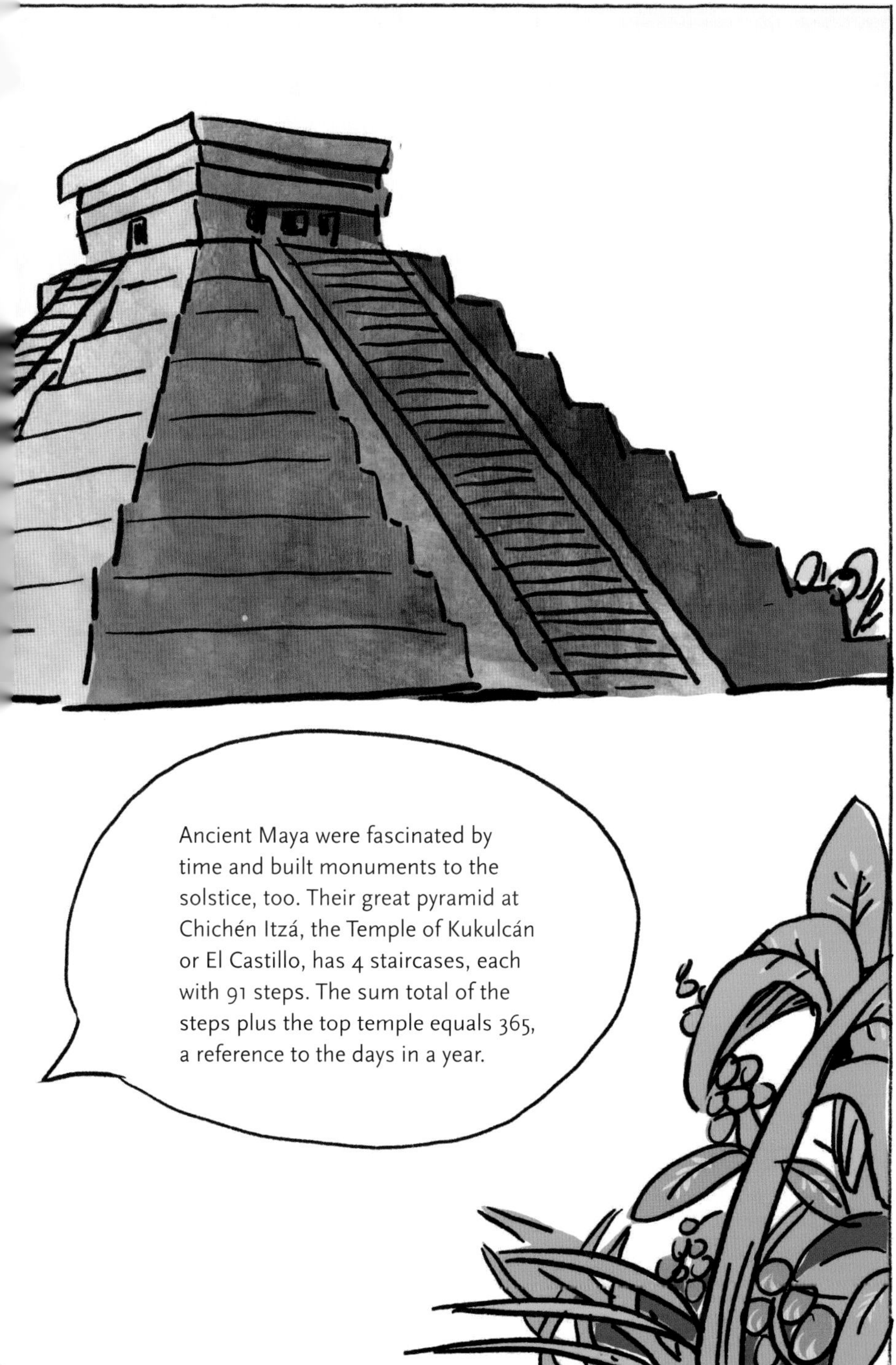
Ancient Maya were fascinated by time and built monuments to the solstice, too. Their great pyramid at Chichén Itzá, the Temple of Kukulcán or El Castillo, has 4 staircases, each with 91 steps. The sum total of the steps plus the top temple equals 365, a reference to the days in a year.

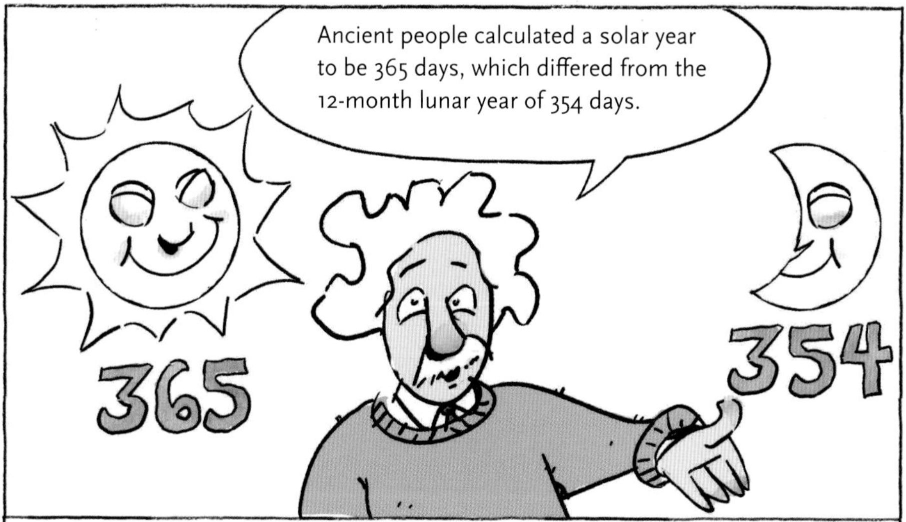
Ancient people calculated a solar year to be 365 days, which differed from the 12-month lunar year of 354 days.
365
354

Getting the two to coincide proved clumsy; Jewish and Chinese lunar calendars add a thirteenth month every few years. The Muslim lunar calendar doesn't bother, letting the difference between it and the solar calendar fall farther and farther out of alignment.

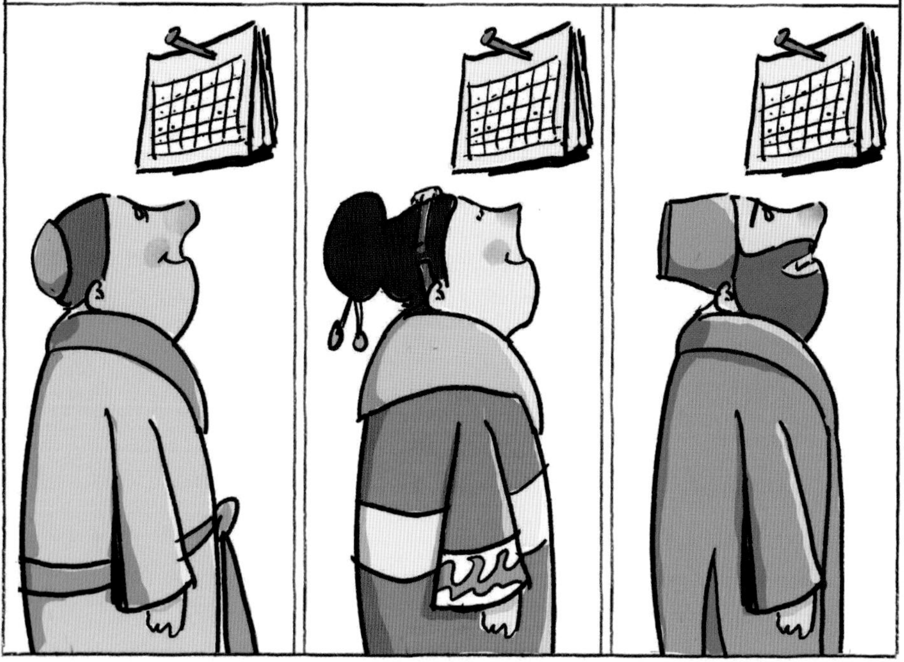

To make matters even more confusing, a solar year is really 365 *and ¼* days. If we ignored the fractional day, eventually January would drift into the heat of summer, and July might find itself under a deluge of winter snow. Or vice versa, depending on whether you live in the Northern Hemisphere (above the equator) or the Southern Hemisphere (below the equator).

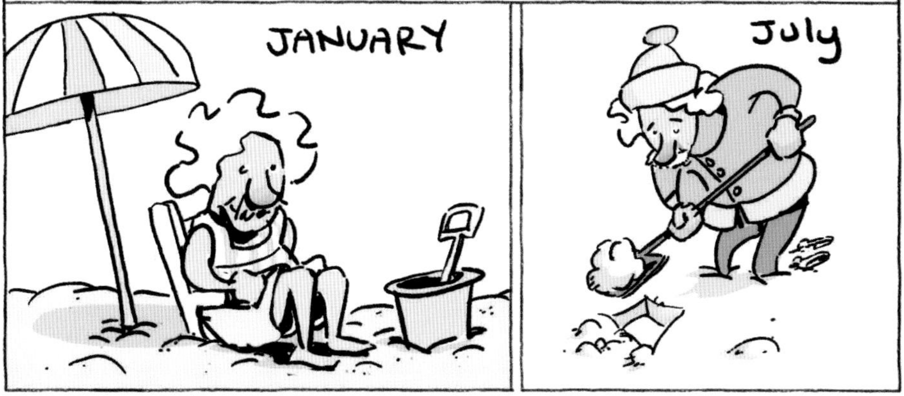
JANUARY
July

To keep the months in their proper seasons, in 1582 Roman Catholic Pope Gregory I proclaimed a calendar that employed months with a varying number of days. Every four years, an extra day would be added to February to account for that extra ¼ of a day. We call that special fourth year a leap year.

The so-called Gregorian calendar is a Big Idea still used across most of the world.

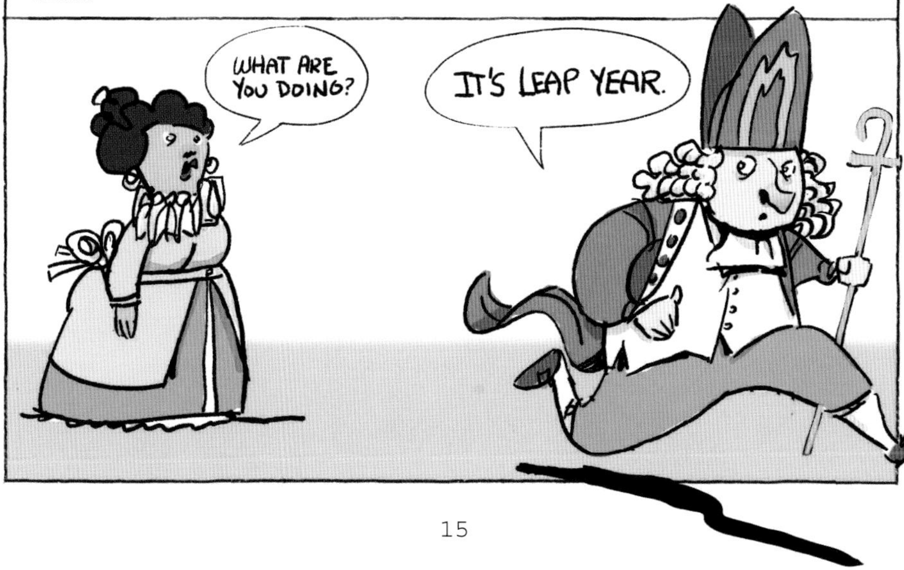
WHAT ARE YOU DOING?
IT'S LEAP YEAR.

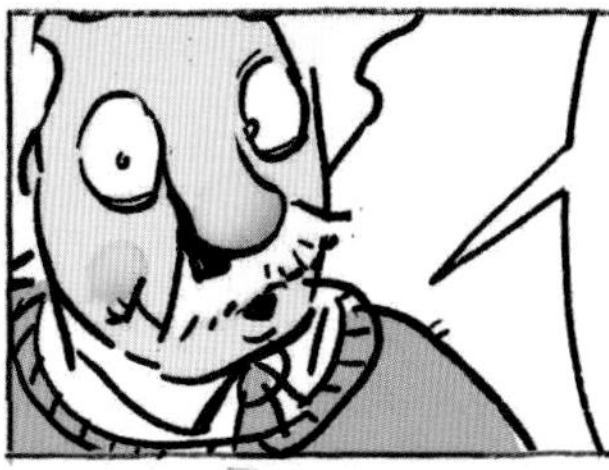

And how did we end up with seven days in a week?

Although the ancient Egyptians used a ten-day week, and the Romans had an eight-day week, it was the ancient Babylonians who had a Big Idea that made the difference.

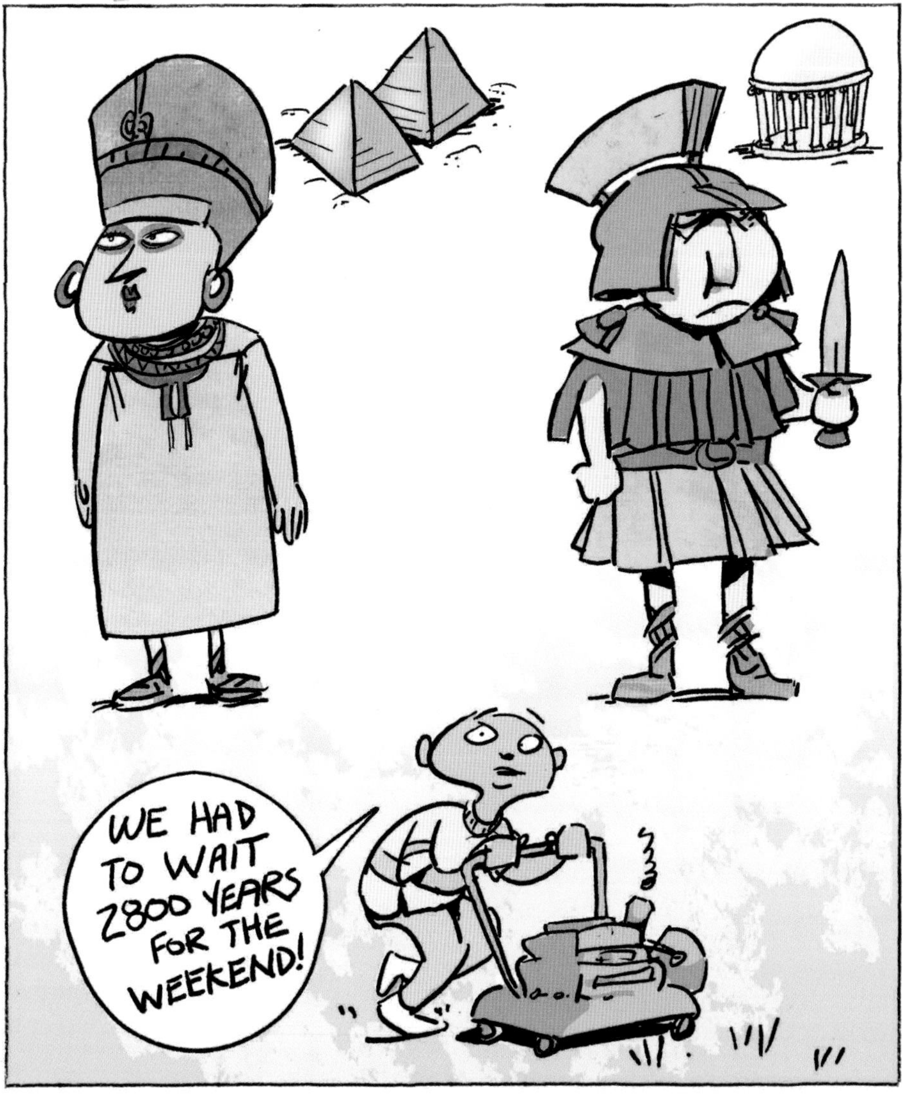
WE HAD TO WAIT 2800 YEARS FOR THE WEEKEND!

Their twenty-eight-day lunar calendar was divided into four parts of seven days each. Three thousand years ago, Babylonian influence across the Middle East was so great that their neighbors adopted the same seven-day week.

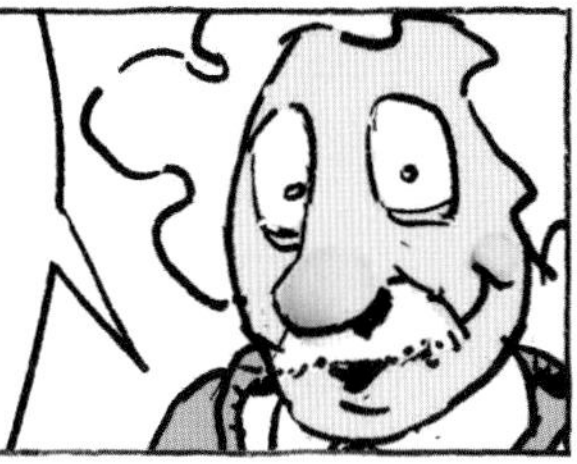

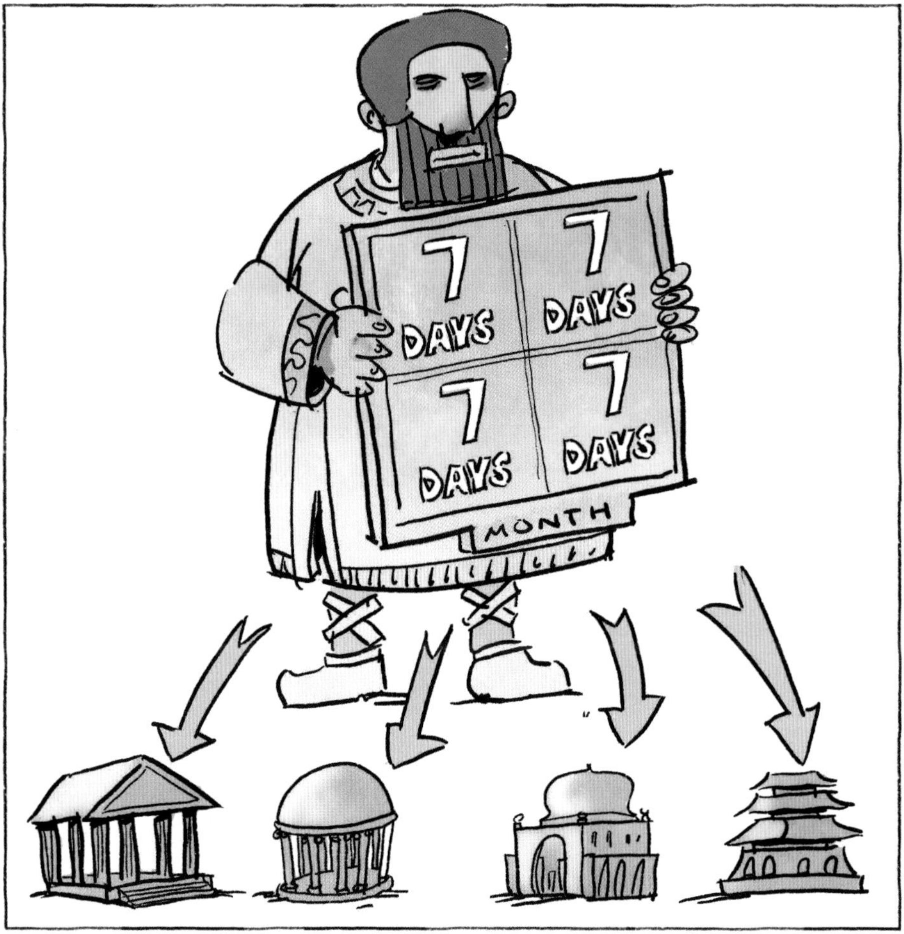
7 DAYS
7 DAYS
7 DAYS
7 DAYS
MONTH

It spread to Greece, Rome, India, and China and is now an international standard, even though the months of a Gregorian calendar are not neatly divided into four weeks of seven days each.

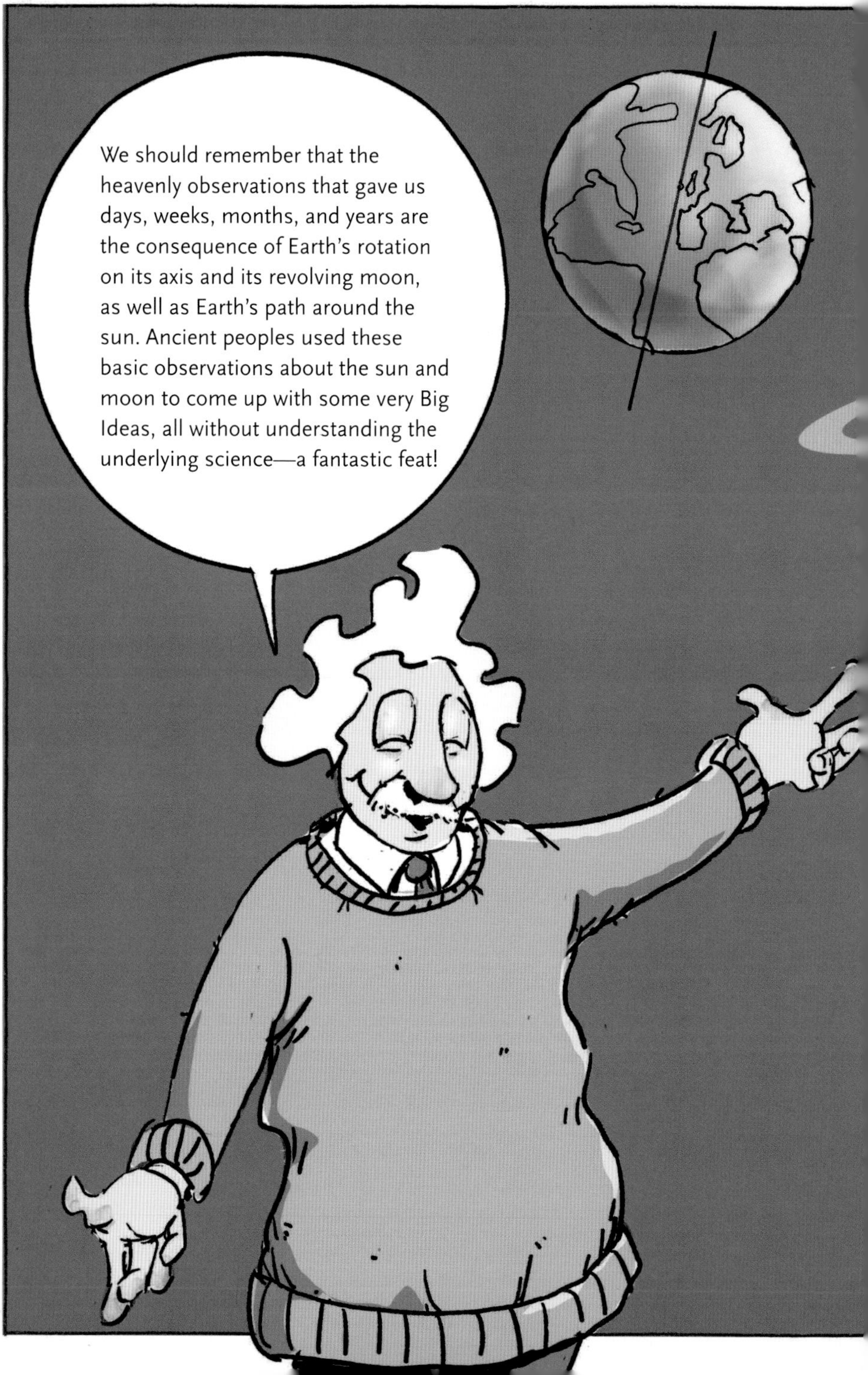
We should remember that the heavenly observations that gave us days, weeks, months, and years are the consequence of Earth's rotation on its axis and its revolving moon, as well as Earth's path around the sun. Ancient peoples used these basic observations about the sun and moon to come up with some very Big Ideas, all without understanding the underlying science—a fantastic feat!

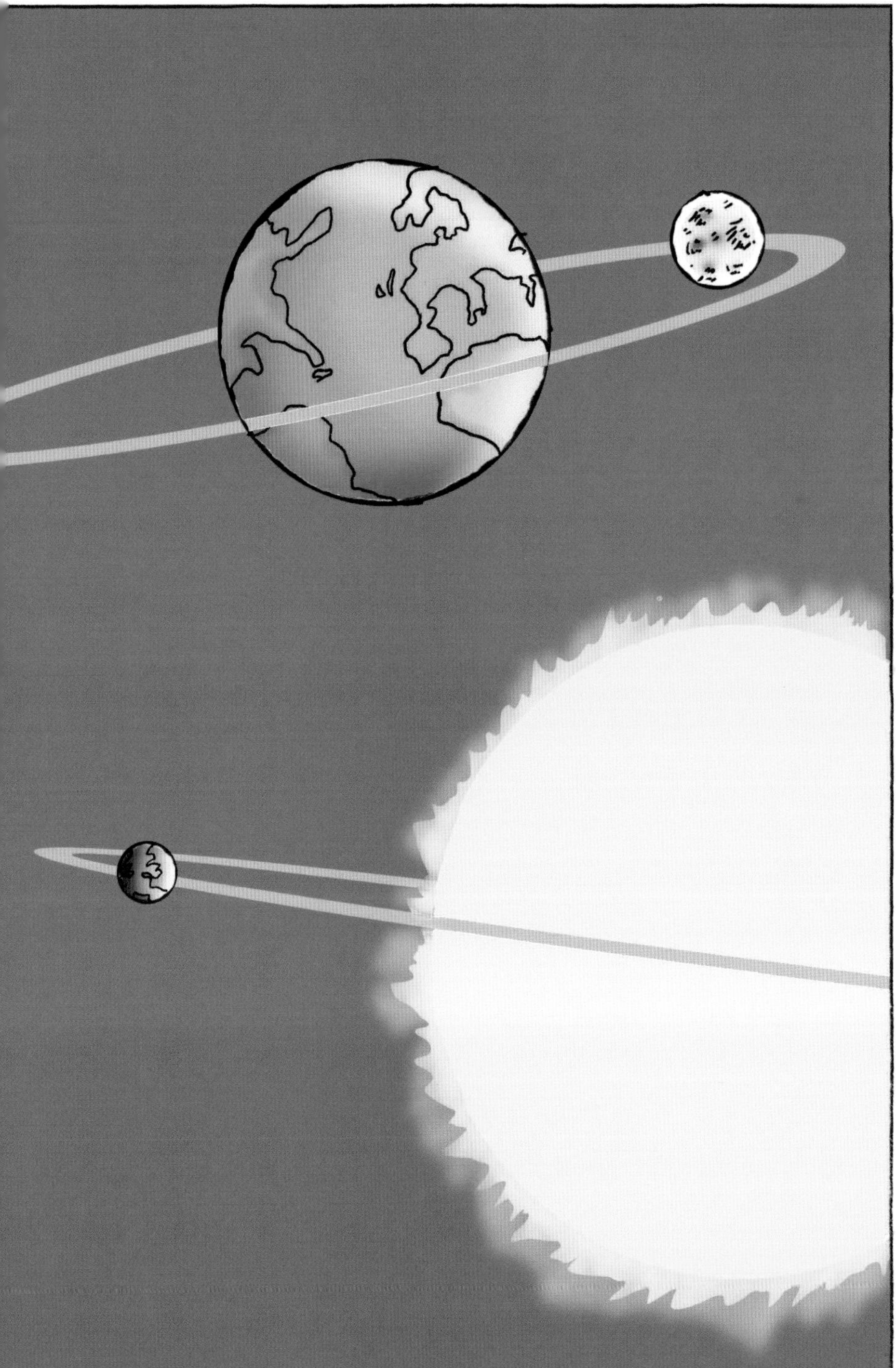

So we've divided time into days, weeks, months, and years . . . but where did hours, minutes, and seconds come from?

About four thousand years ago, an unknown Egyptian placed a stick upright into the ground and noticed its shadow change direction and length as the sun moved across the sky over the course of a day. Someone figured out the shadows corresponded to time of day—say, late morning, or early afternoon. The Egyptians then decided to divide the day into twelve parts.

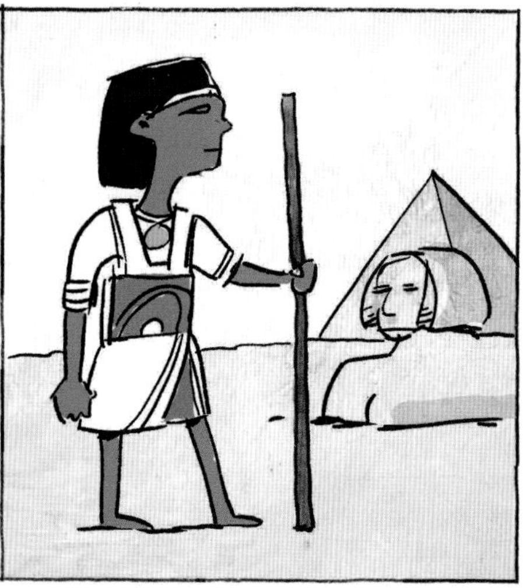

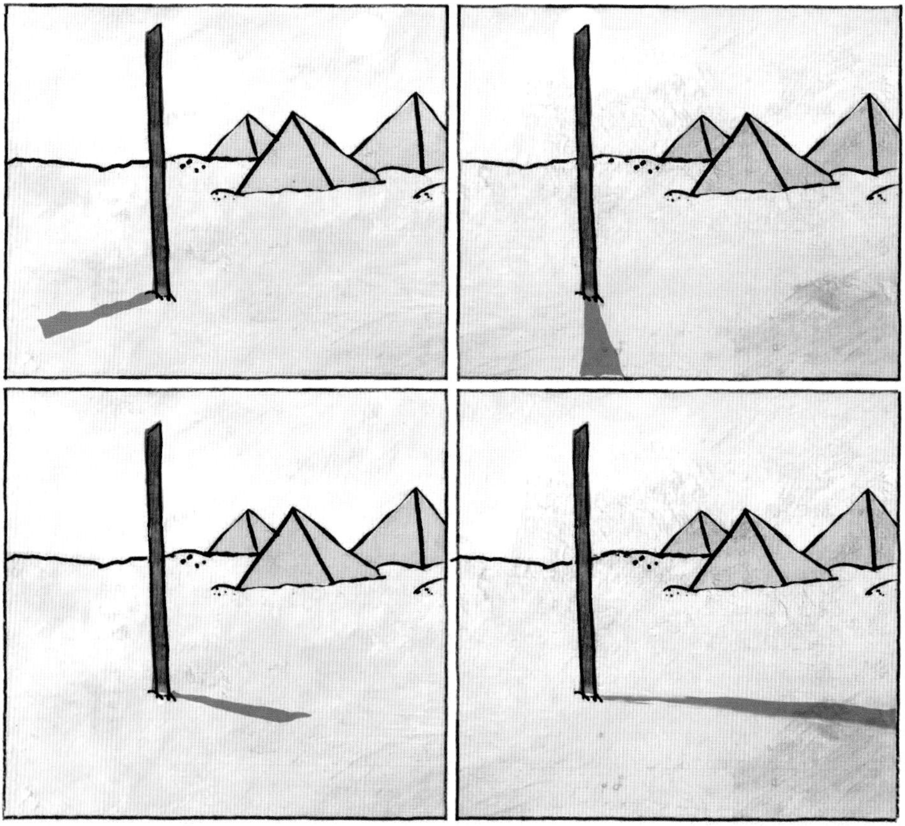

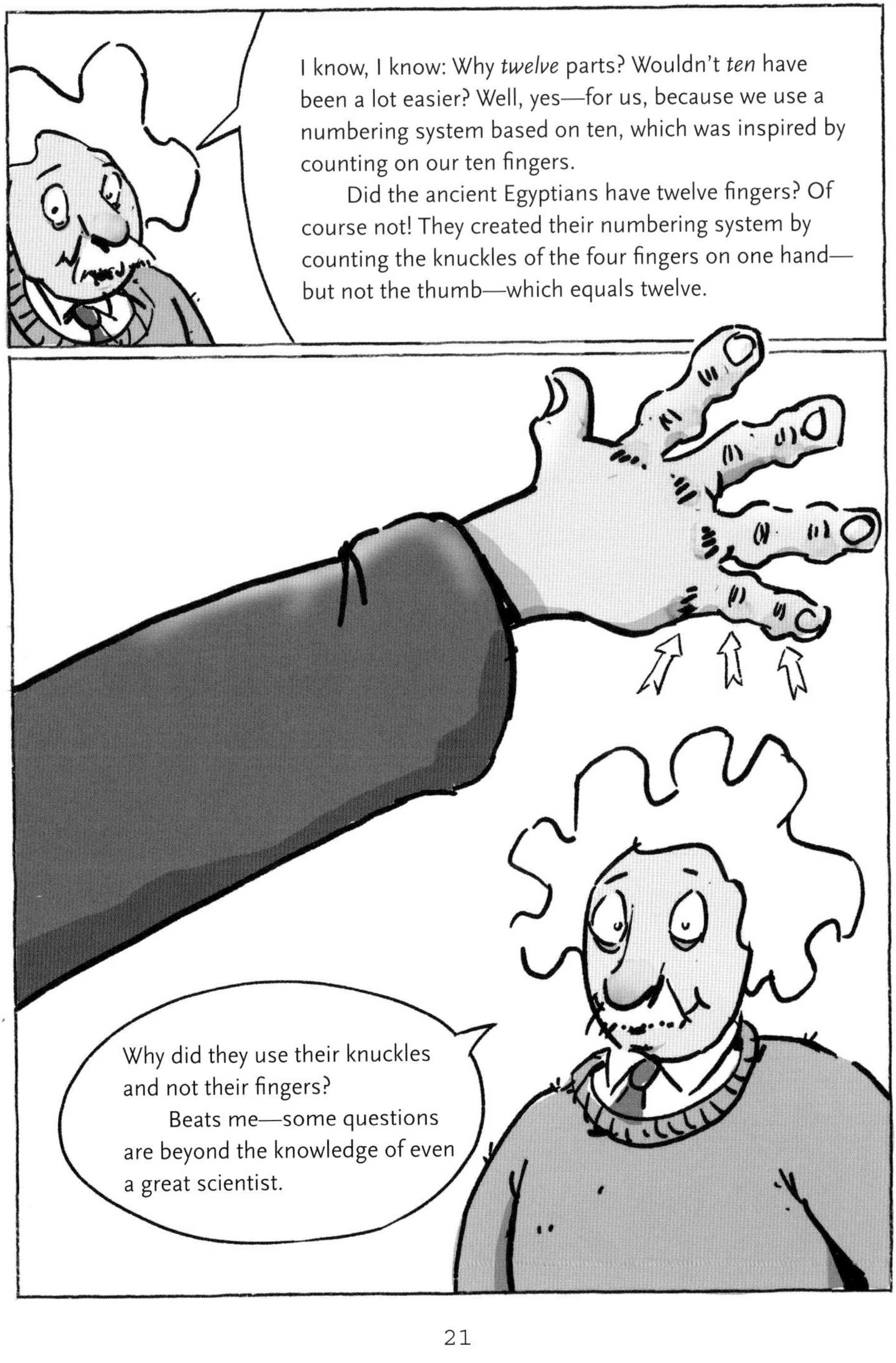
I know, I know: Why *twelve* parts? Wouldn't *ten* have been a lot easier? Well, yes—for us, because we use a numbering system based on ten, which was inspired by counting on our ten fingers.
Did the ancient Egyptians have twelve fingers? Of course not! They created their numbering system by counting the knuckles of the four fingers on one hand—but not the thumb—which equals twelve.
Why did they use their knuckles and not their fingers?
Beats me—some questions are beyond the knowledge of even a great scientist.

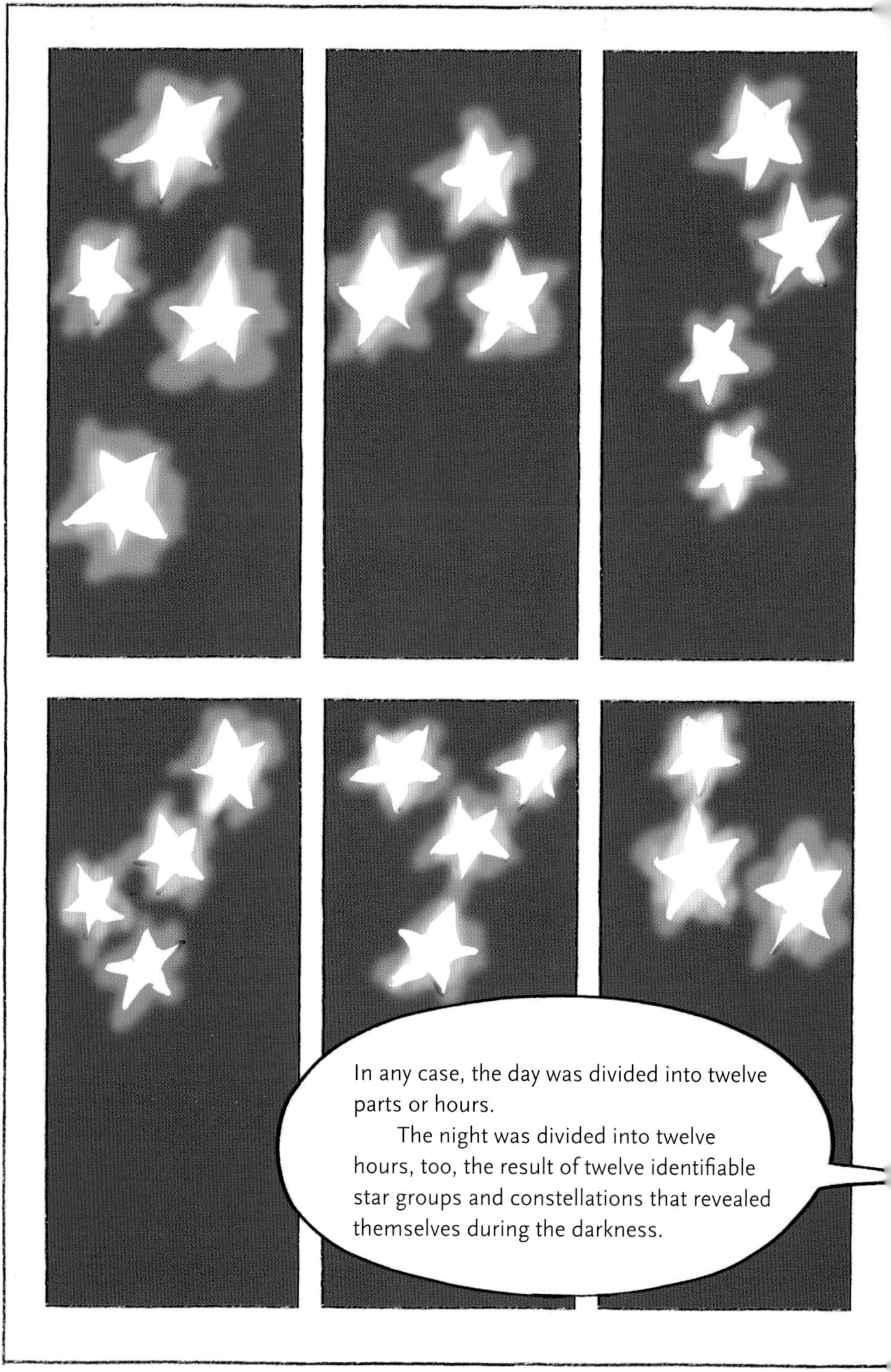
In any case, the day was divided into twelve parts or hours.
The night was divided into twelve hours, too, the result of twelve identifiable star groups and constellations that revealed themselves during the darkness.

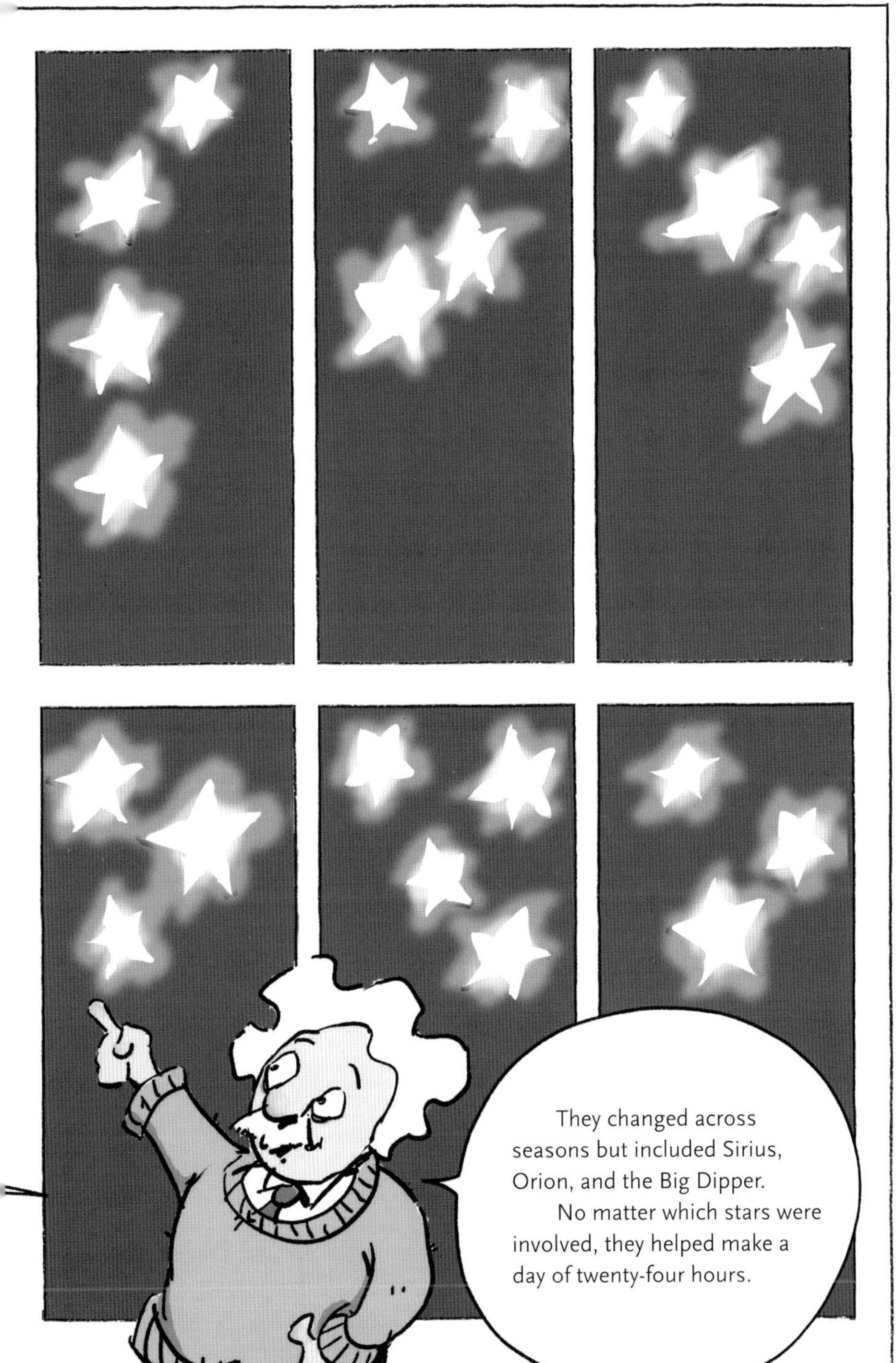
They changed across seasons but included Sirius, Orion, and the Big Dipper.
No matter which stars were involved, they helped make a day of twenty-four hours.

And minutes and seconds?

An ancient Greek scientist, taking inspiration from our old friends the Babylonians—who used a counting system based on sixty—divided an hour into sixty pieces that we call minutes, and then sliced each minute into another sixty pieces that we call seconds.

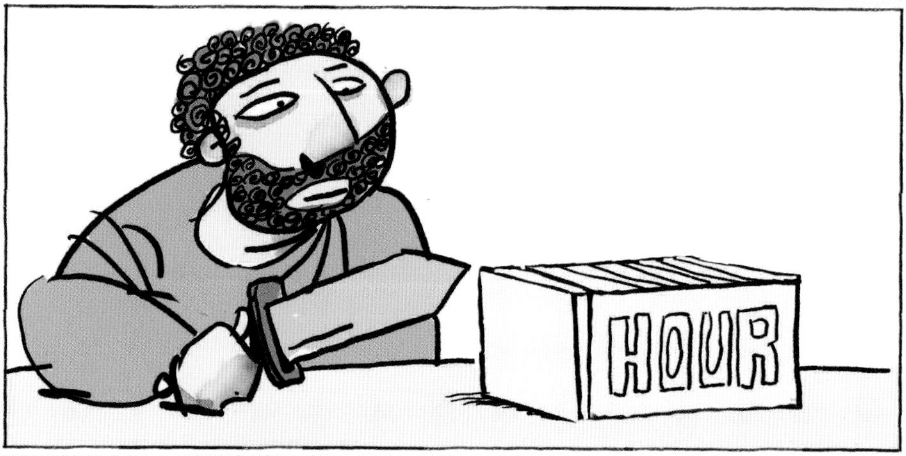
HOUR

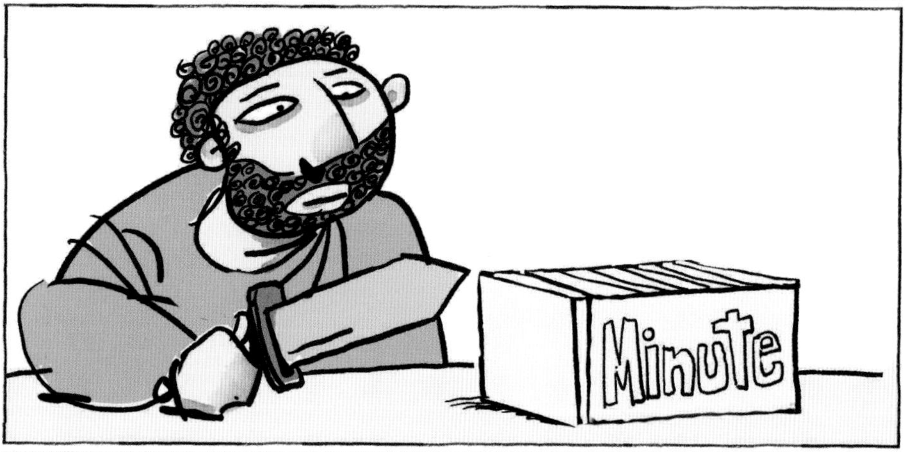
Minute

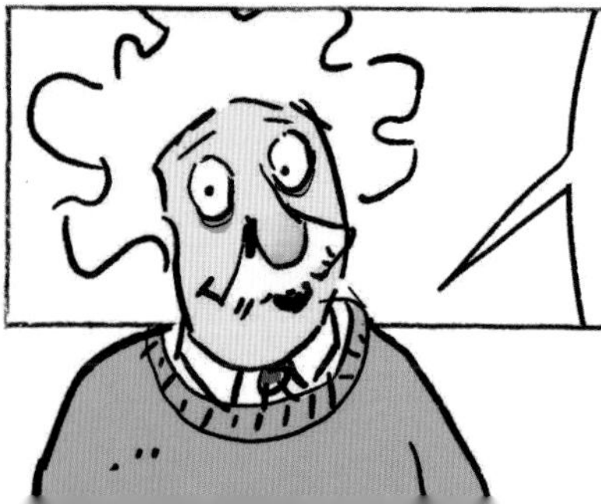

Why a counting system of sixty? What happened to ten or twelve?

Again, I'm stumped, as are many other people.

Now that people had hours, seconds, and minutes, they needed a device to keep track of them all. Since we people have a knack for invention, we thought up timekeepers.

I've already mentioned early sundials. There were water clocks, too, that used the water level of a container into which water slowly dripped to mark time. Water clocks were especially handy at night, when a sundial would be useless. Native Americans and early Africans were among those who used them.

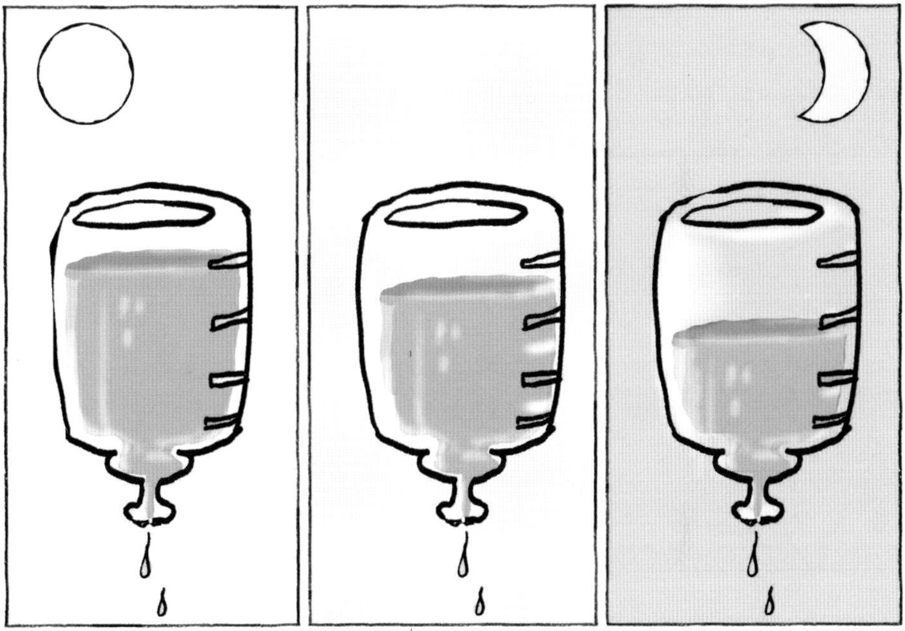

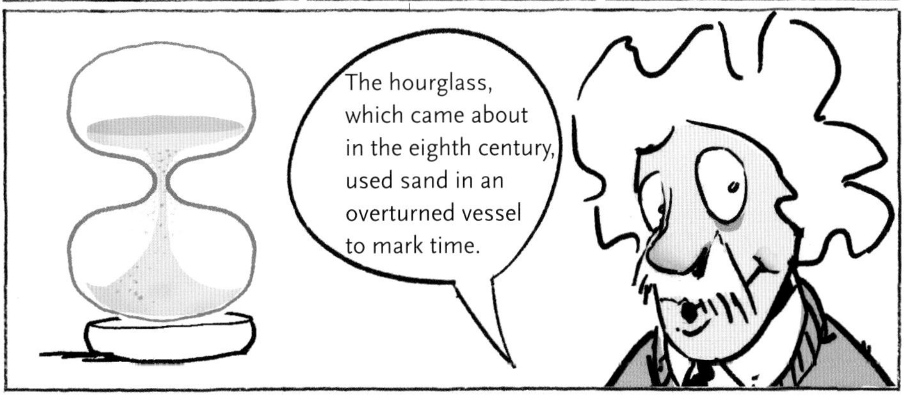
The hourglass, which came about in the eighth century, used sand in an overturned vessel to mark time.

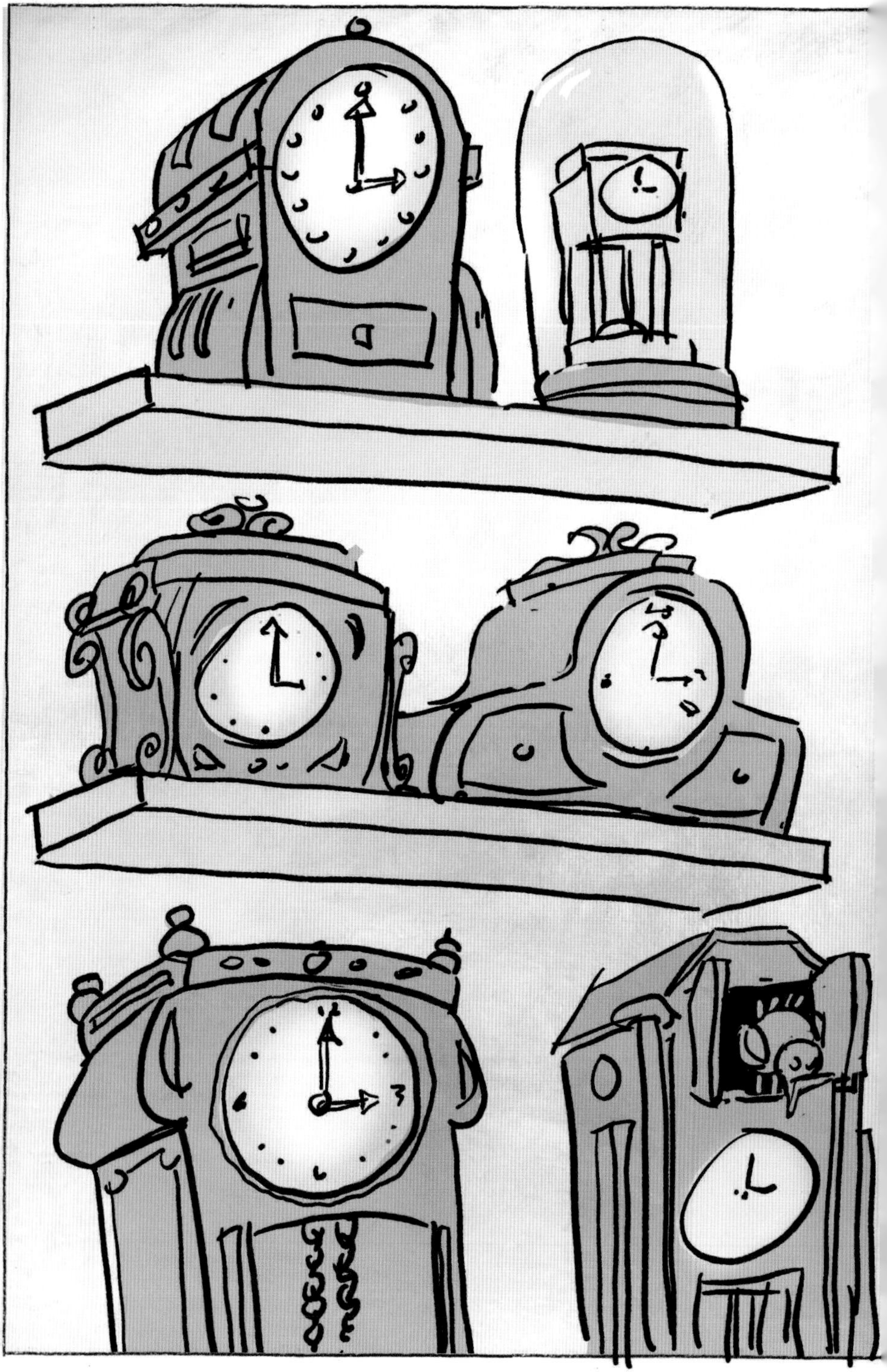

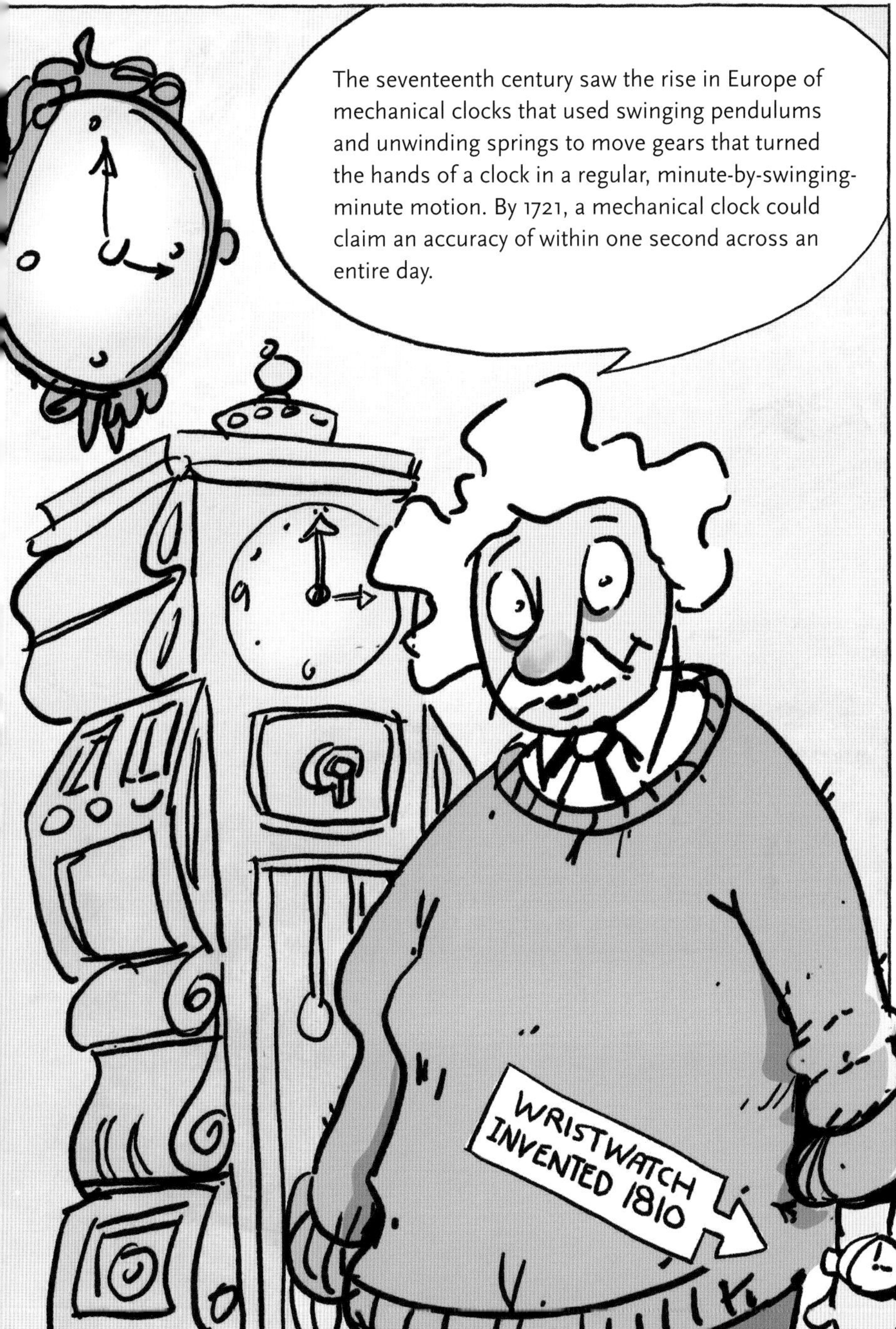
The seventeenth century saw the rise in Europe of mechanical clocks that used swinging pendulums and unwinding springs to move gears that turned the hands of a clock in a regular, minute-by-swinging-minute motion. By 1721, a mechanical clock could claim an accuracy of within one second across an entire day.
WRISTWATCH INVENTED 1810

One of the most important clocks was invented in the mid-eighteenth century by self-taught English clockmaker John Harrison.

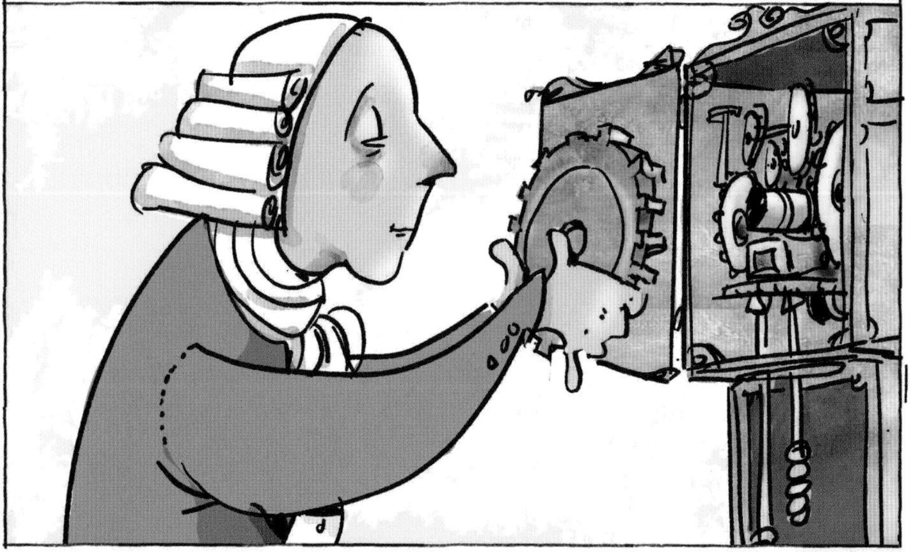

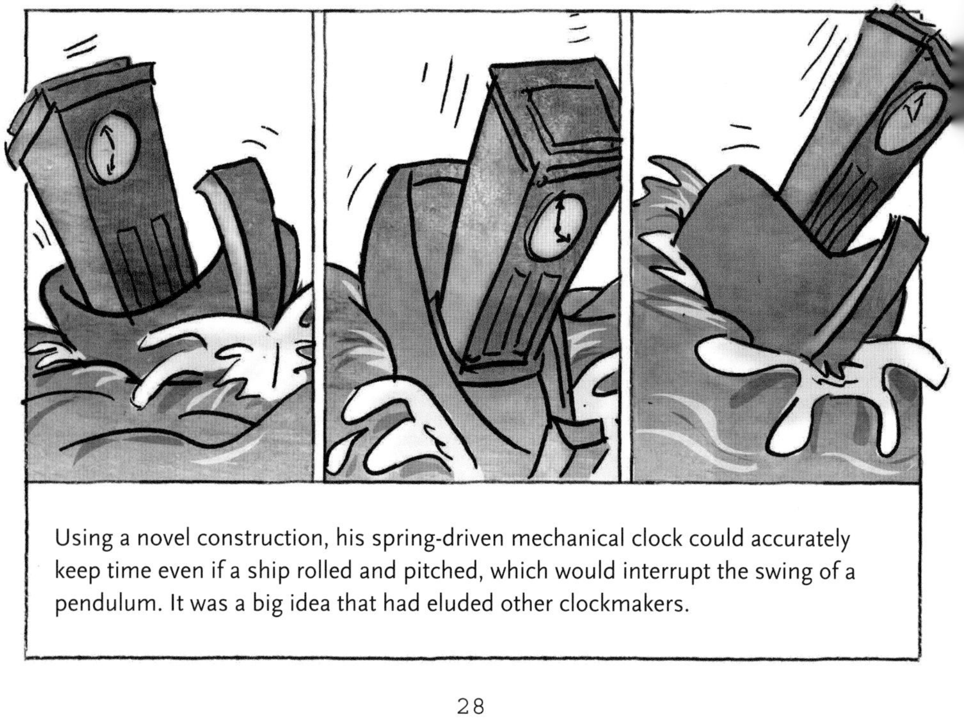

Using a novel construction, his spring-driven mechanical clock could accurately keep time even if a ship rolled and pitched, which would interrupt the swing of a pendulum. It was a big idea that had eluded other clockmakers.

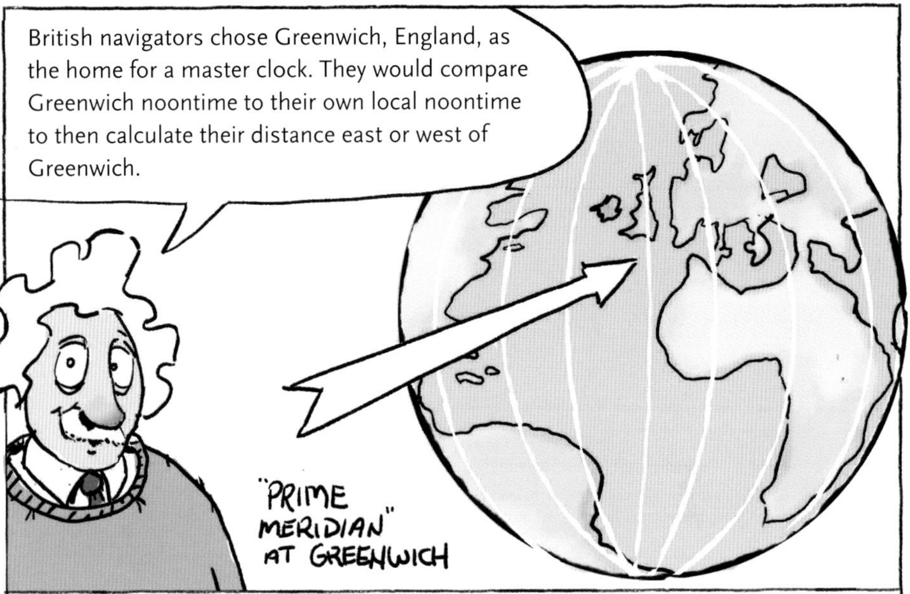
British navigators chose Greenwich, England, as the home for a master clock. They would compare Greenwich noontime to their own local noontime to then calculate their distance east or west of Greenwich.
"PRIME MERIDIAN" AT GREENWICH

Longitude lines divide Earth into regular east-west segments. Along with lines of *latitude,* which divide Earth into north-south segments, a traveler can use the imaginary grid created by lines of longitude and latitude to accurately mark their location.

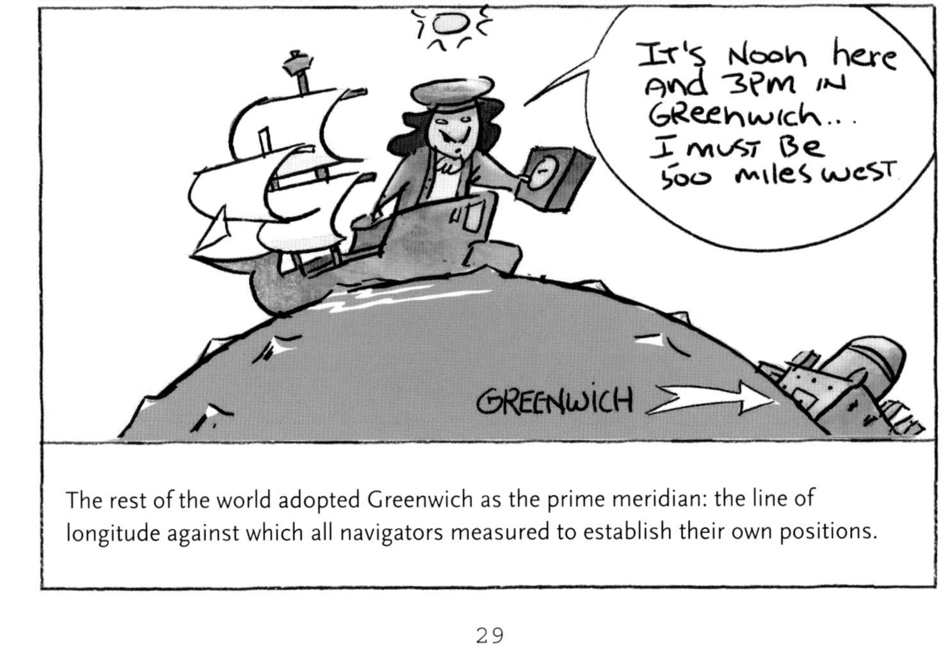
IT'S NOON HERE AND 3PM IN GREENWICH... I MUST BE 500 MILES WEST
GREENWICH

The rest of the world adopted Greenwich as the prime meridian: the line of longitude against which all navigators measured to establish their own positions.

People realized the day had to start and end somewhere. In 1884, that dividing line was decided to be at a line of longitude crossing the Pacific Ocean. A traveler crossing the international date line adds a day going west and loses a day going east.

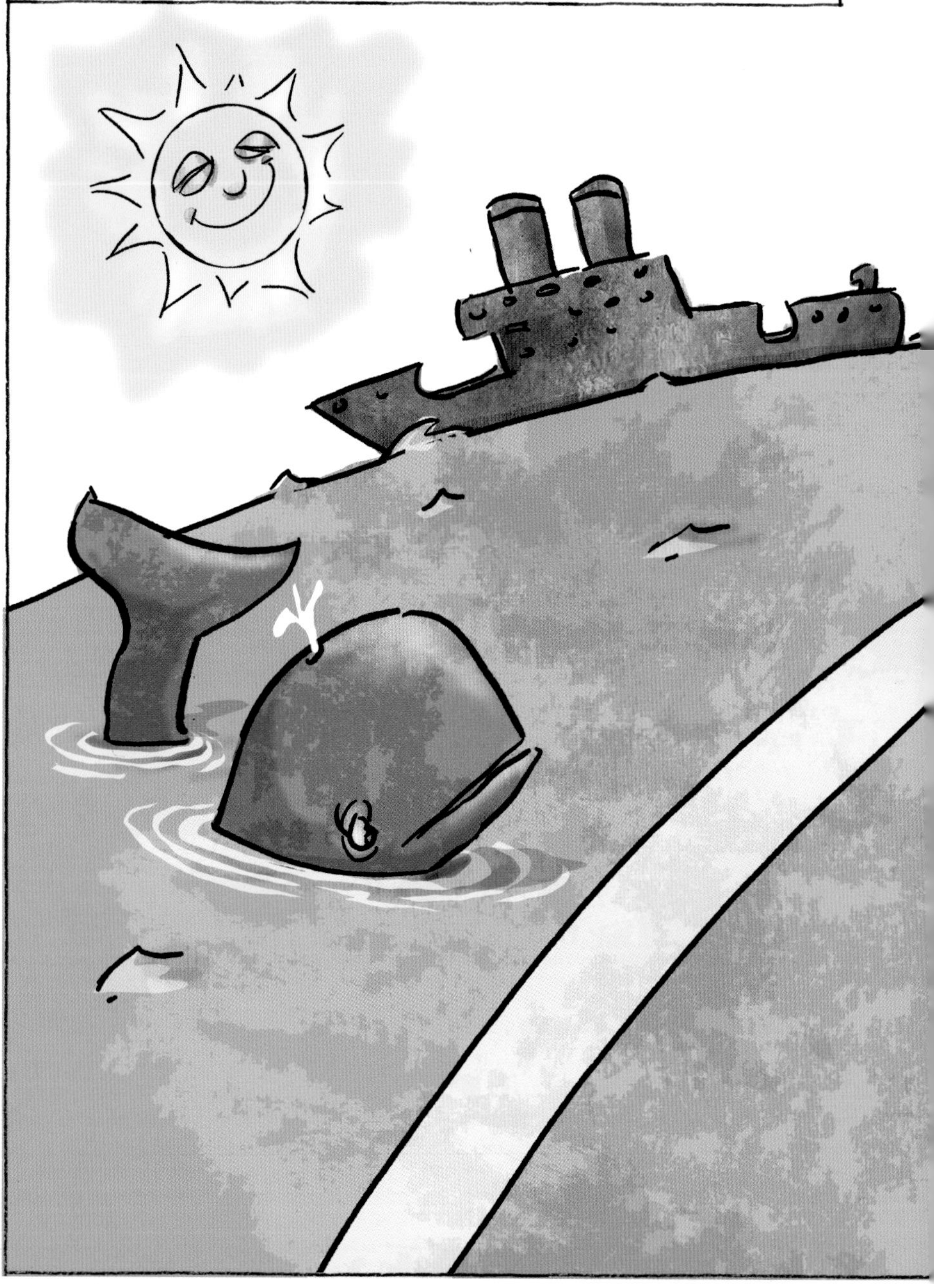

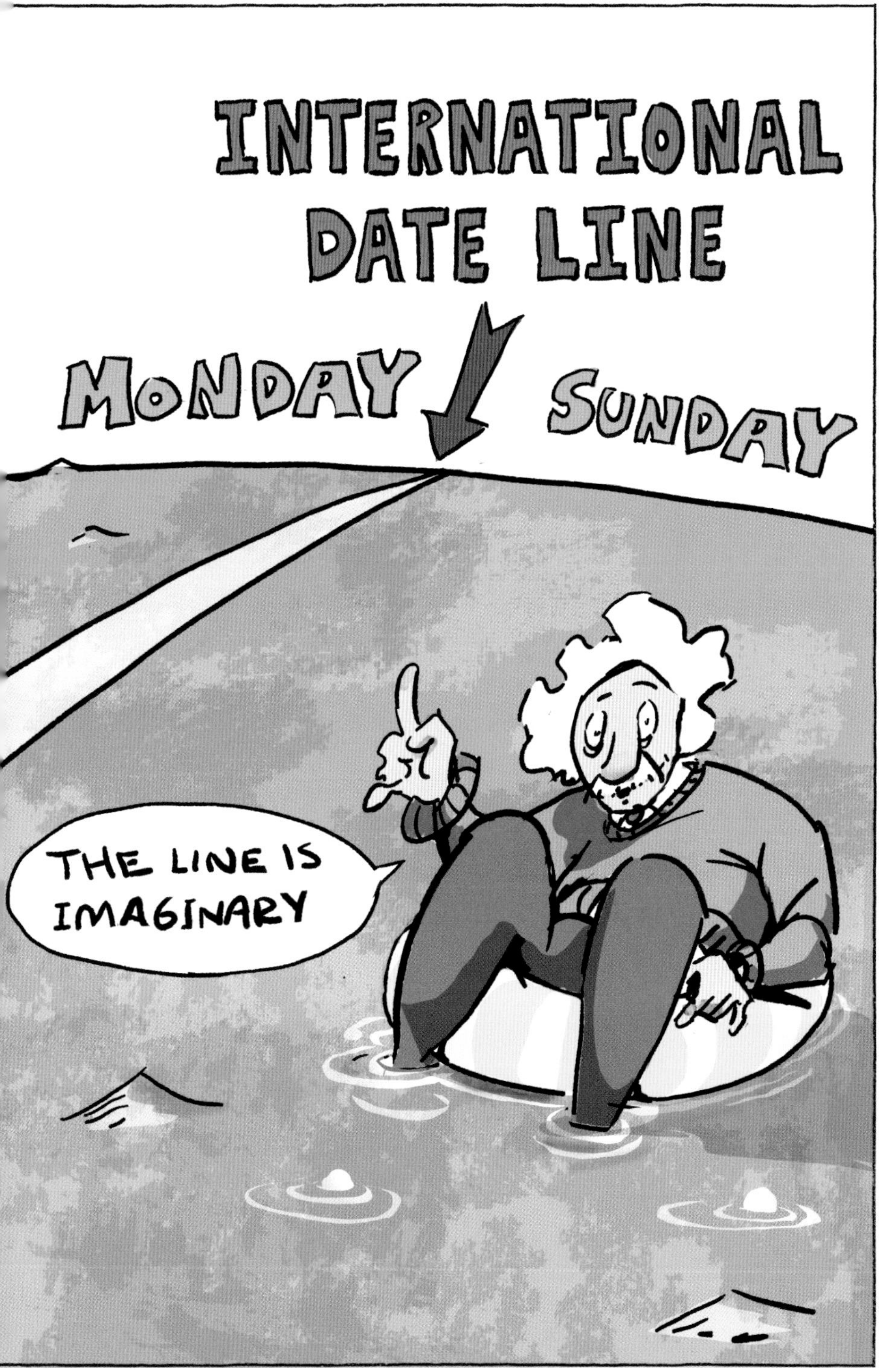
INTERNATIONAL DATE LINE
MONDAY
SUNDAY
THE LINE IS IMAGINARY

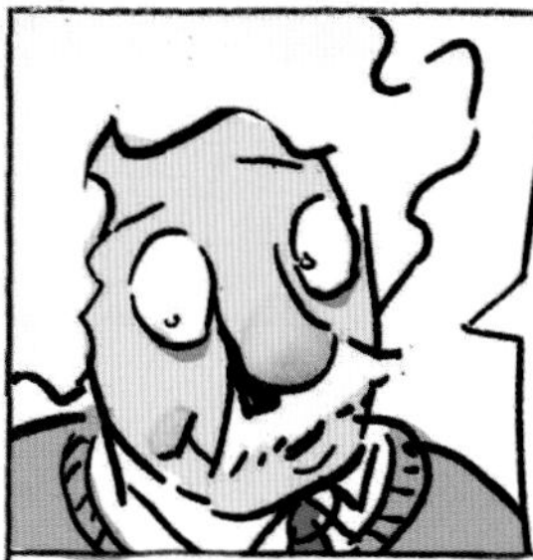

Clocks helped to foster the idea that time is uniform and continuous—and that it moved in one direction: a straight line from the past to the present and into the future.

Galileo Galilei believed it. He was a brilliant Italian scientist who studied all sorts of things, including the Big Idea that Earth revolved around the sun, an idea opposed by the powerful Catholic Church at the time.

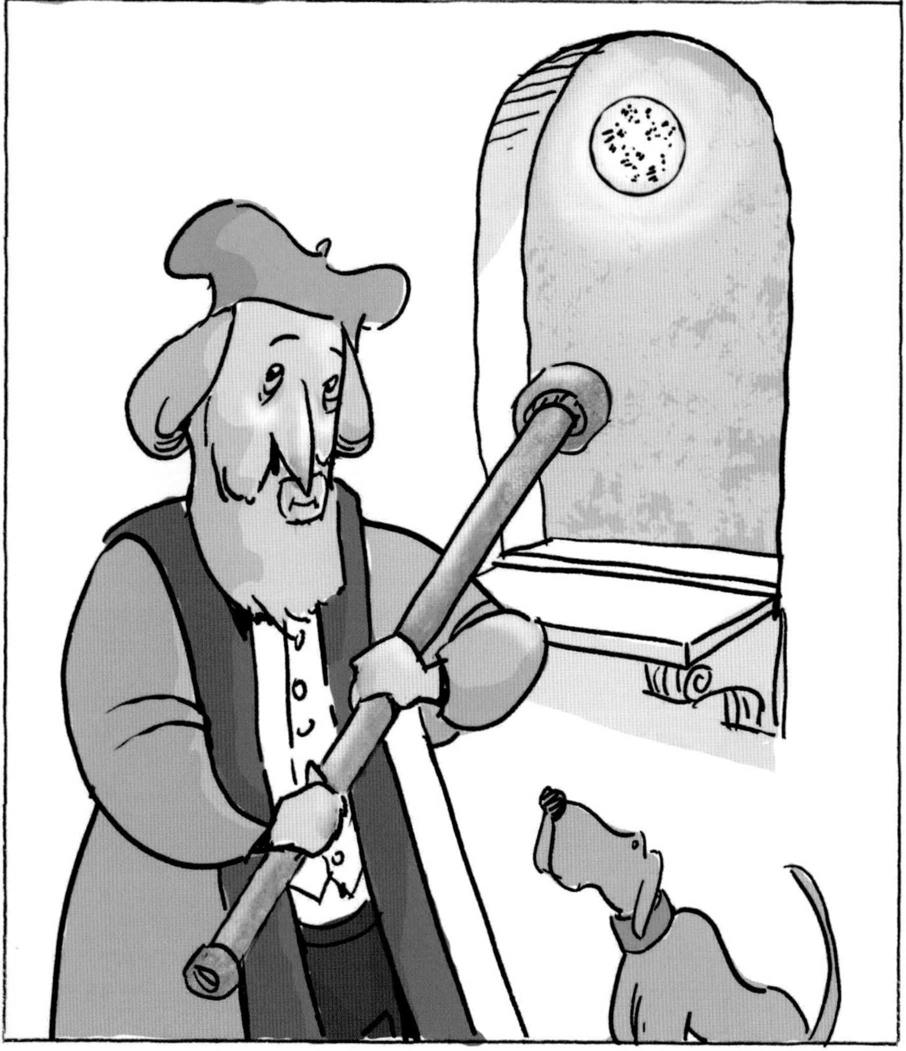

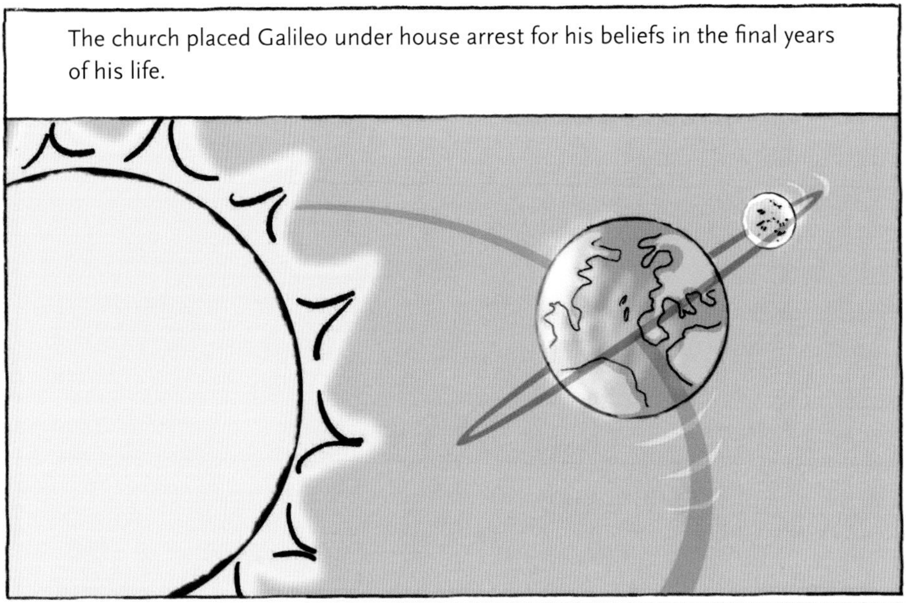
The church placed Galileo under house arrest for his beliefs in the final years of his life.

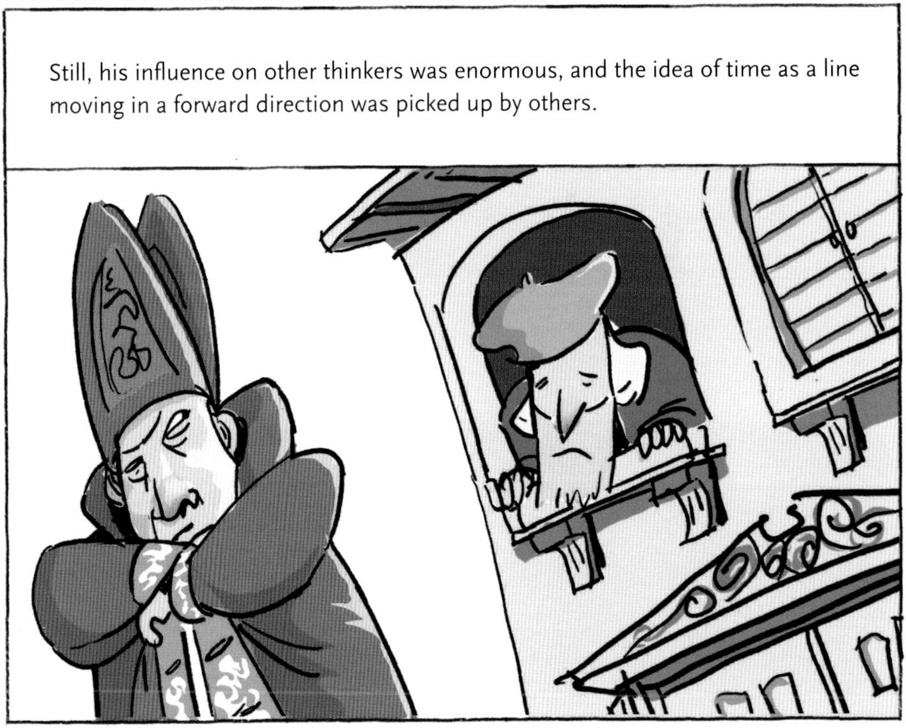
Still, his influence on other thinkers was enormous, and the idea of time as a line moving in a forward direction was picked up by others.

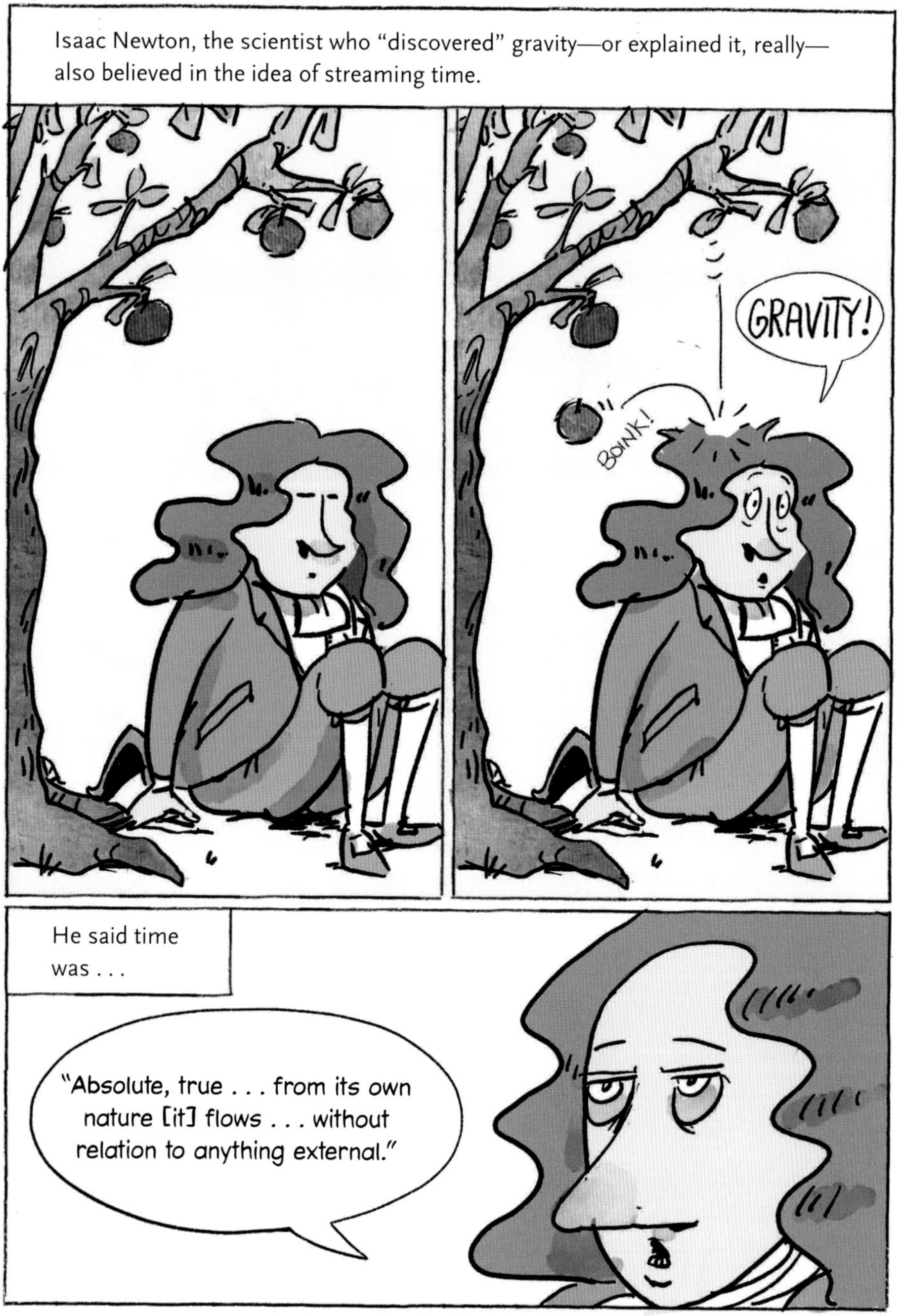
Isaac Newton, the scientist who "discovered" gravity—or explained it, really—also believed in the idea of streaming time.
BOINK!
GRAVITY!
He said time was . . .
"Absolute, true . . . from its own nature [it] flows . . . without relation to anything external."

That is, time goes on independent of everyday events. It has no beginning or end.

Others expanded on the idea, saying absolute time is everywhere.

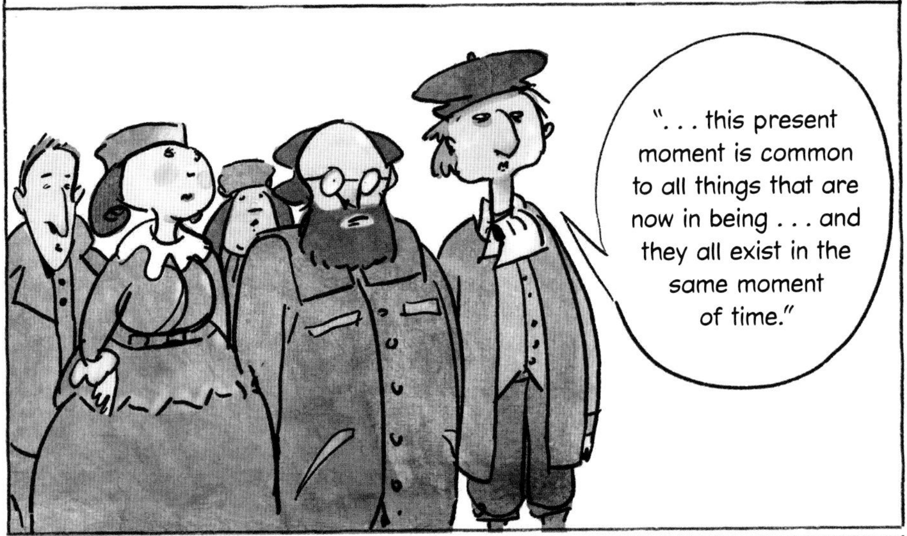
". . . this present moment is common to all things that are now in being . . . and they all exist in the same moment of time."

That is, a moment of time is the same no matter where you are, whether you're in Thailand or Switzerland, Argentina or the Arctic, on the moon, Jupiter, or Halley's Comet.

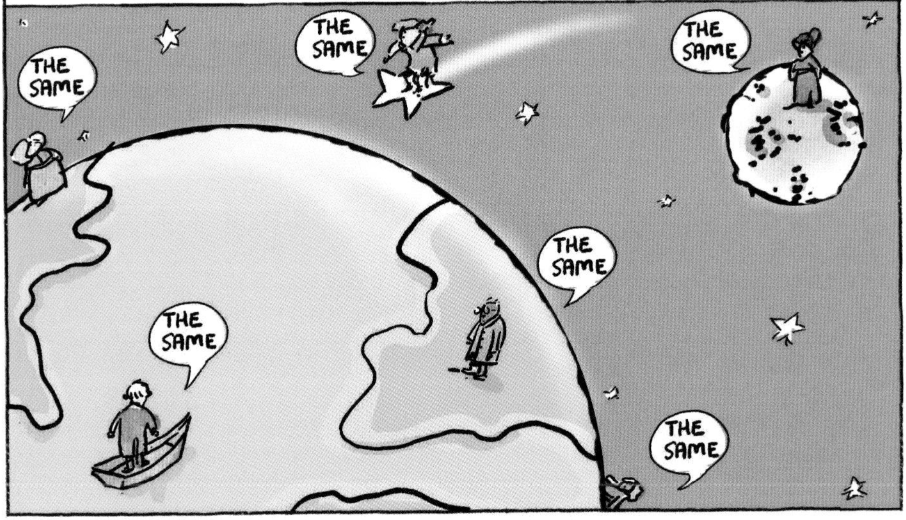
THE SAME
THE SAME
THE SAME
THE SAME
THE SAME
THE SAME

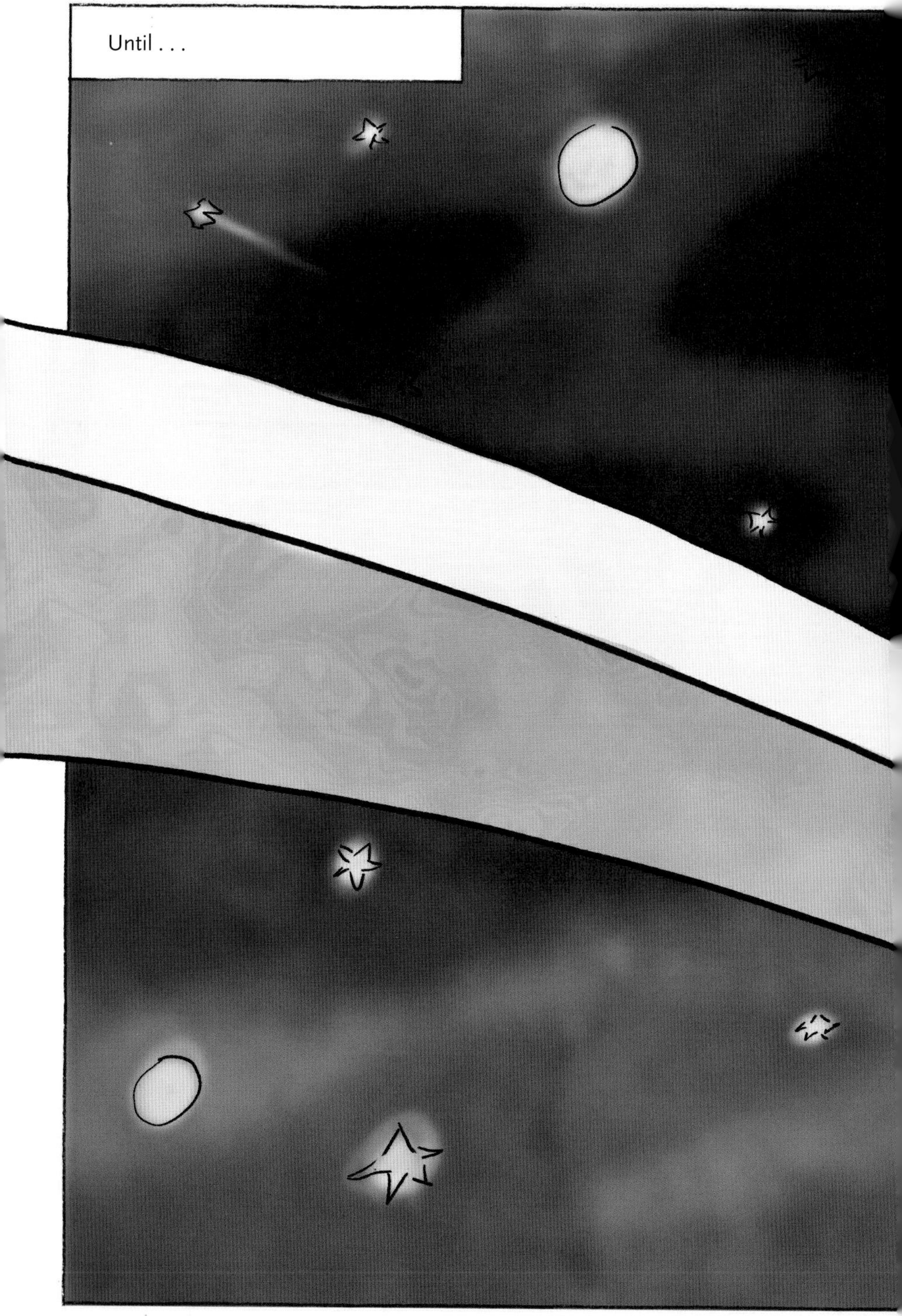
Until . . .

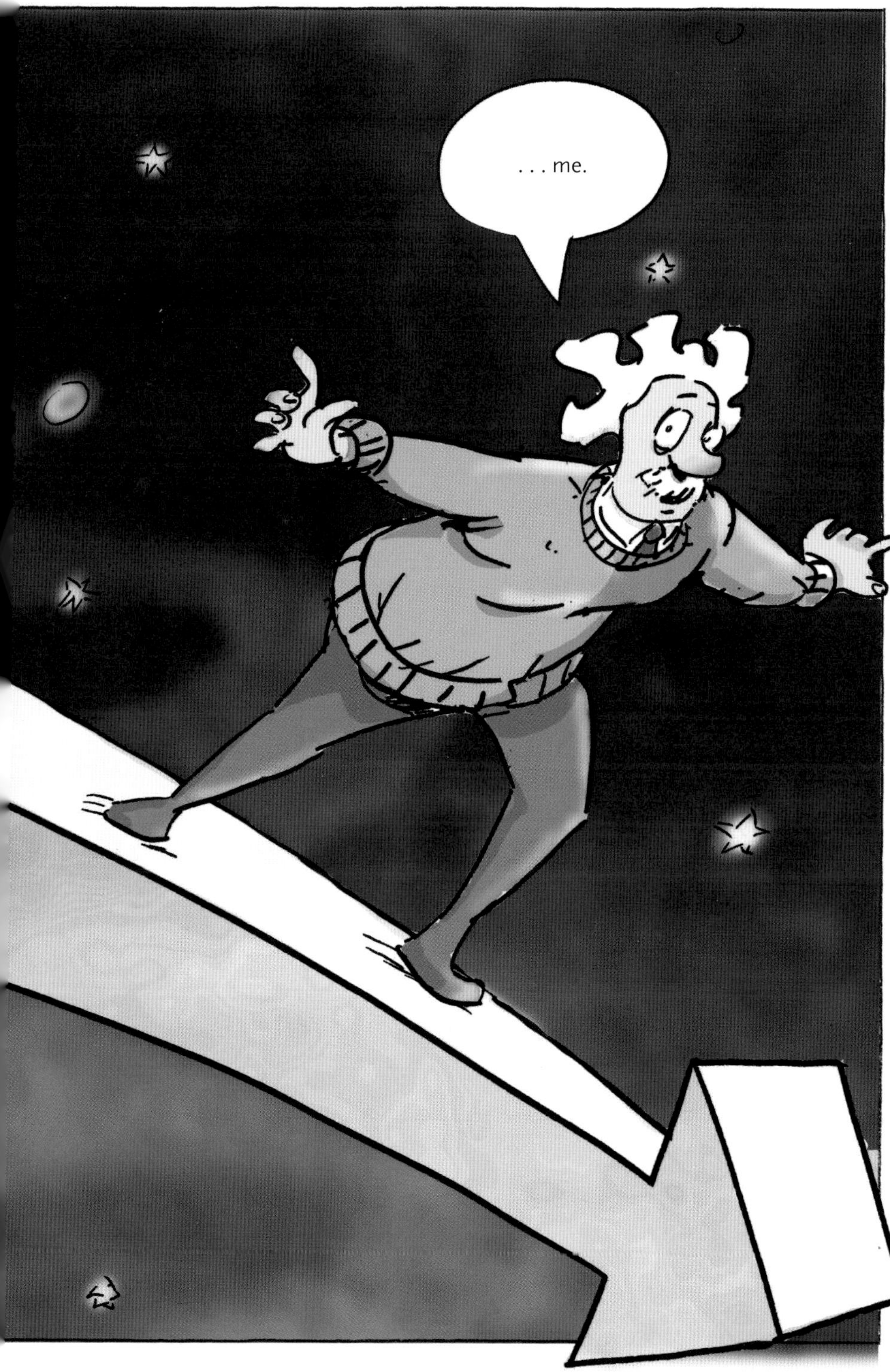
. . . me.

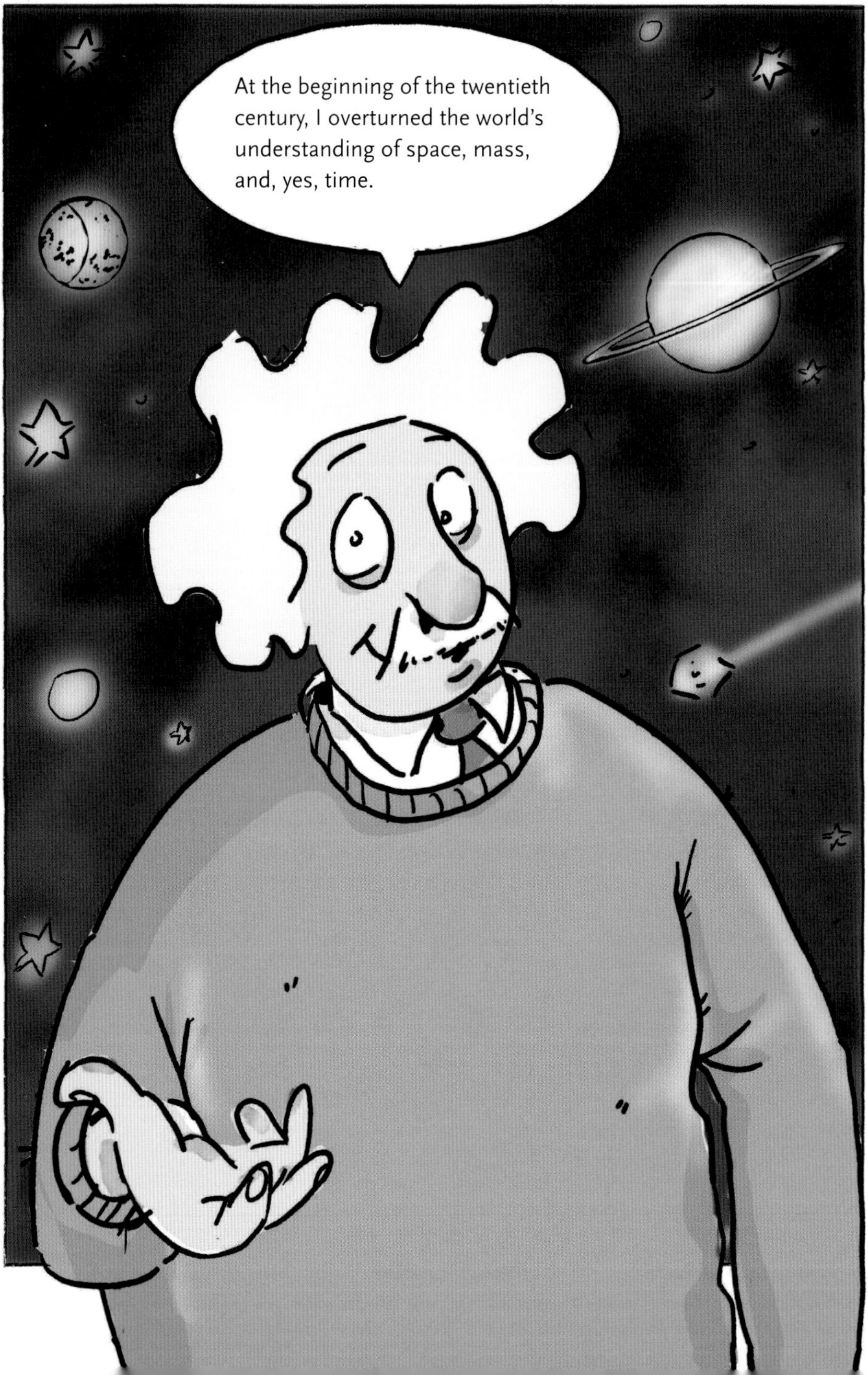
At the beginning of the twentieth century, I overturned the world's understanding of space, mass, and, yes, time.

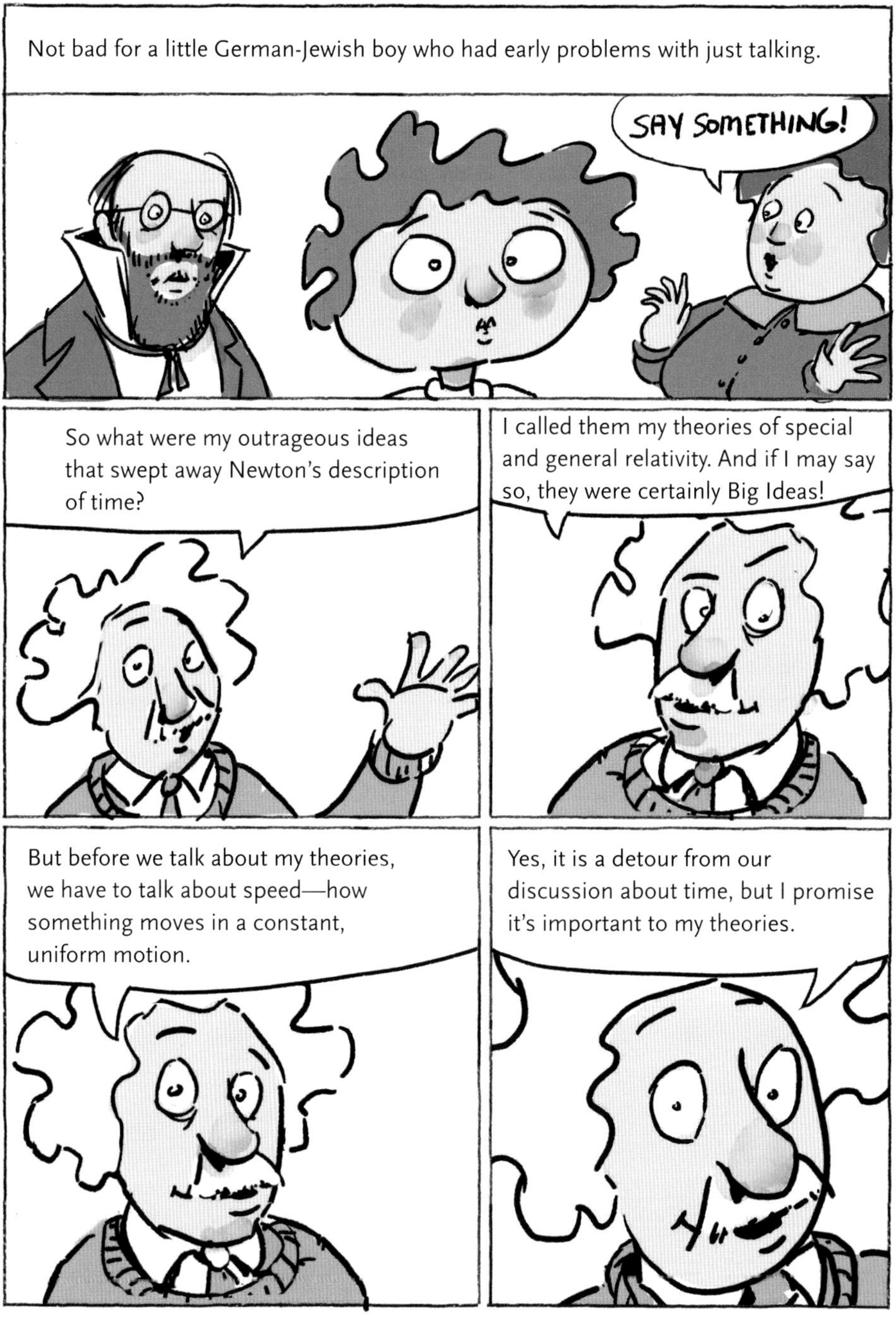
Not bad for a little German-Jewish boy who had early problems with just talking.
SAY SOMETHING!
So what were my outrageous ideas that swept away Newton's description of time?
I called them my theories of special and general relativity. And if I may say so, they were certainly Big Ideas!
But before we talk about my theories, we have to talk about speed—how something moves in a constant, uniform motion.
Yes, it is a detour from our discussion about time, but I promise it's important to my theories.

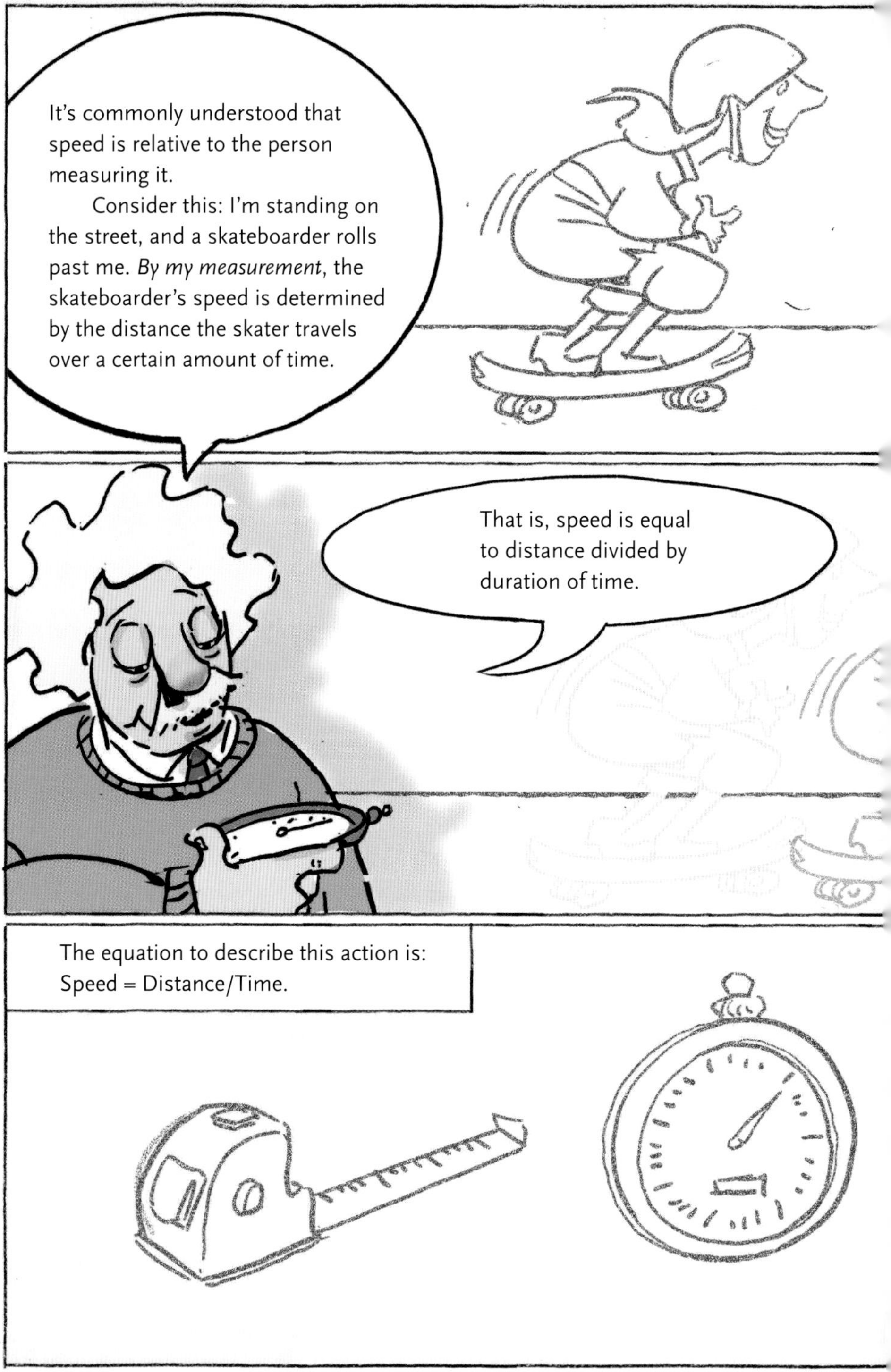
It's commonly understood that speed is relative to the person measuring it.
Consider this: I'm standing on the street, and a skateboarder rolls past me. *By my measurement*, the skateboarder's speed is determined by the distance the skater travels over a certain amount of time.
That is, speed is equal to distance divided by duration of time.
The equation to describe this action is: Speed = Distance/Time.

So if the skateboarder goes twenty miles in one hour, we can say the skater's speed is twenty miles an hour.

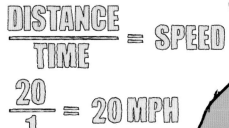

$$\frac{\text{DISTANCE}}{\text{TIME}} = \text{SPEED}$$

$$\frac{20}{1} = 20 \text{ MPH}$$

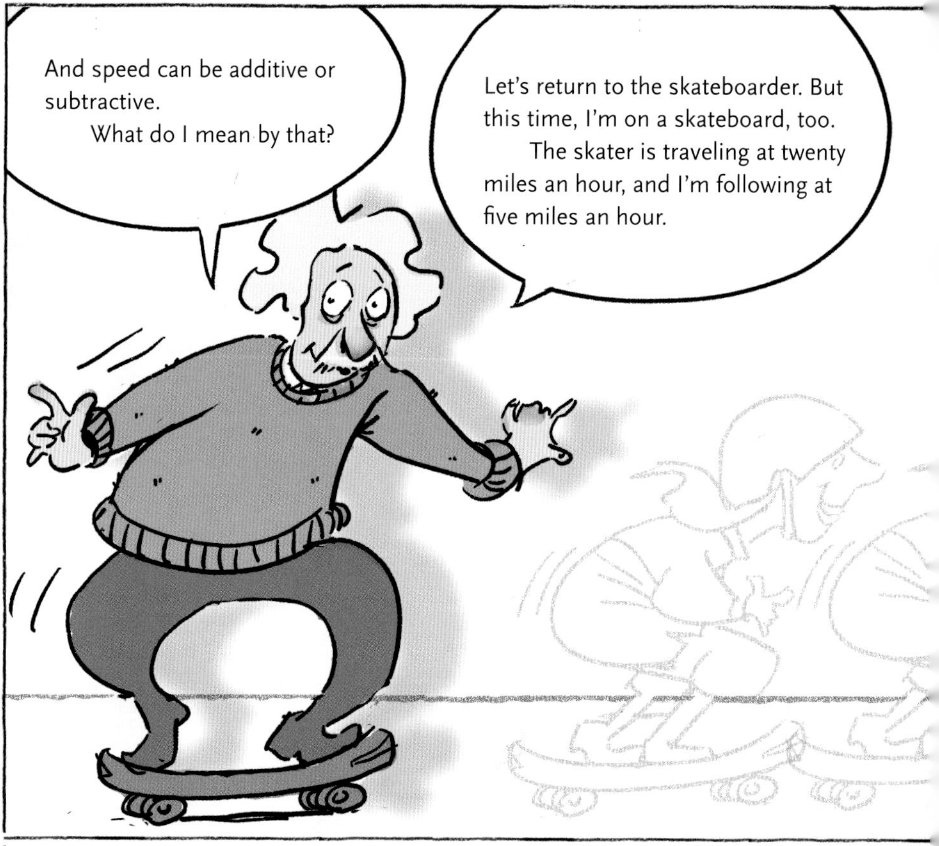
And speed can be additive or subtractive. What do I mean by that?
Let's return to the skateboarder. But this time, I'm on a skateboard, too. The skater is traveling at twenty miles an hour, and I'm following at five miles an hour.

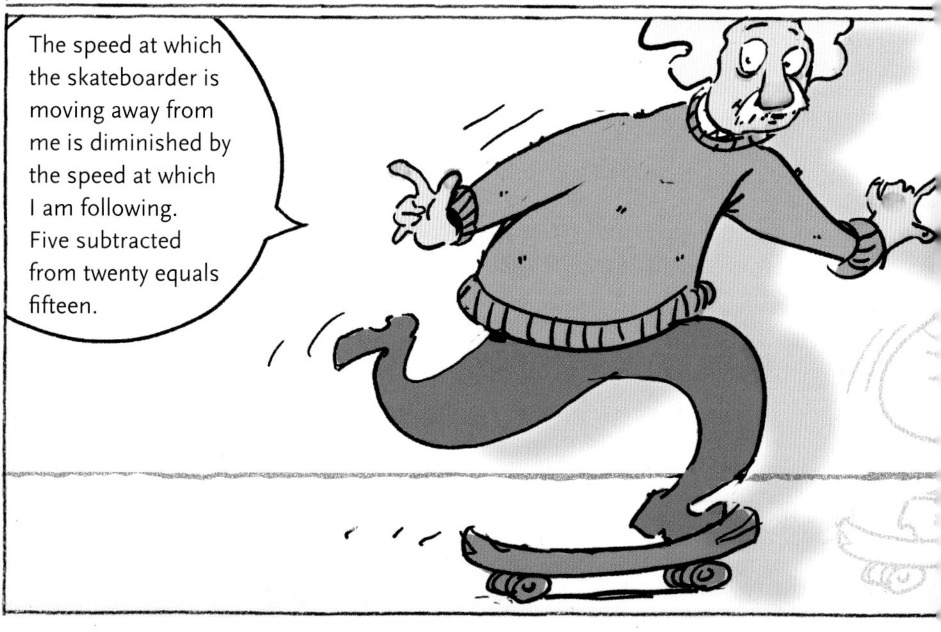
The speed at which the skateboarder is moving away from me is diminished by the speed at which I am following. Five subtracted from twenty equals fifteen.

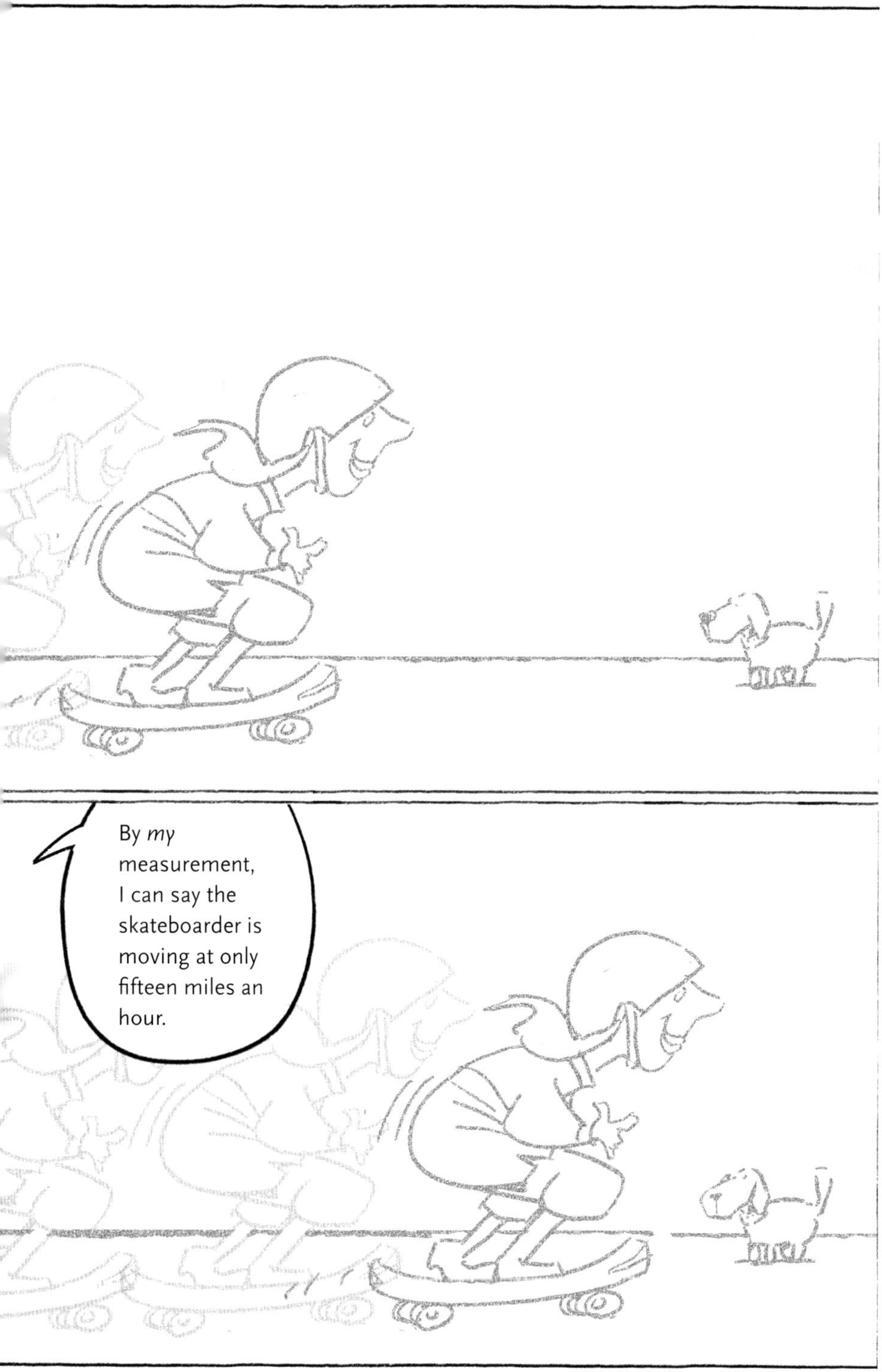
By *my* measurement, I can say the skateboarder is moving at only fifteen miles an hour.

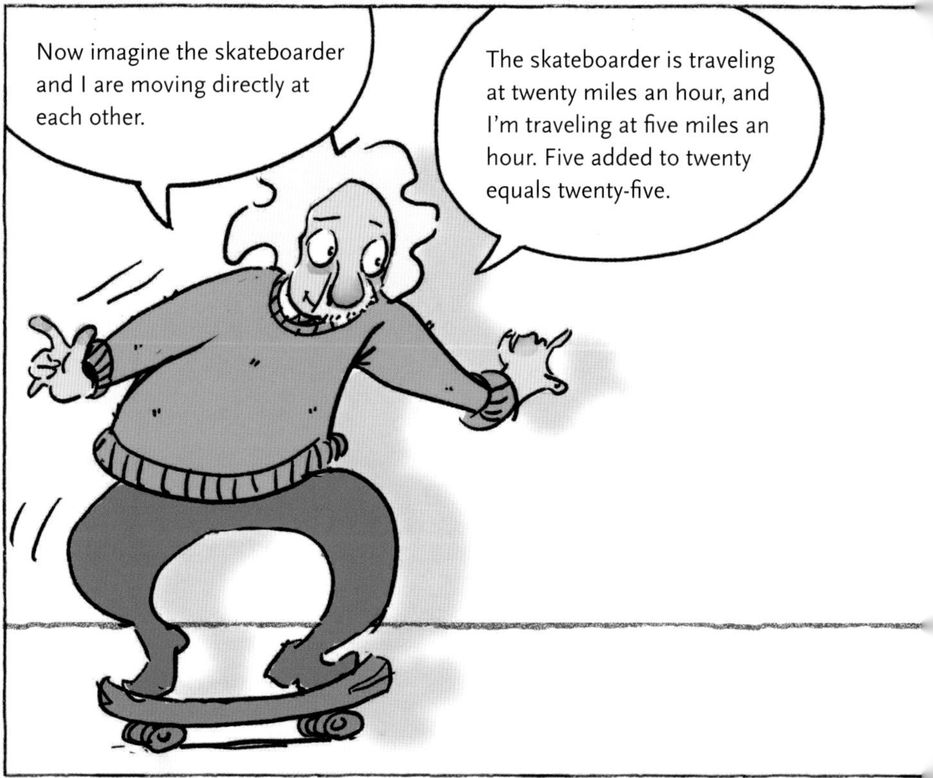
Now imagine the skateboarder and I are moving directly at each other.
The skateboarder is traveling at twenty miles an hour, and I'm traveling at five miles an hour. Five added to twenty equals twenty-five.

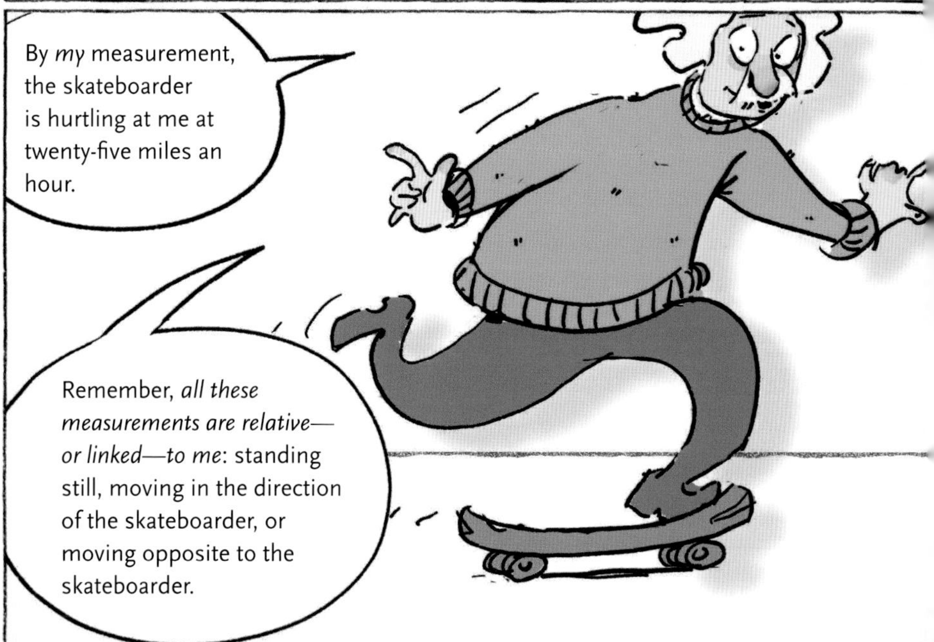
By *my* measurement, the skateboarder is hurtling at me at twenty-five miles an hour.
Remember, *all these measurements are relative—or linked—to me*: standing still, moving in the direction of the skateboarder, or moving opposite to the skateboarder.

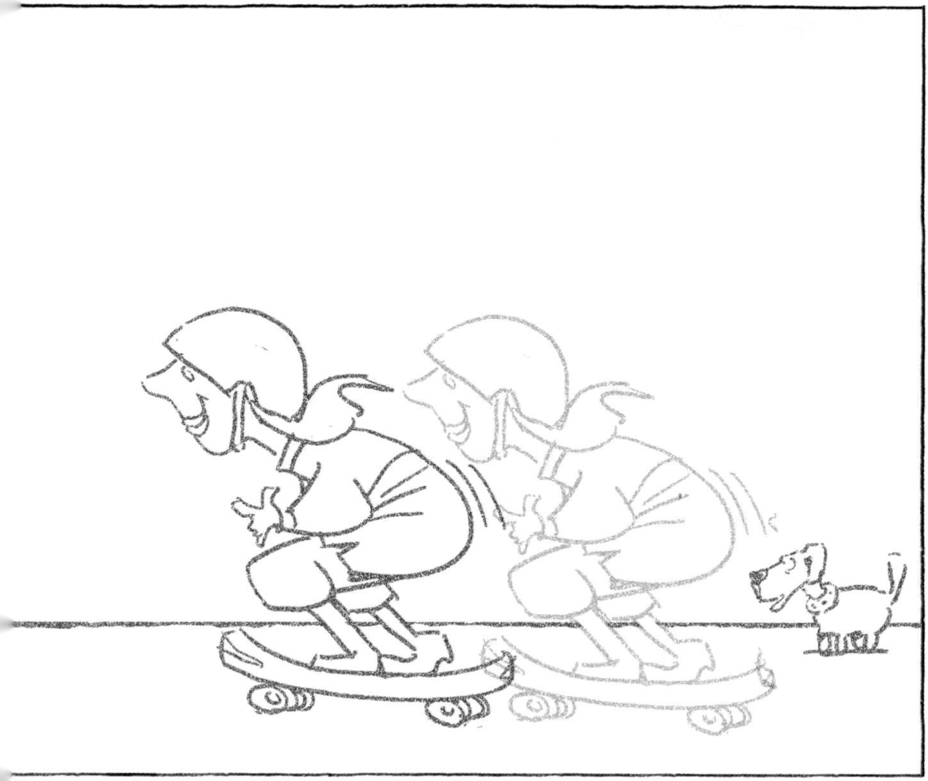
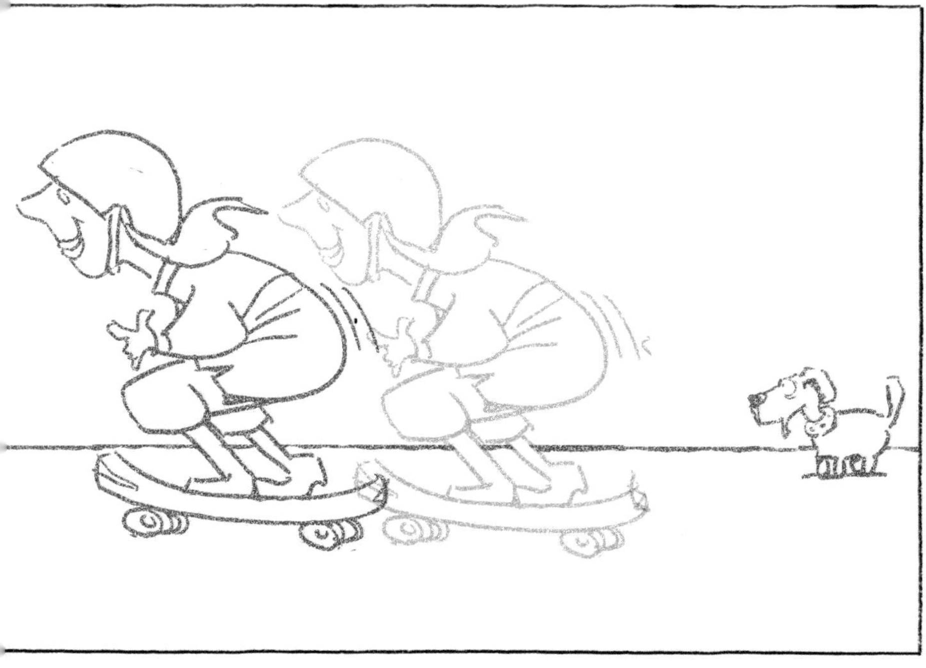

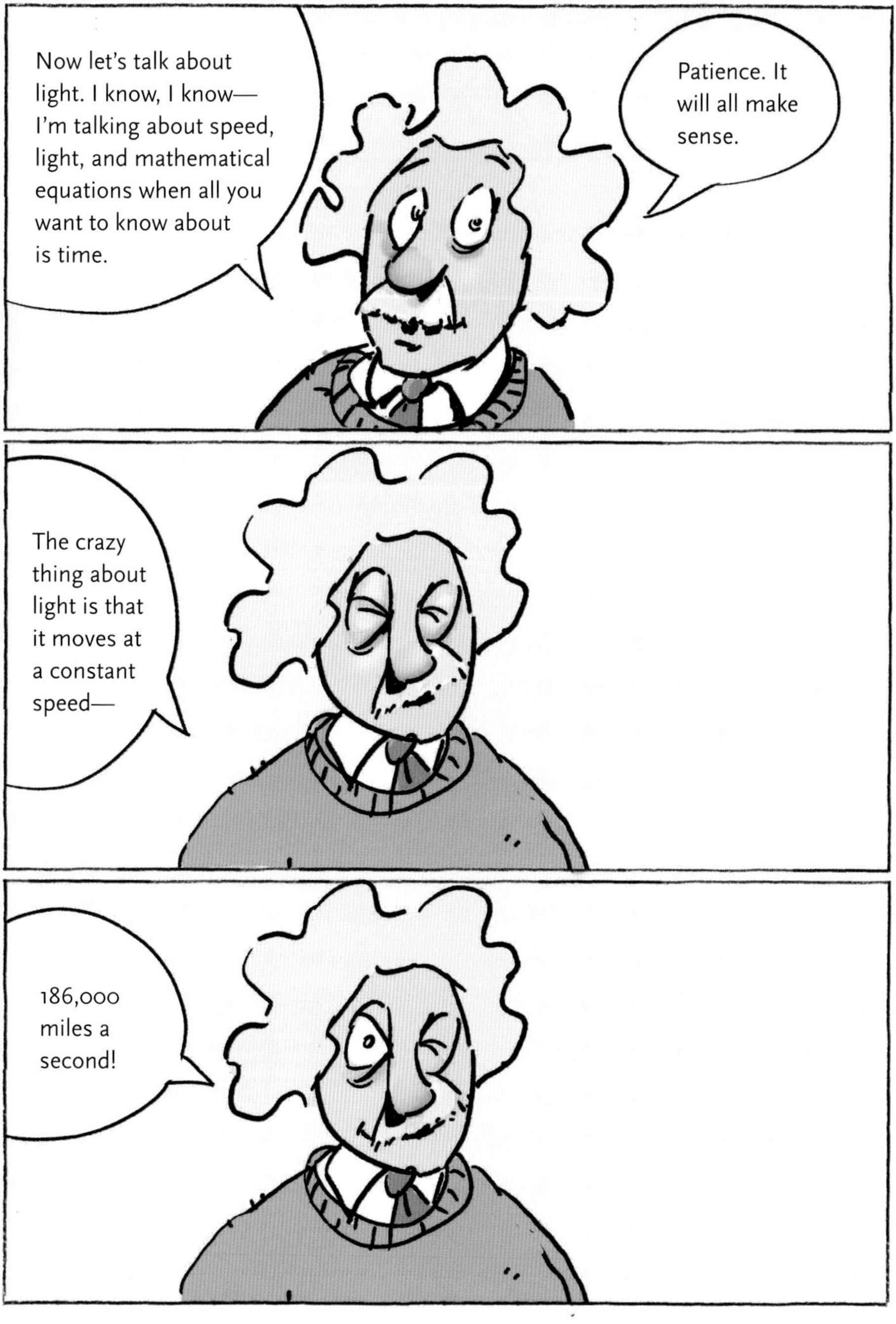
Now let's talk about light. I know, I know— I'm talking about speed, light, and mathematical equations when all you want to know about is time.
Patience. It will all make sense.
The crazy thing about light is that it moves at a constant speed—
186,000 miles a second!

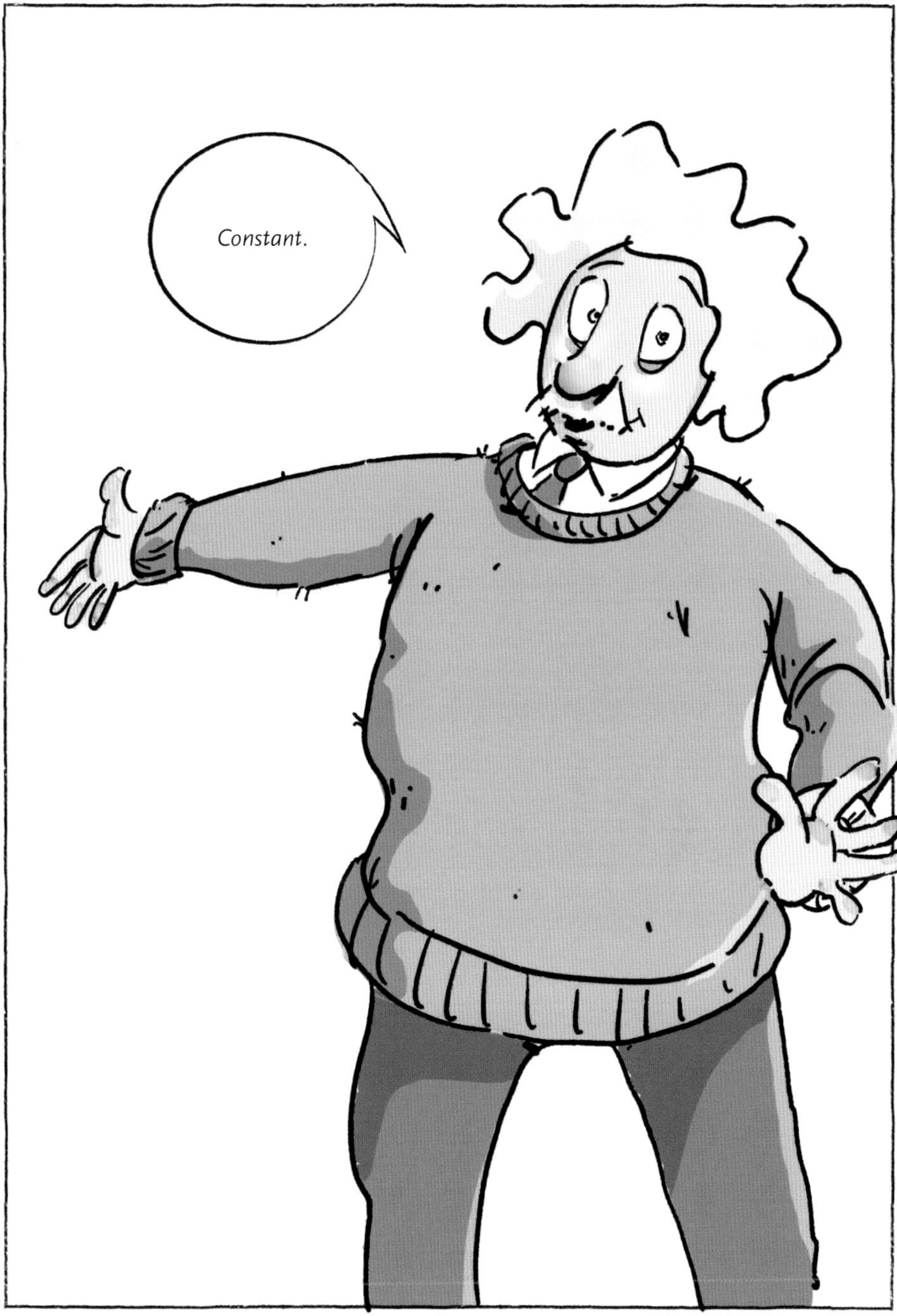
Constant.

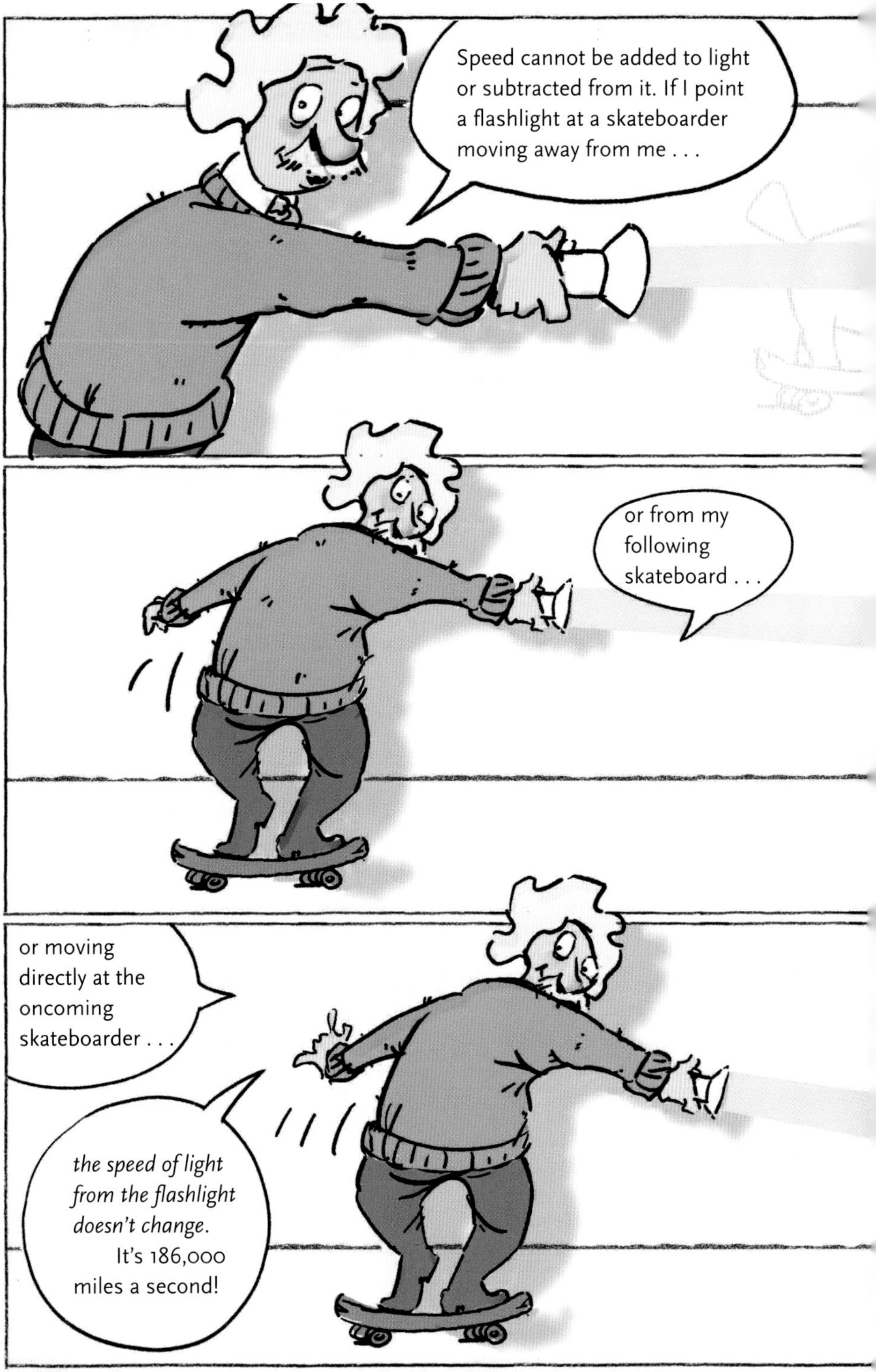
Speed cannot be added to light or subtracted from it. If I point a flashlight at a skateboarder moving away from me . . .
or from my following skateboard . . .
or moving directly at the oncoming skateboarder . . .
the speed of light from the flashlight doesn't change. It's 186,000 miles a second!

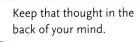

Keep that thought in the back of your mind.

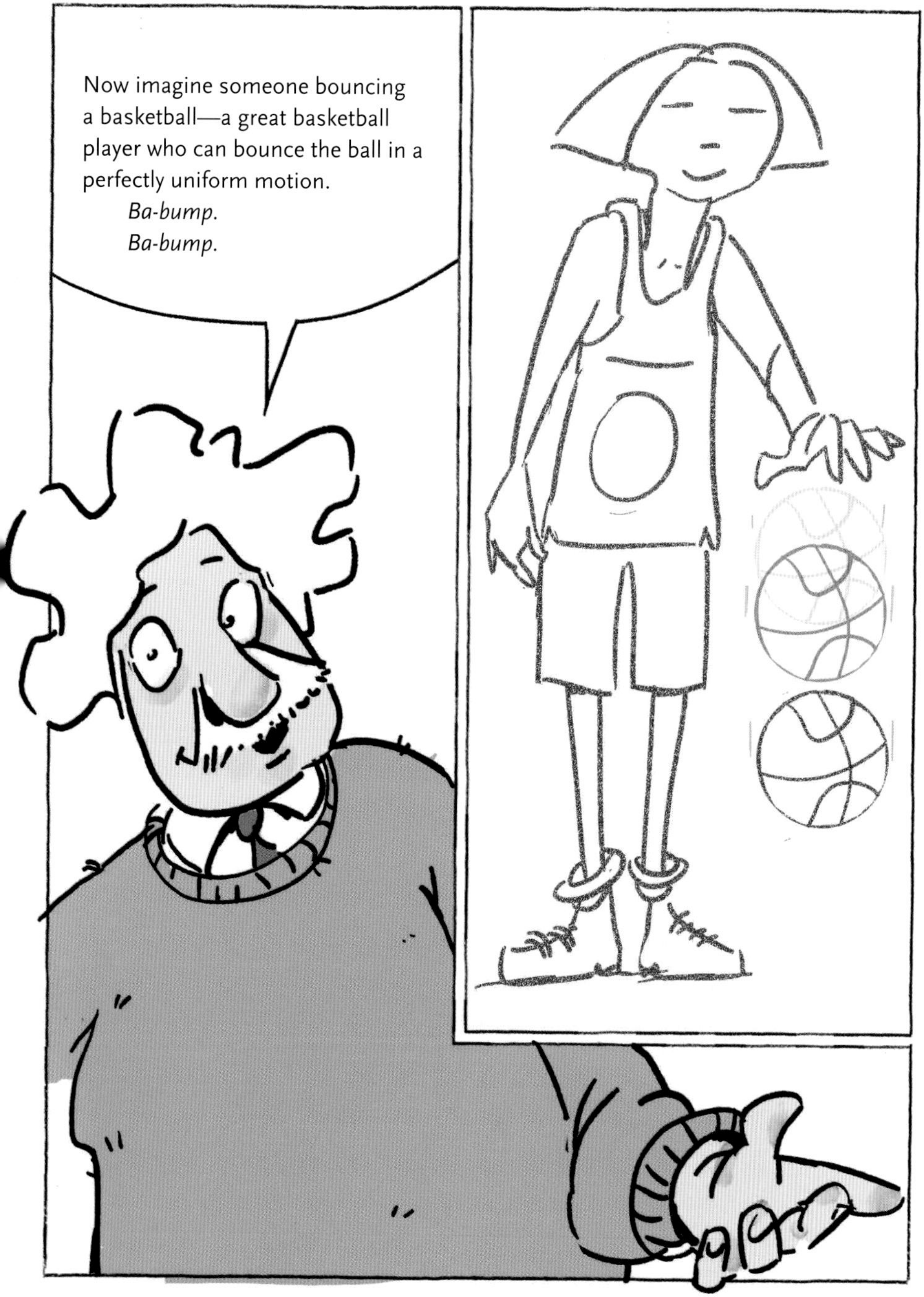
Now imagine someone bouncing a basketball—a great basketball player who can bounce the ball in a perfectly uniform motion.
Ba-bump.
Ba-bump.

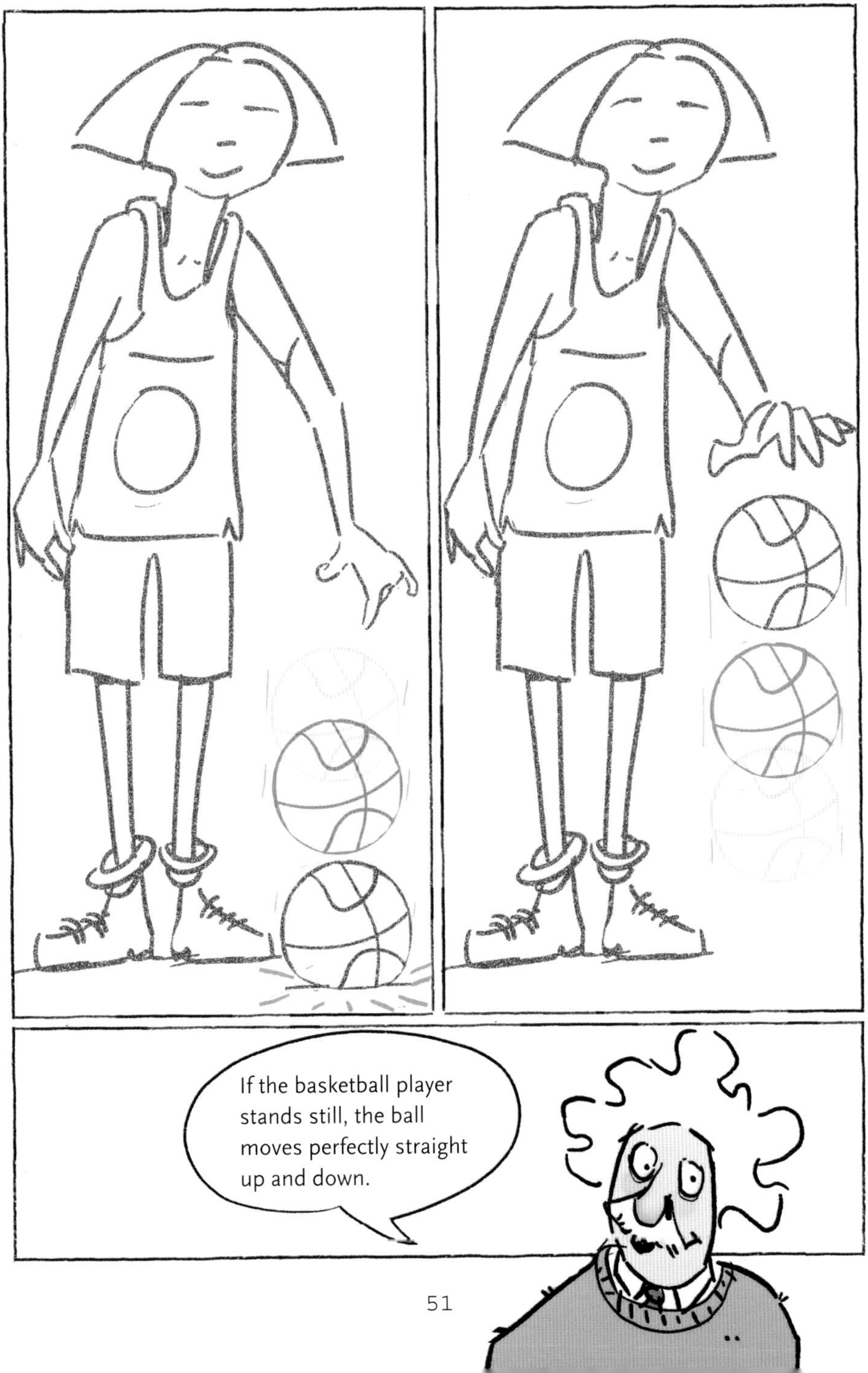
If the basketball player stands still, the ball moves perfectly straight up and down.

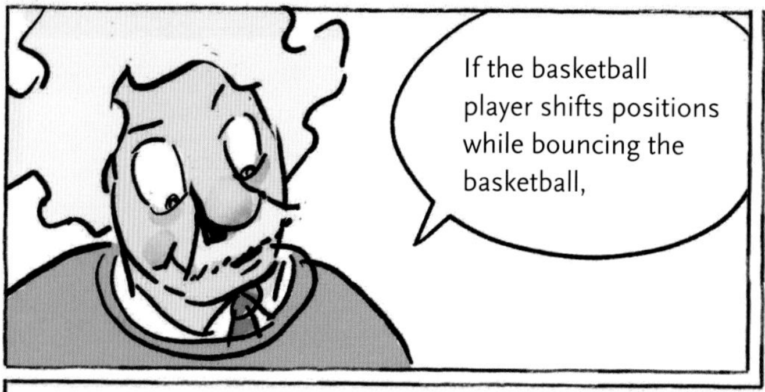
If the basketball player shifts positions while bouncing the basketball,

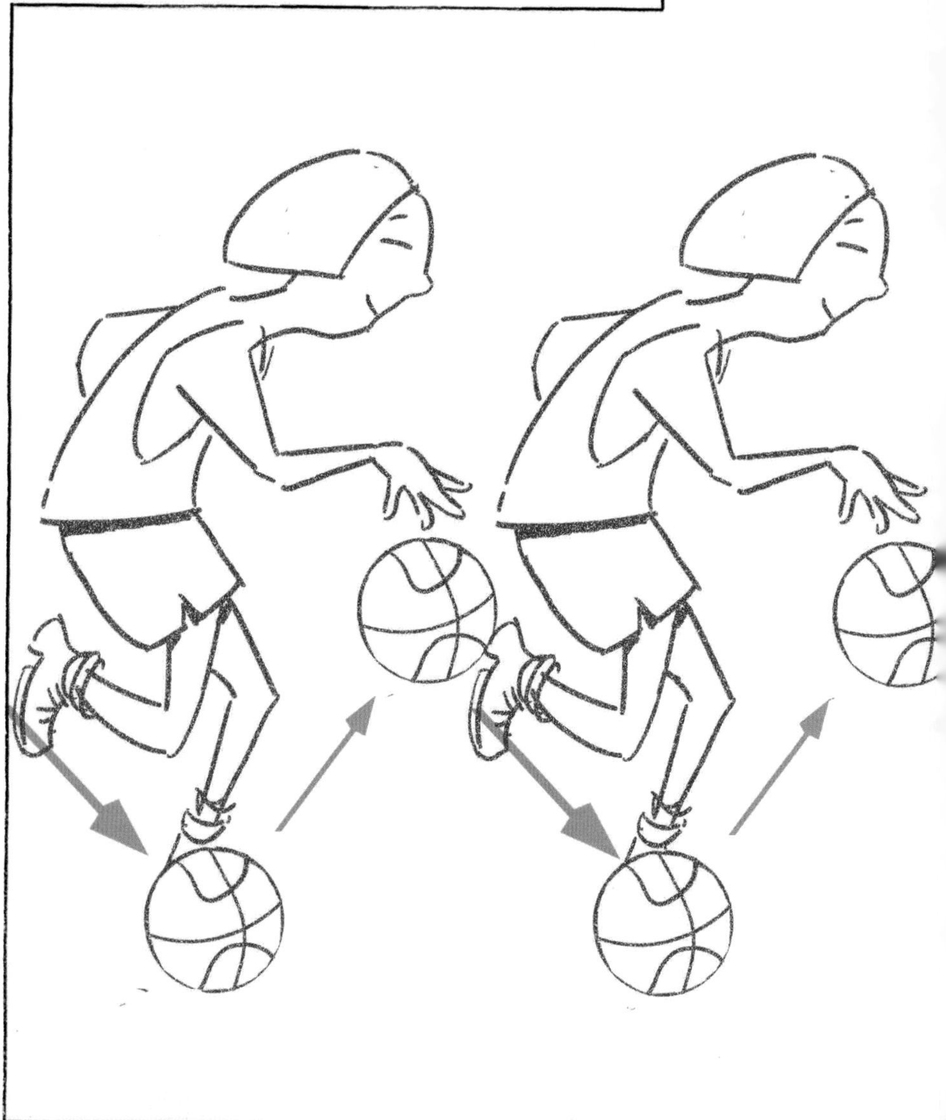

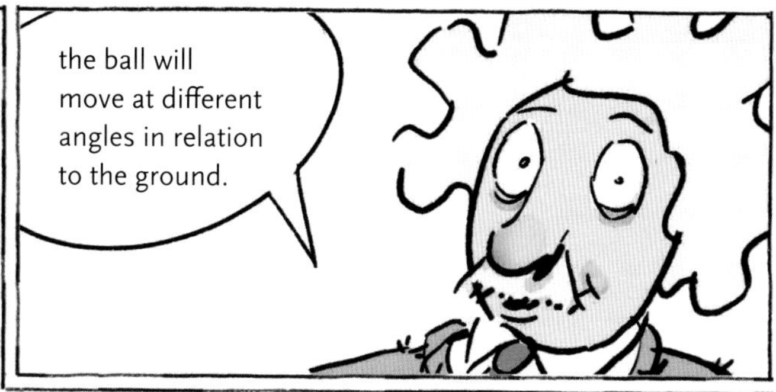
the ball will move at different angles in relation to the ground.

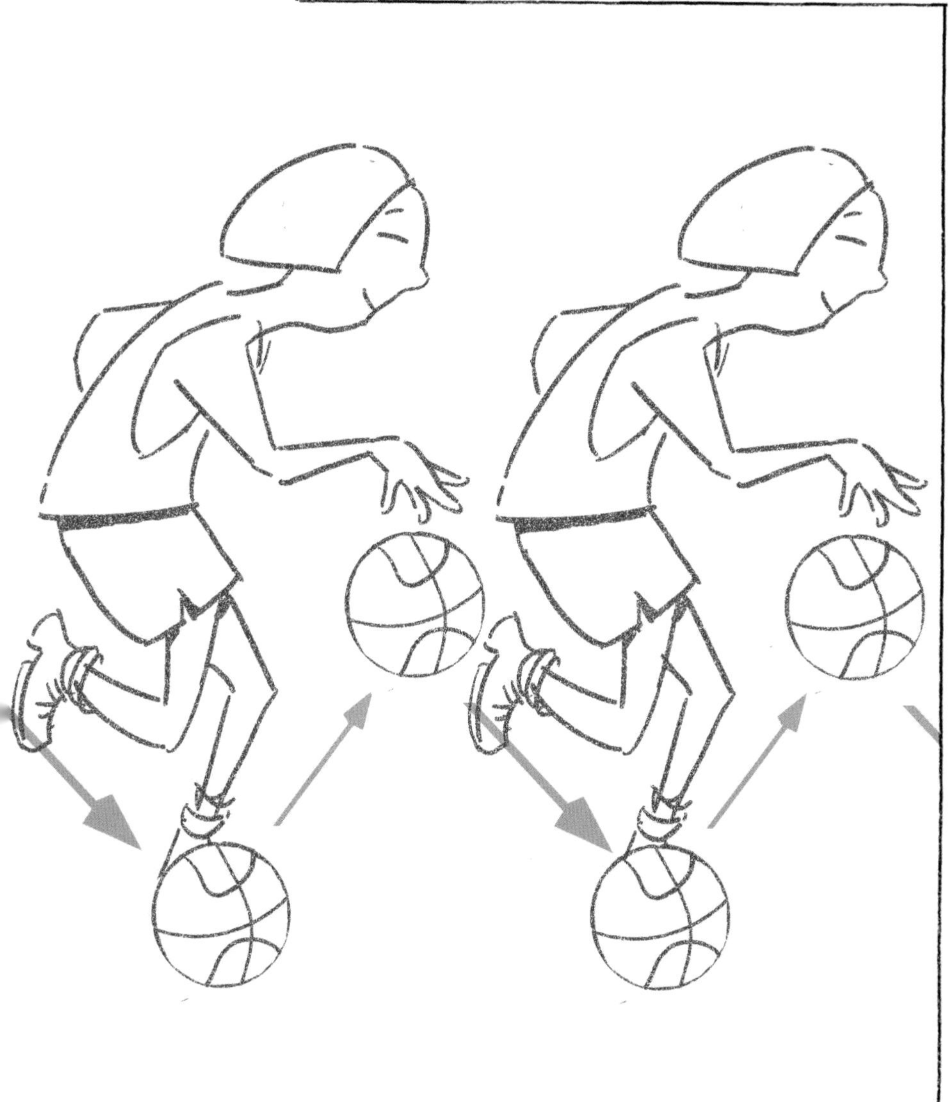

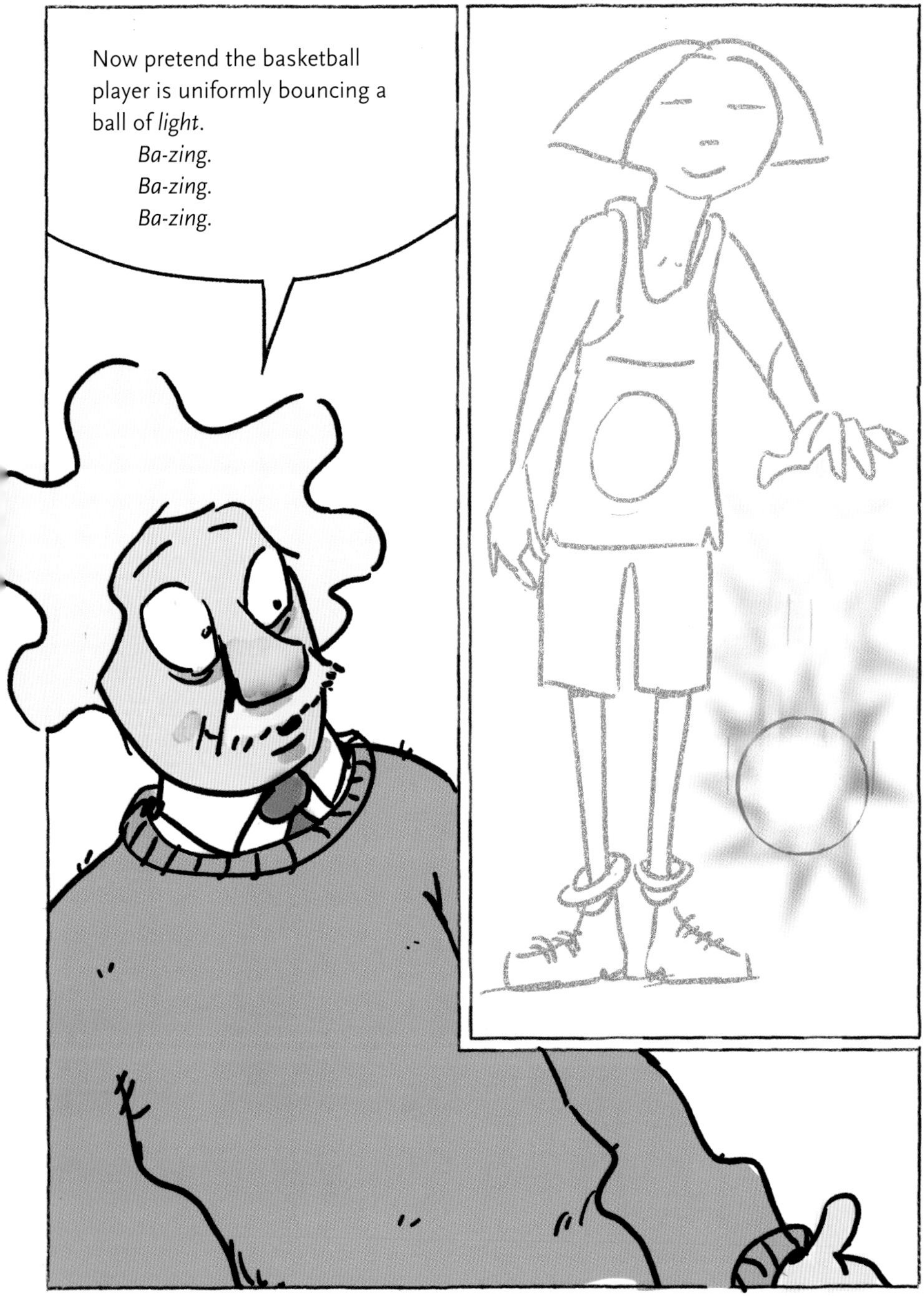
Now pretend the basketball player is uniformly bouncing a ball of *light*.
Ba-zing.
Ba-zing.
Ba-zing.

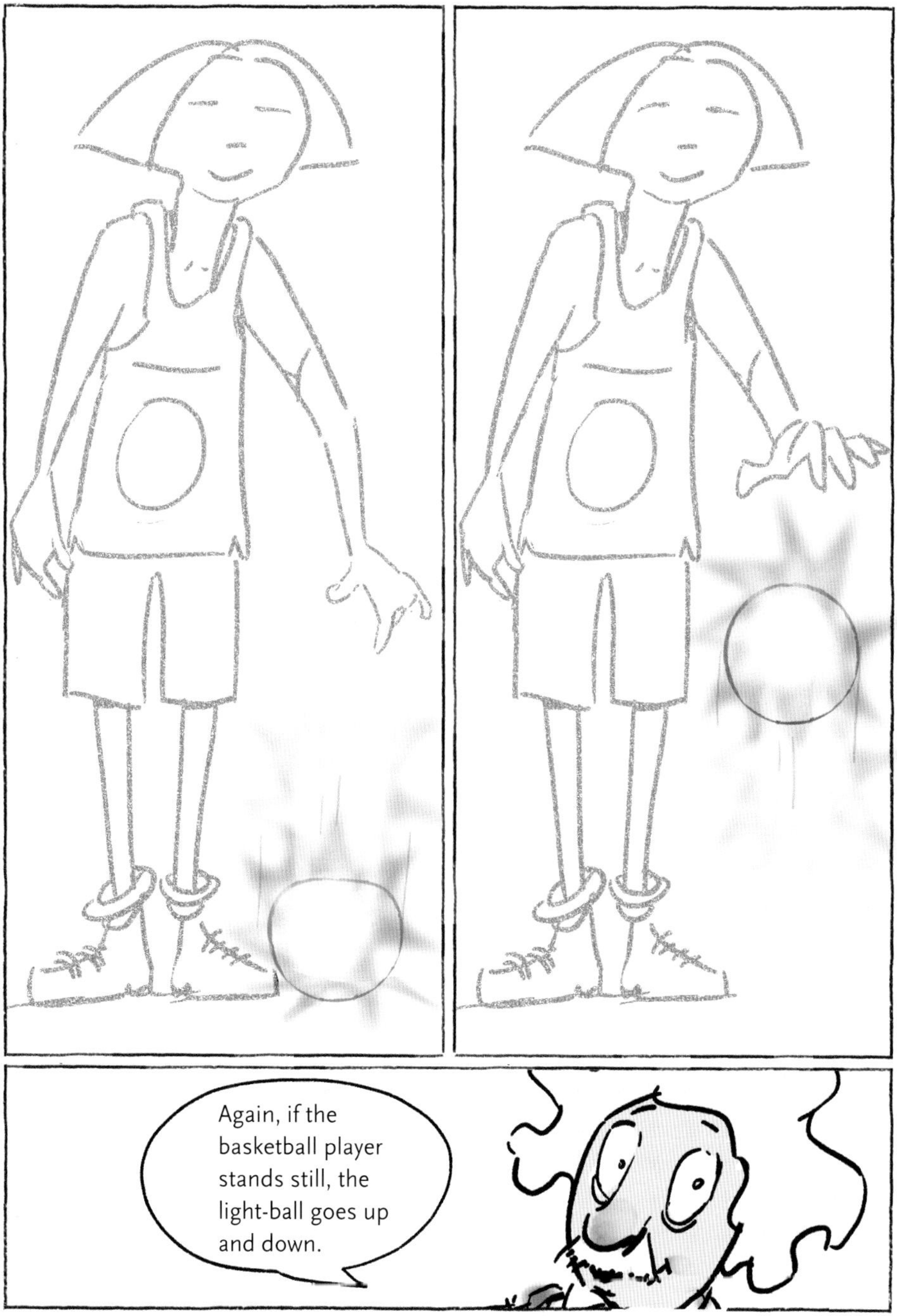
Again, if the basketball player stands still, the light-ball goes up and down.

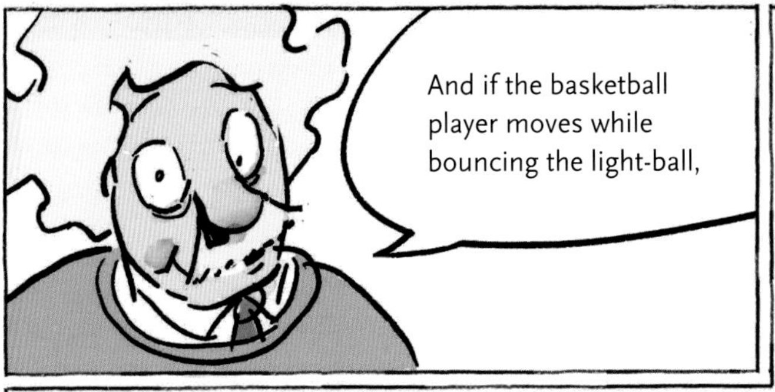
And if the basketball player moves while bouncing the light-ball,

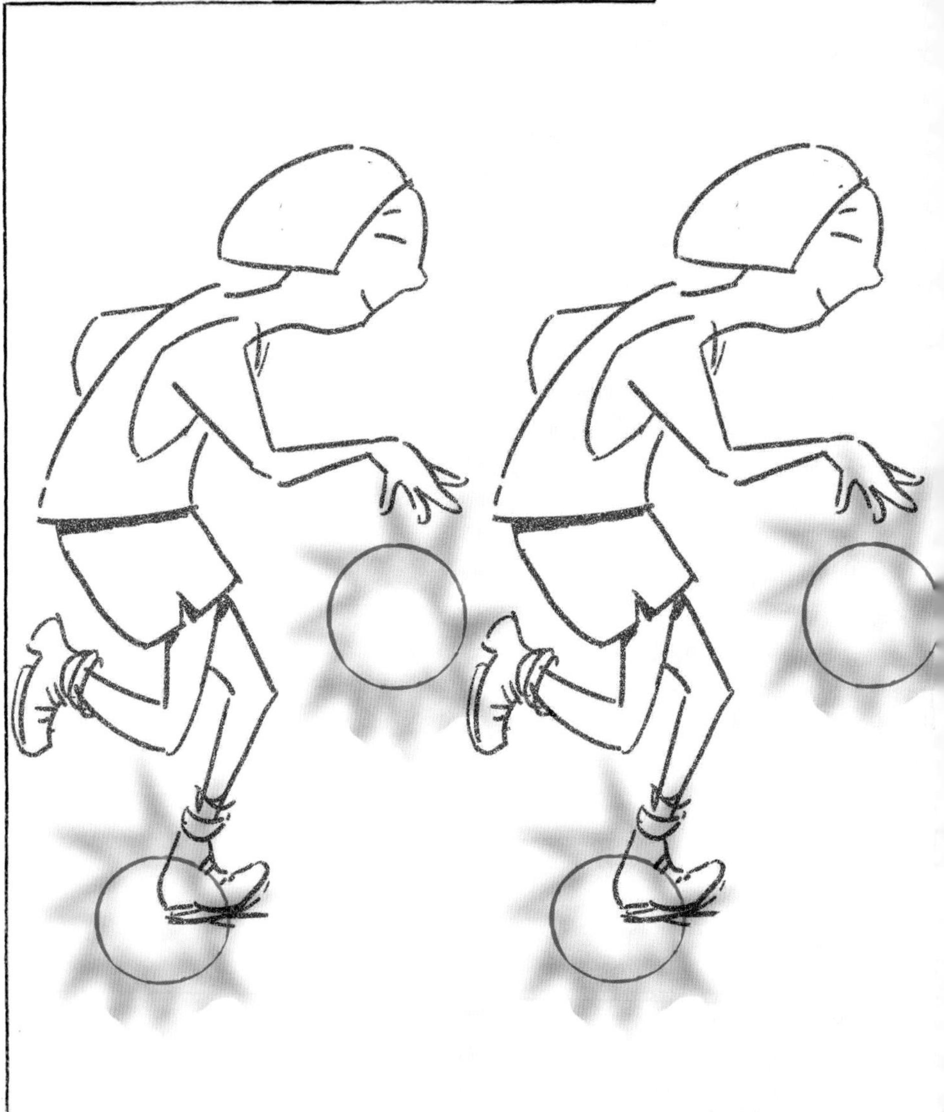

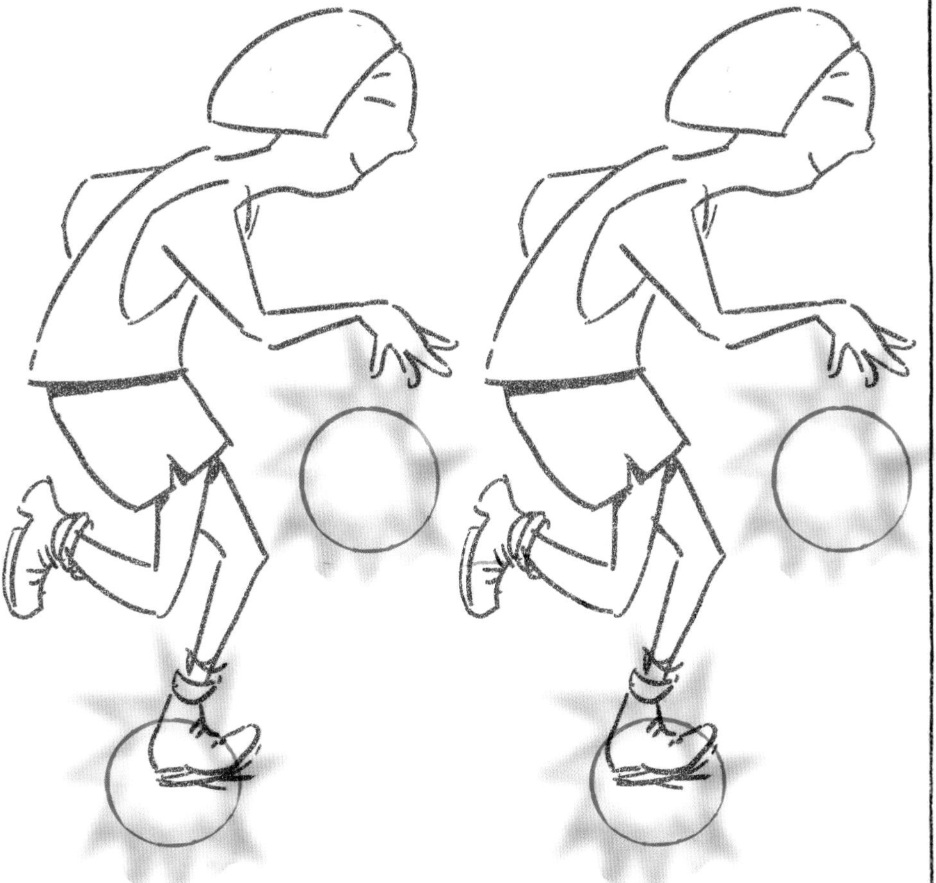

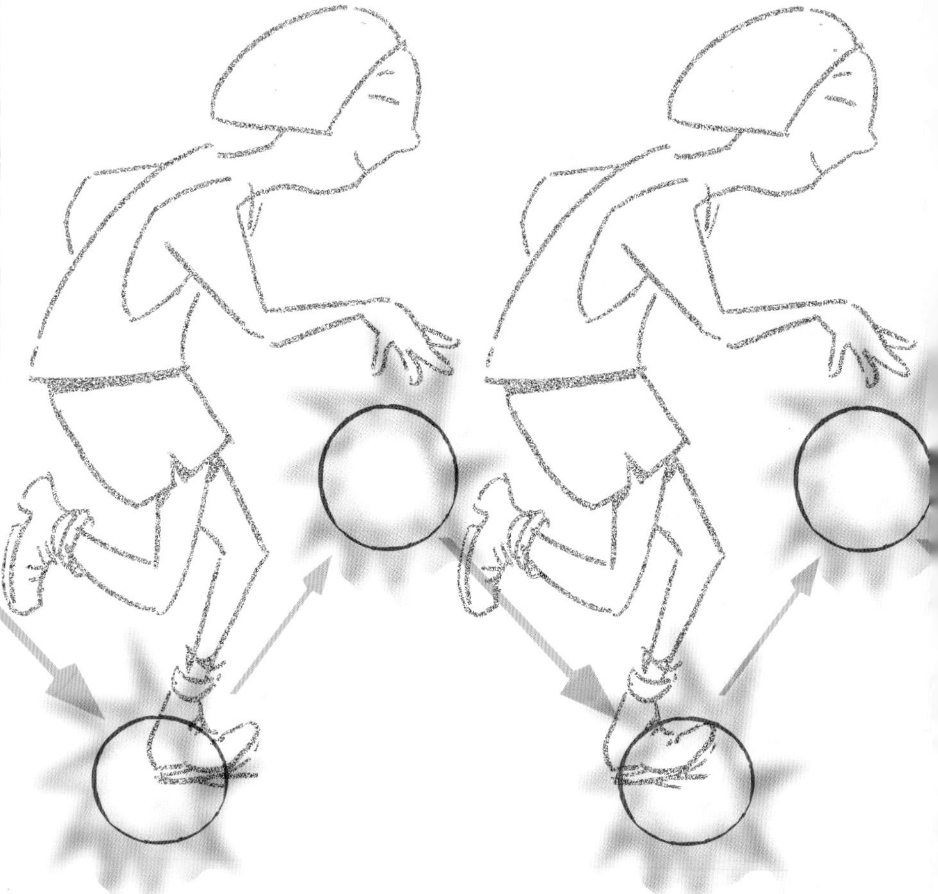

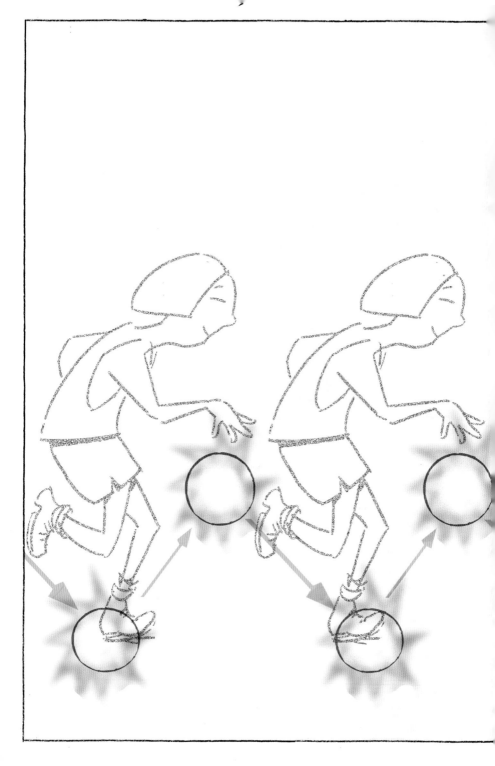

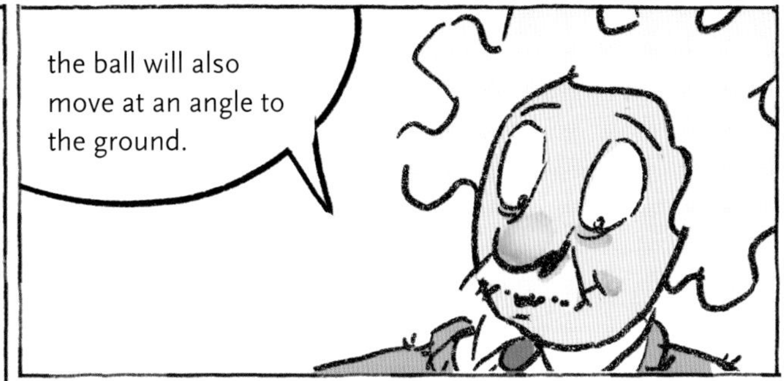
the ball will also move at an angle to the ground.

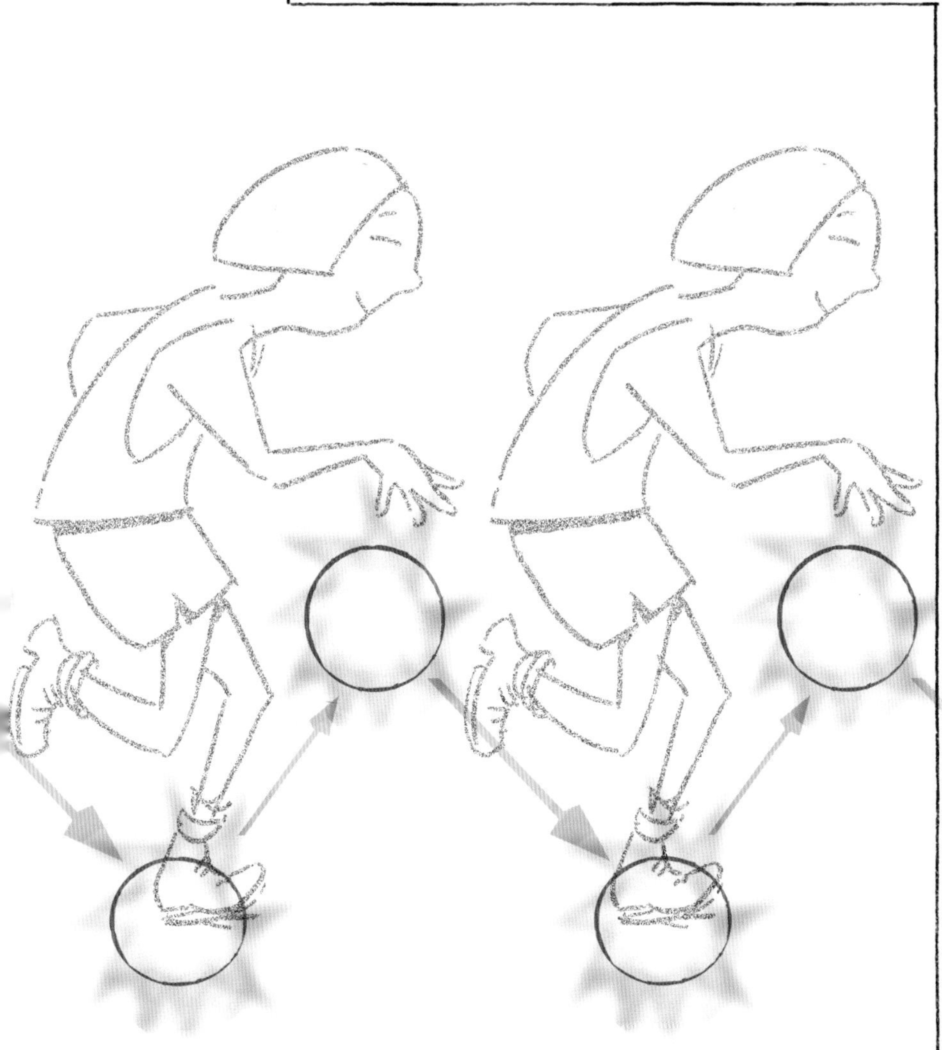

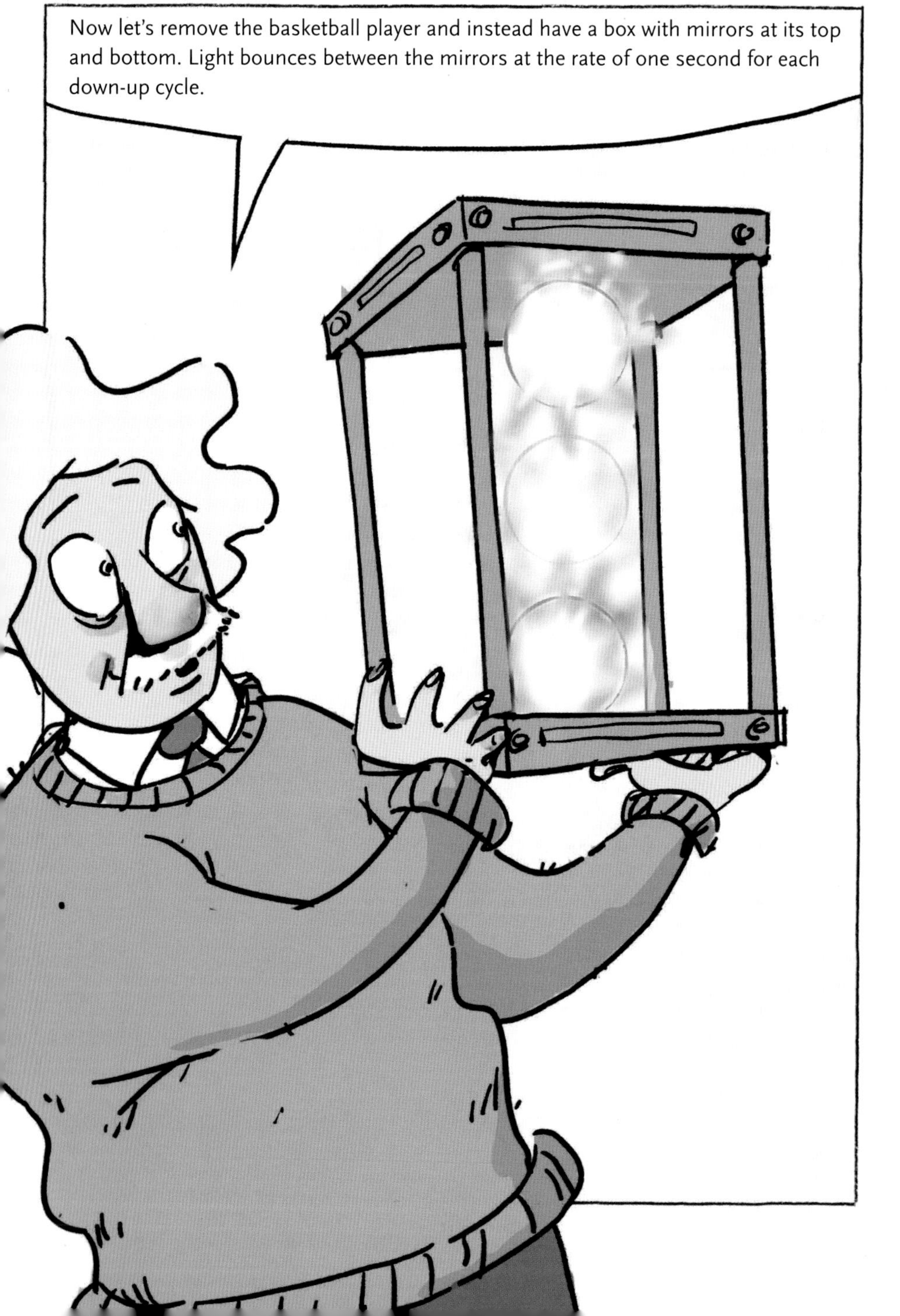
Now let's remove the basketball player and instead have a box with mirrors at its top and bottom. Light bounces between the mirrors at the rate of one second for each down-up cycle.

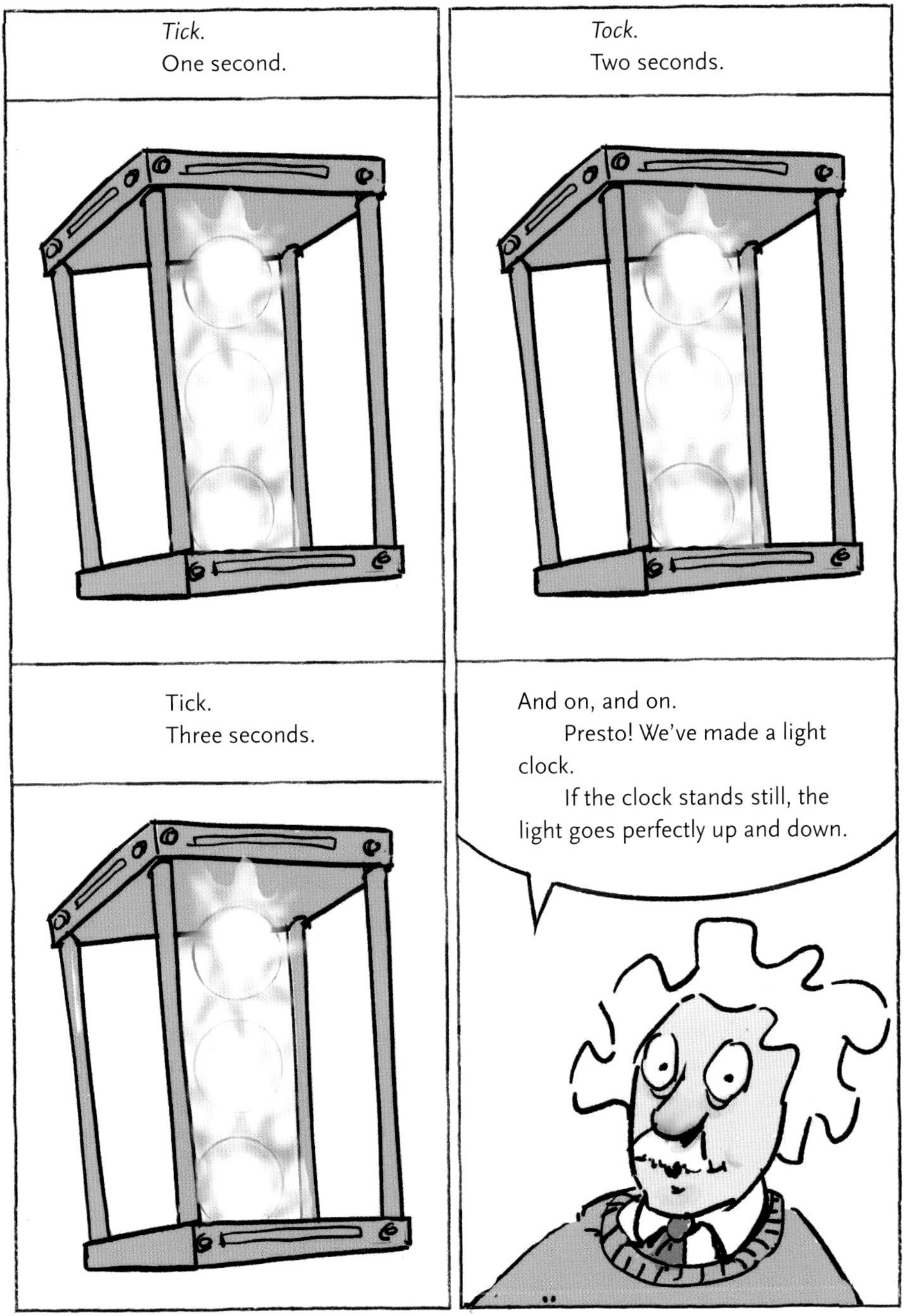
Tick.
One second.
Tock.
Two seconds.
Tick.
Three seconds.
And on, and on.
Presto! We've made a light clock.
If the clock stands still, the light goes perfectly up and down.

And if the light box moves while the light bounces between mirrors,

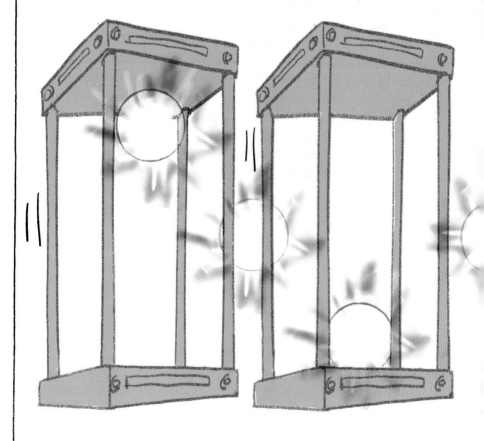

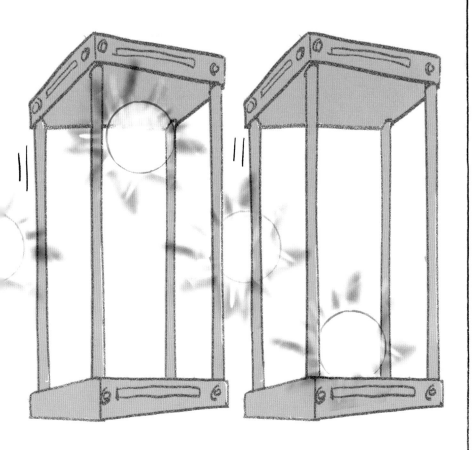

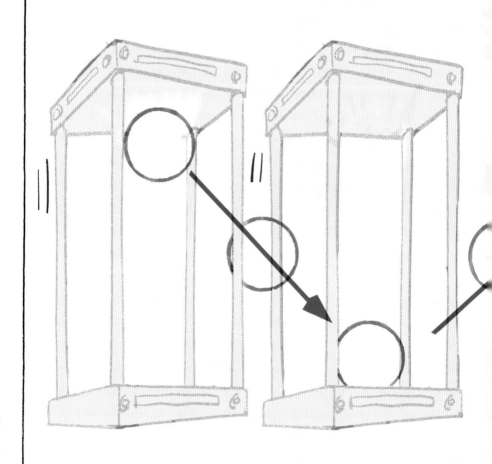

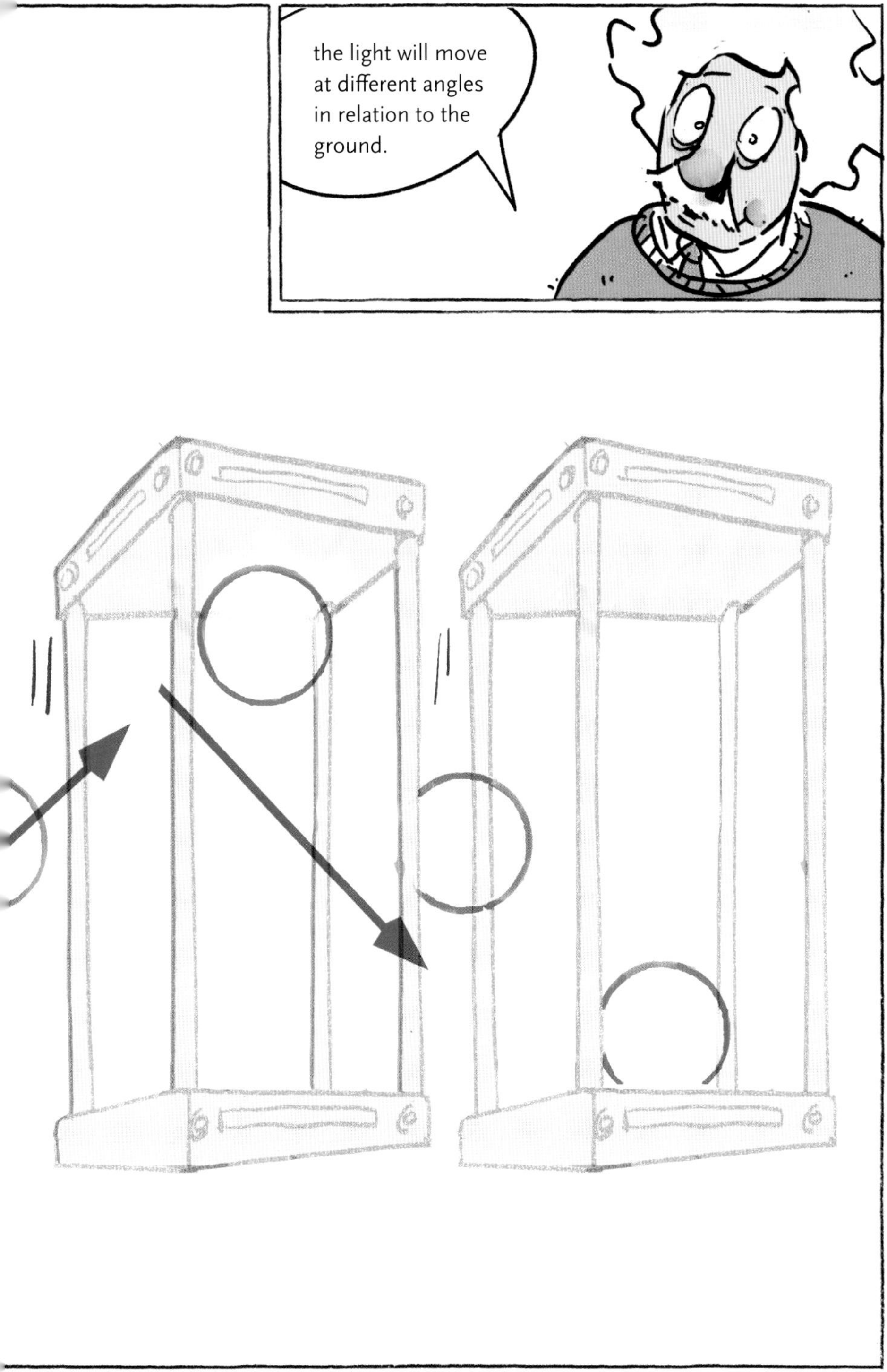
the light will move
at different angles
in relation to the
ground.

The distance the light travels at angles is *longer* than the distance light travels when it is only going up and down.

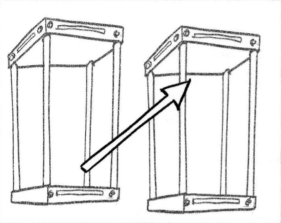

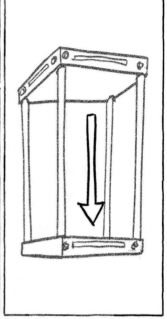

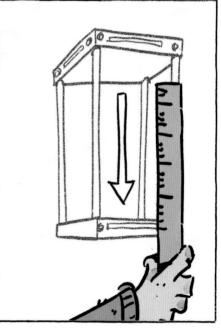

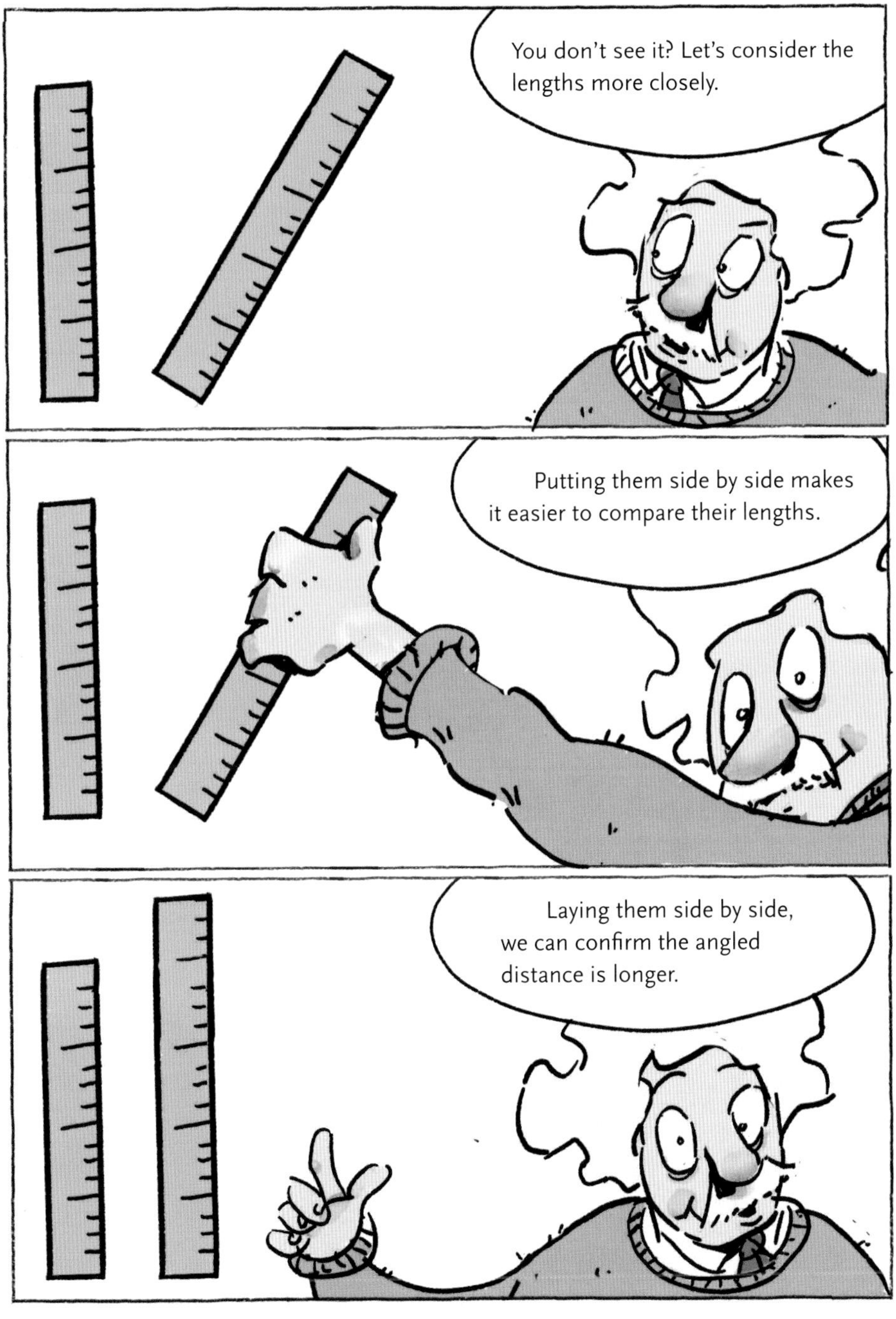
You don't see it? Let's consider the lengths more closely.
Putting them side by side makes it easier to compare their lengths.
Laying them side by side, we can confirm the angled distance is longer.

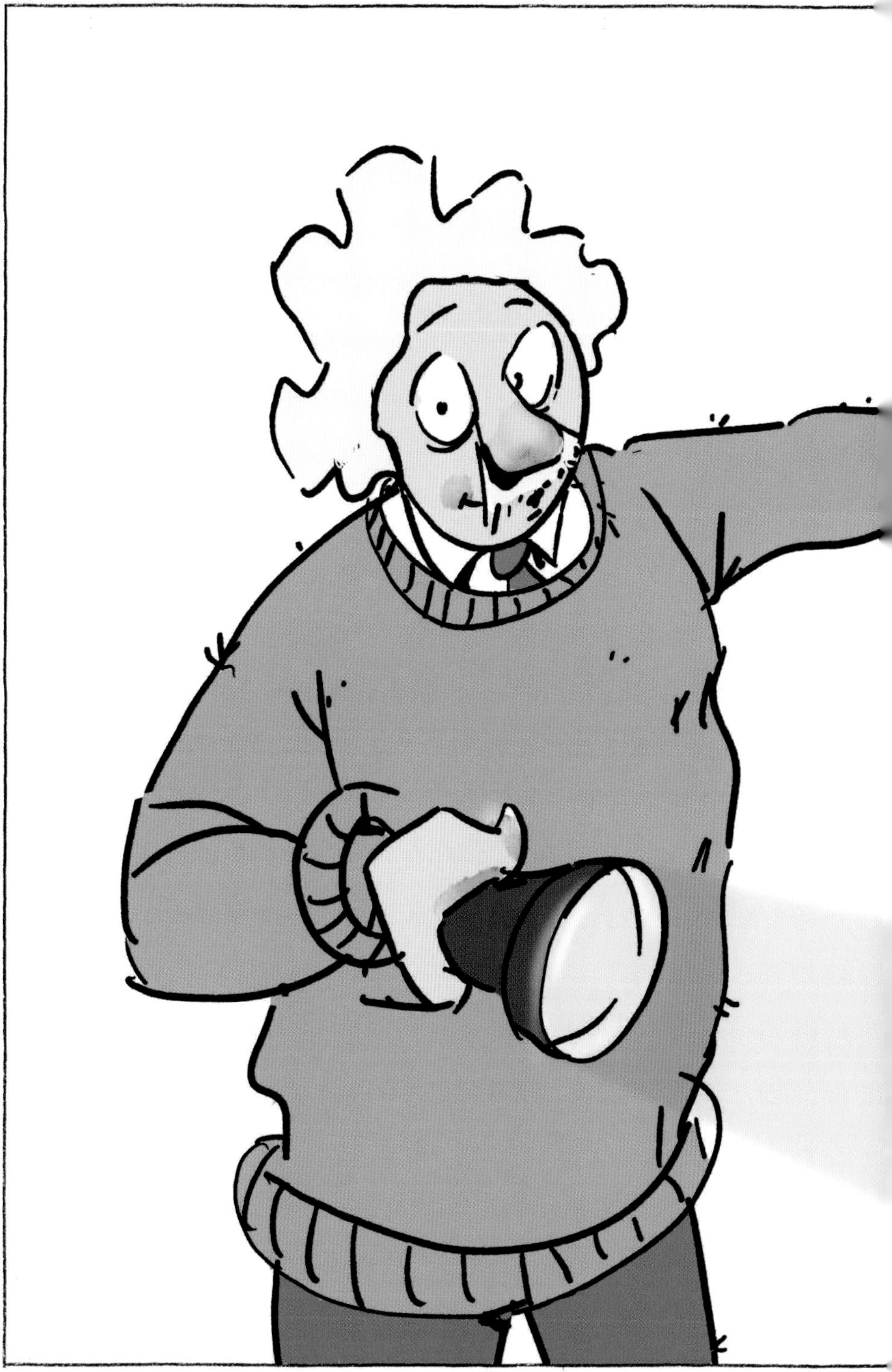

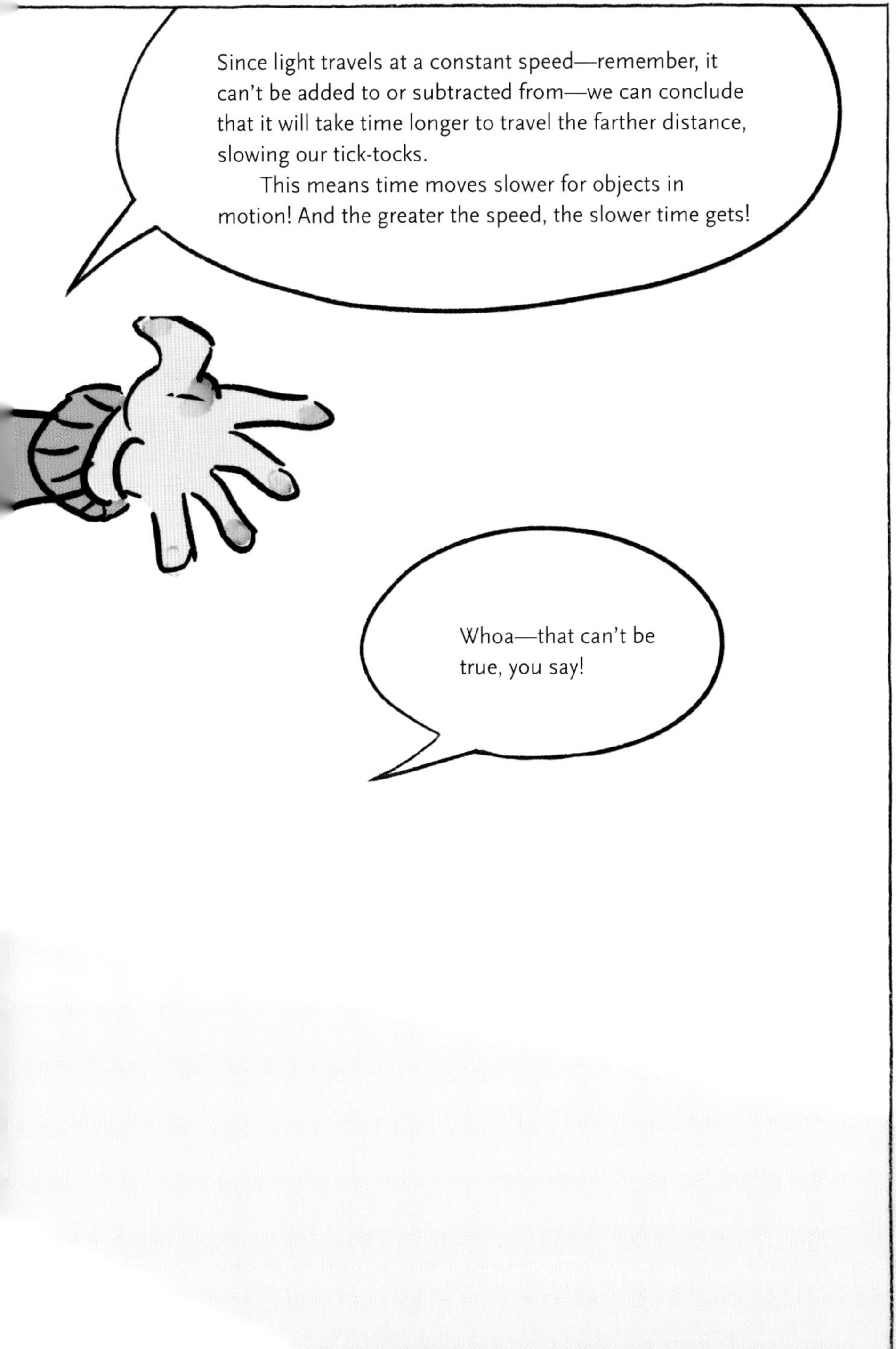
Since light travels at a constant speed—remember, it can't be added to or subtracted from—we can conclude that it will take time longer to travel the farther distance, slowing our tick-tocks.
This means time moves slower for objects in motion! And the greater the speed, the slower time gets!
Whoa—that can't be true, you say!

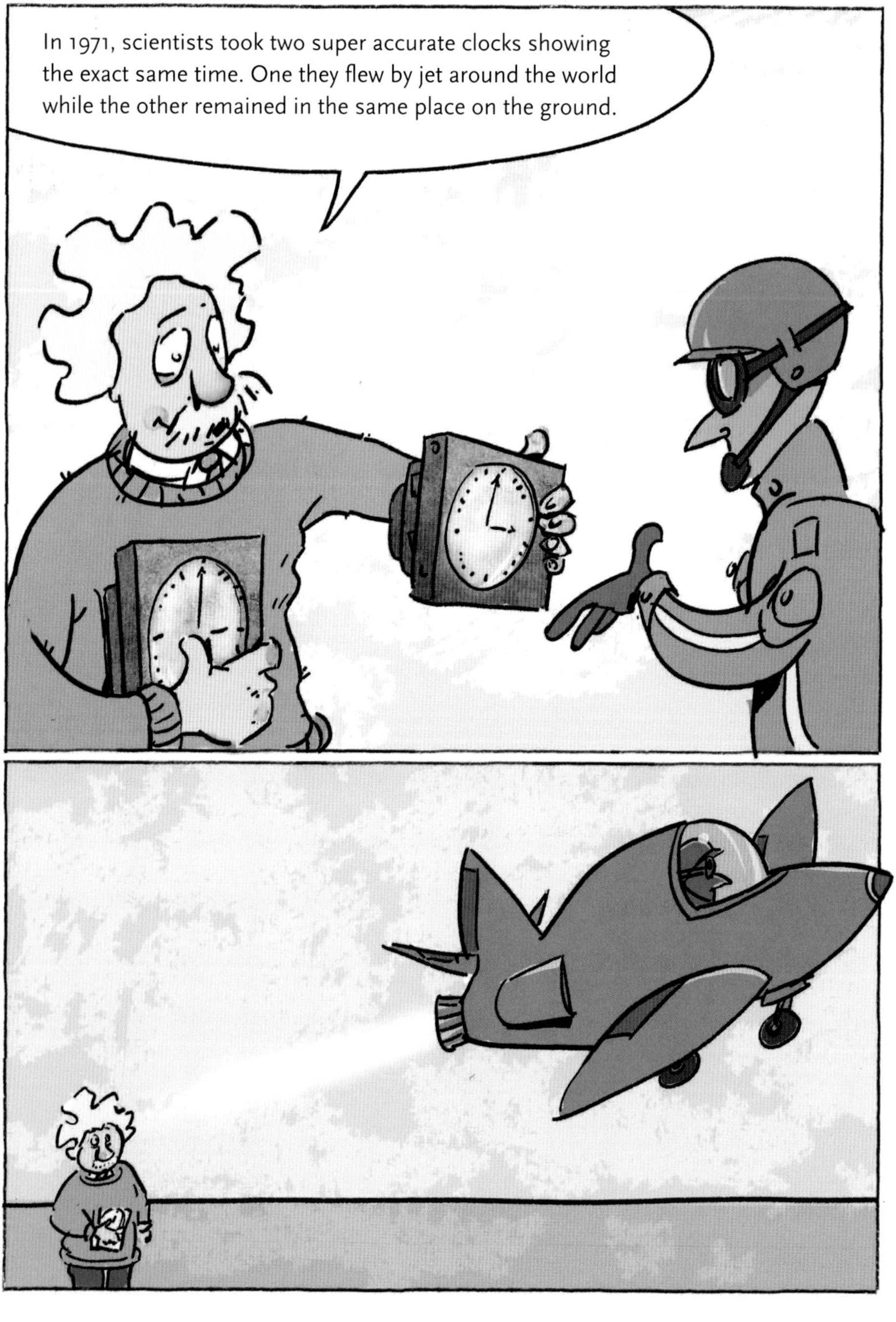
In 1971, scientists took two super accurate clocks showing the exact same time. One they flew by jet around the world while the other remained in the same place on the ground.

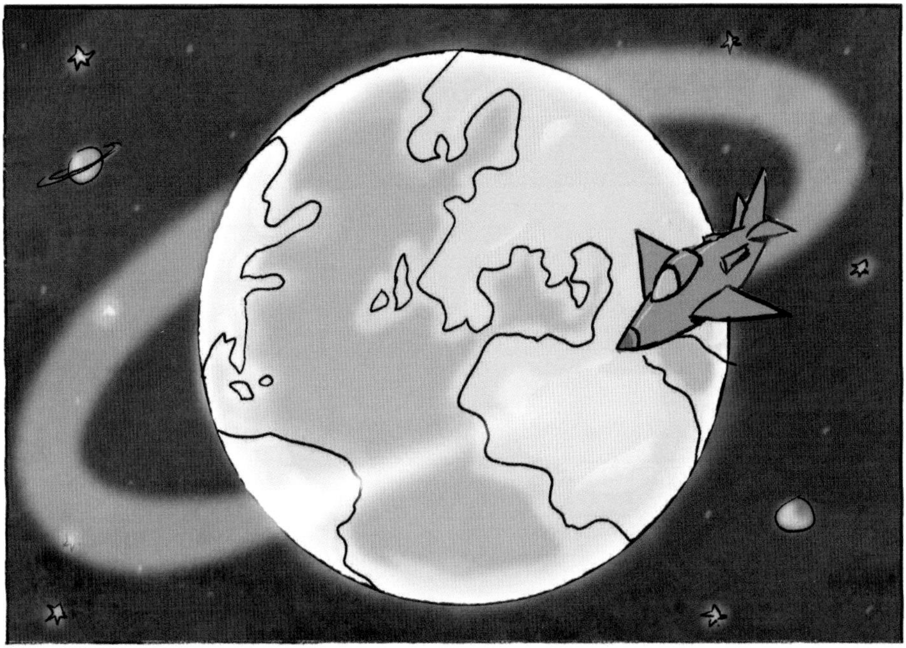

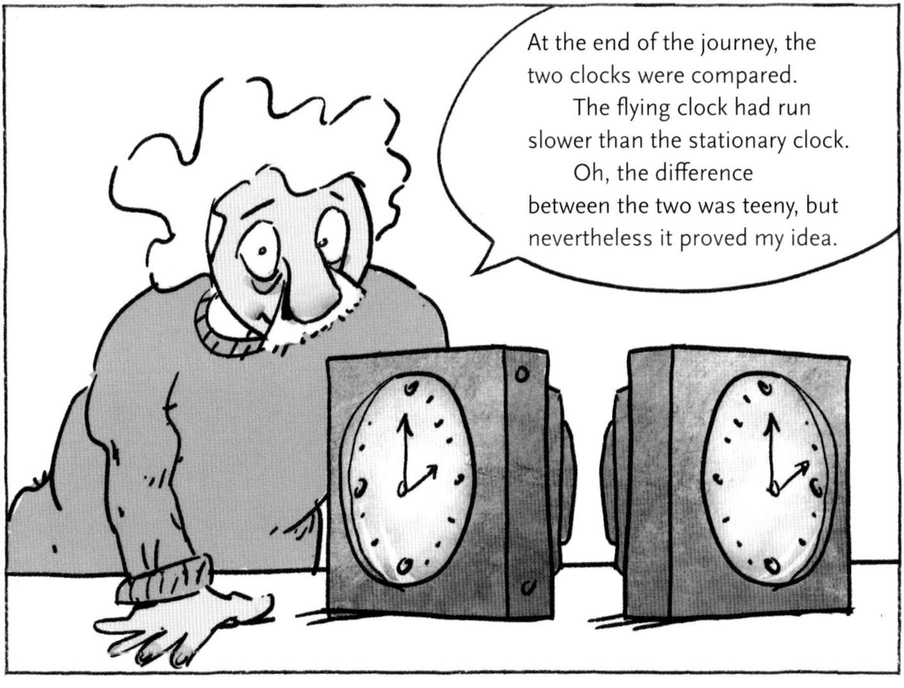
At the end of the journey, the two clocks were compared.
The flying clock had run slower than the stationary clock.
Oh, the difference between the two was teeny, but nevertheless it proved my idea.

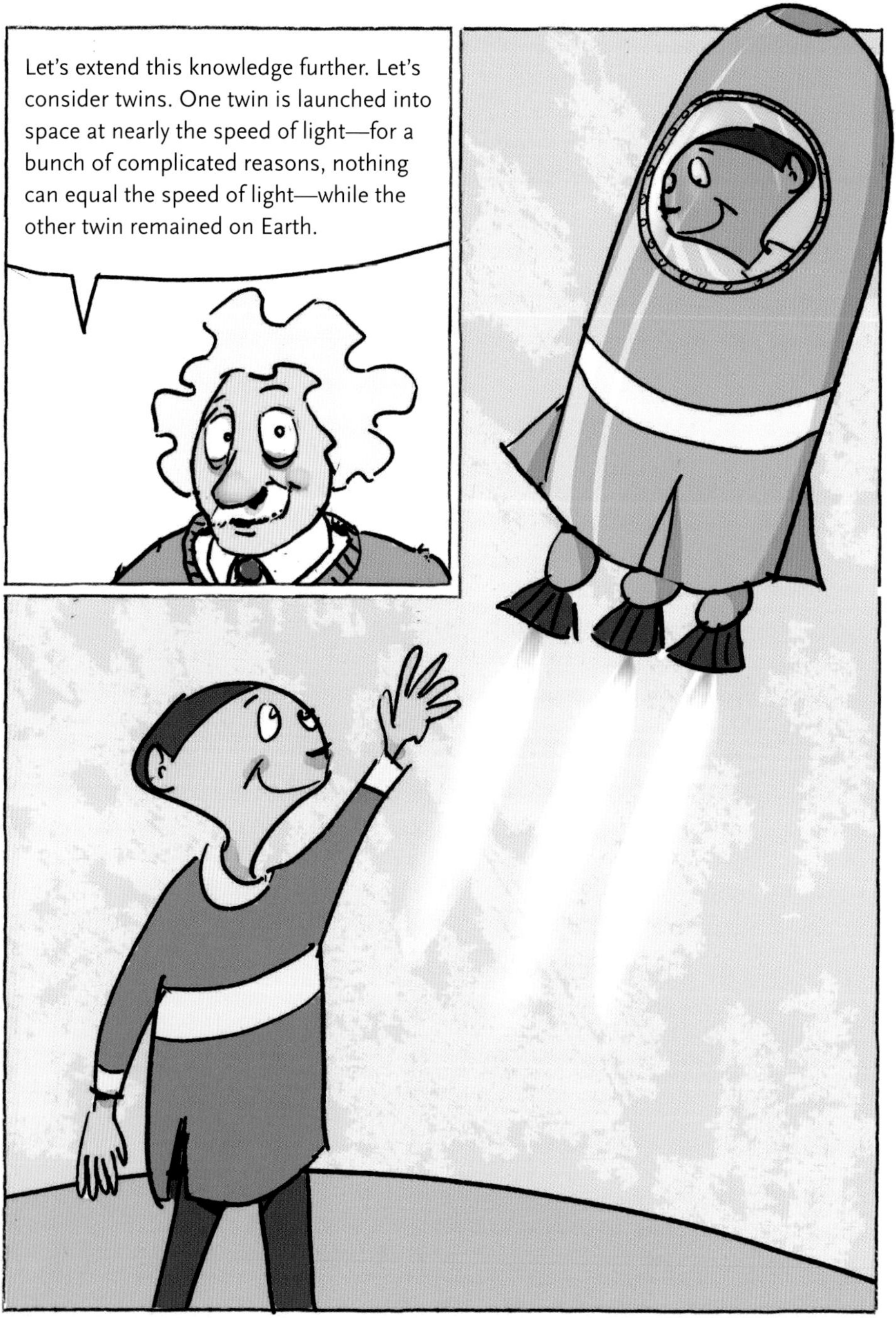
Let's extend this knowledge further. Let's consider twins. One twin is launched into space at nearly the speed of light—for a bunch of complicated reasons, nothing can equal the speed of light—while the other twin remained on Earth.

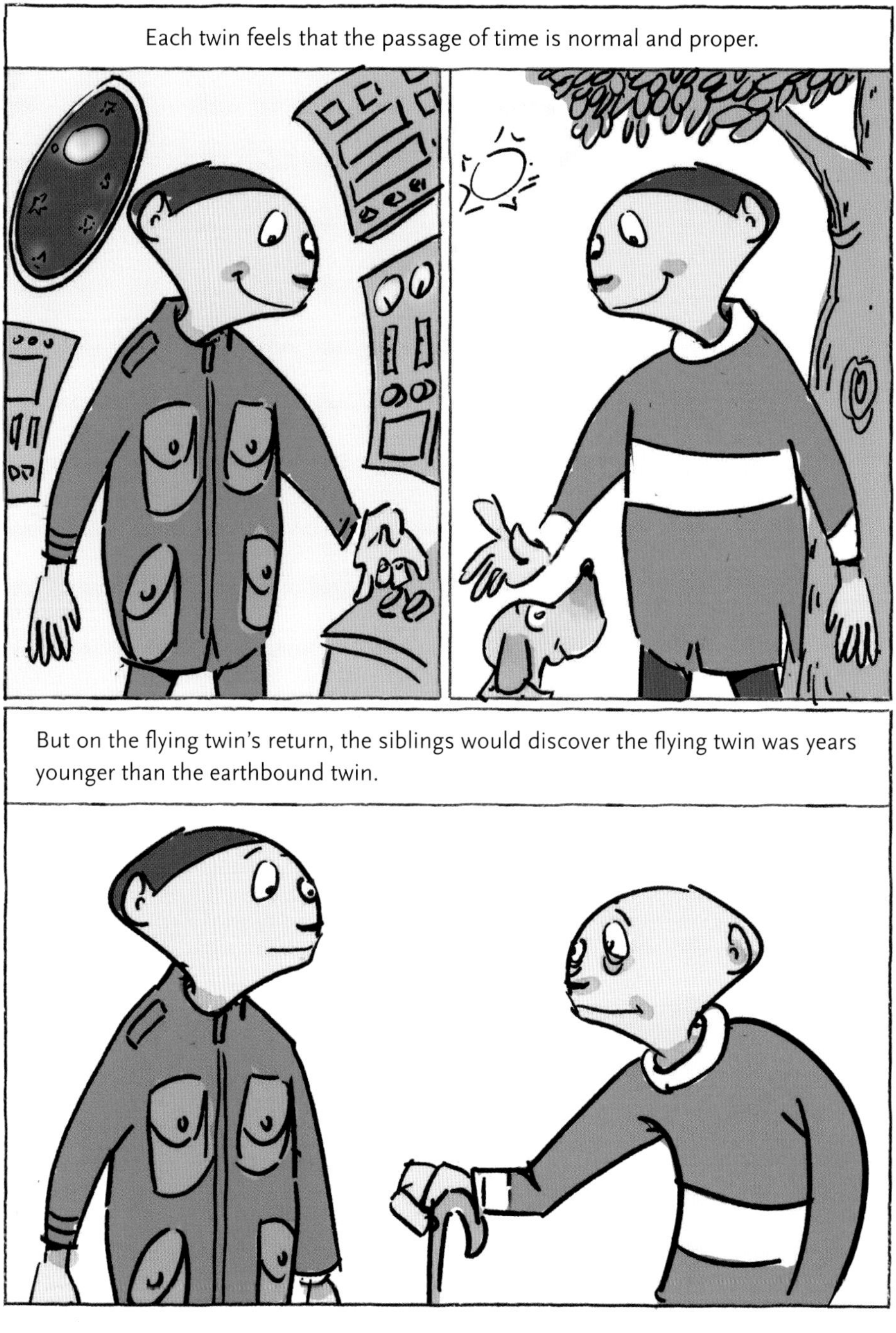
Each twin feels that the passage of time is normal and proper.
But on the flying twin's return, the siblings would discover the flying twin was years younger than the earthbound twin.

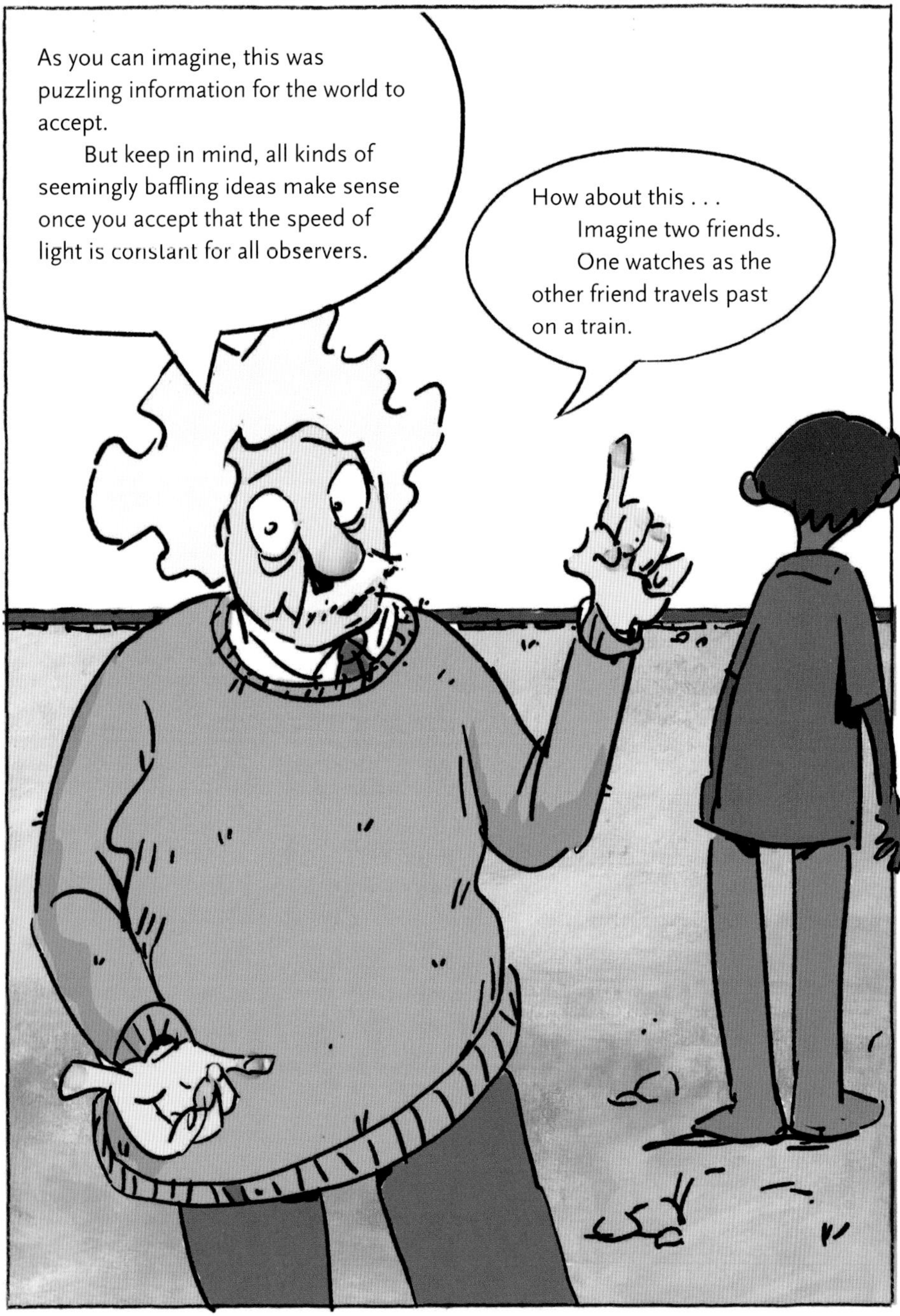
As you can imagine, this was puzzling information for the world to accept.
But keep in mind, all kinds of seemingly baffling ideas make sense once you accept that the speed of light is constant for all observers.
How about this . . .
Imagine two friends.
One watches as the other friend travels past on a train.

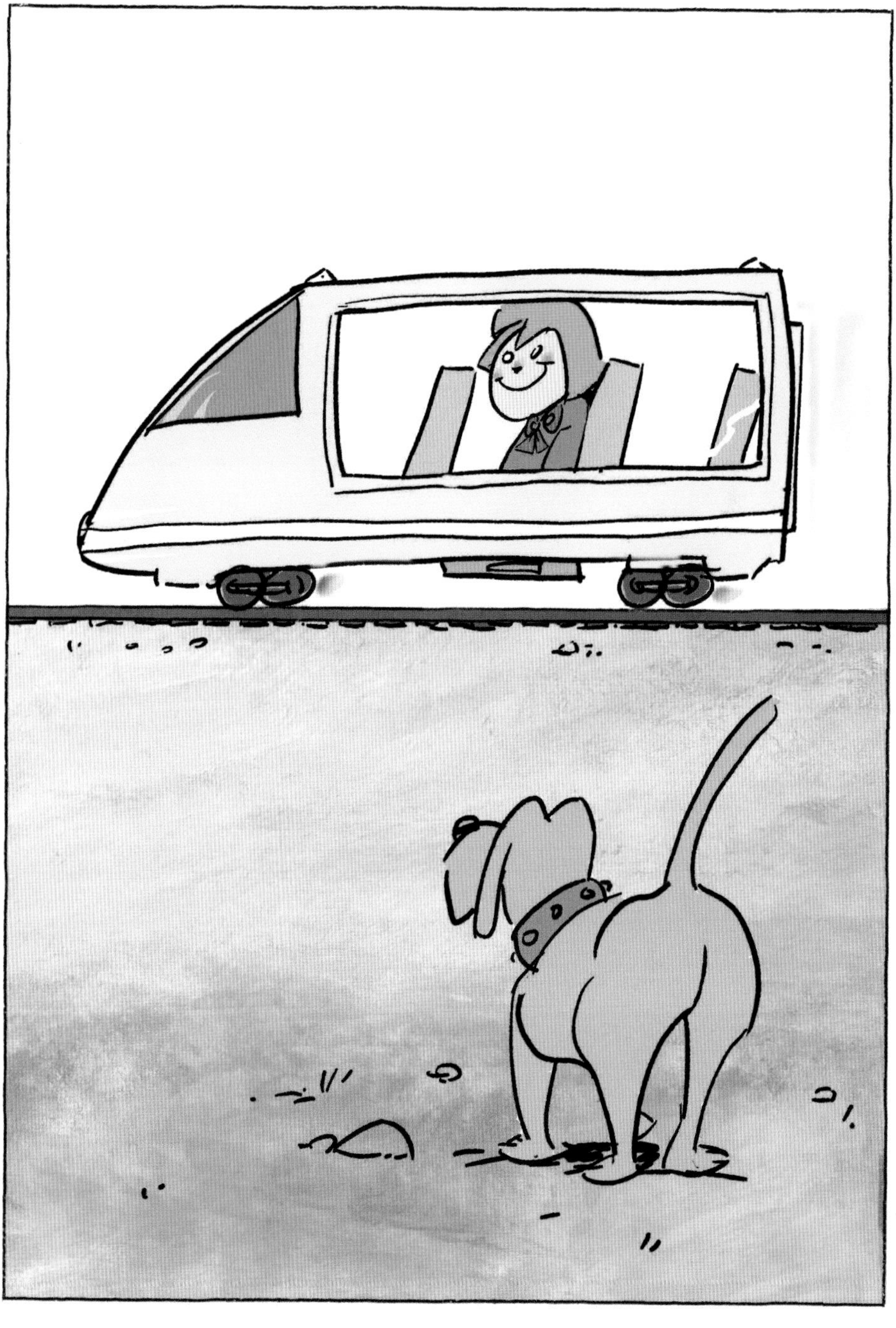

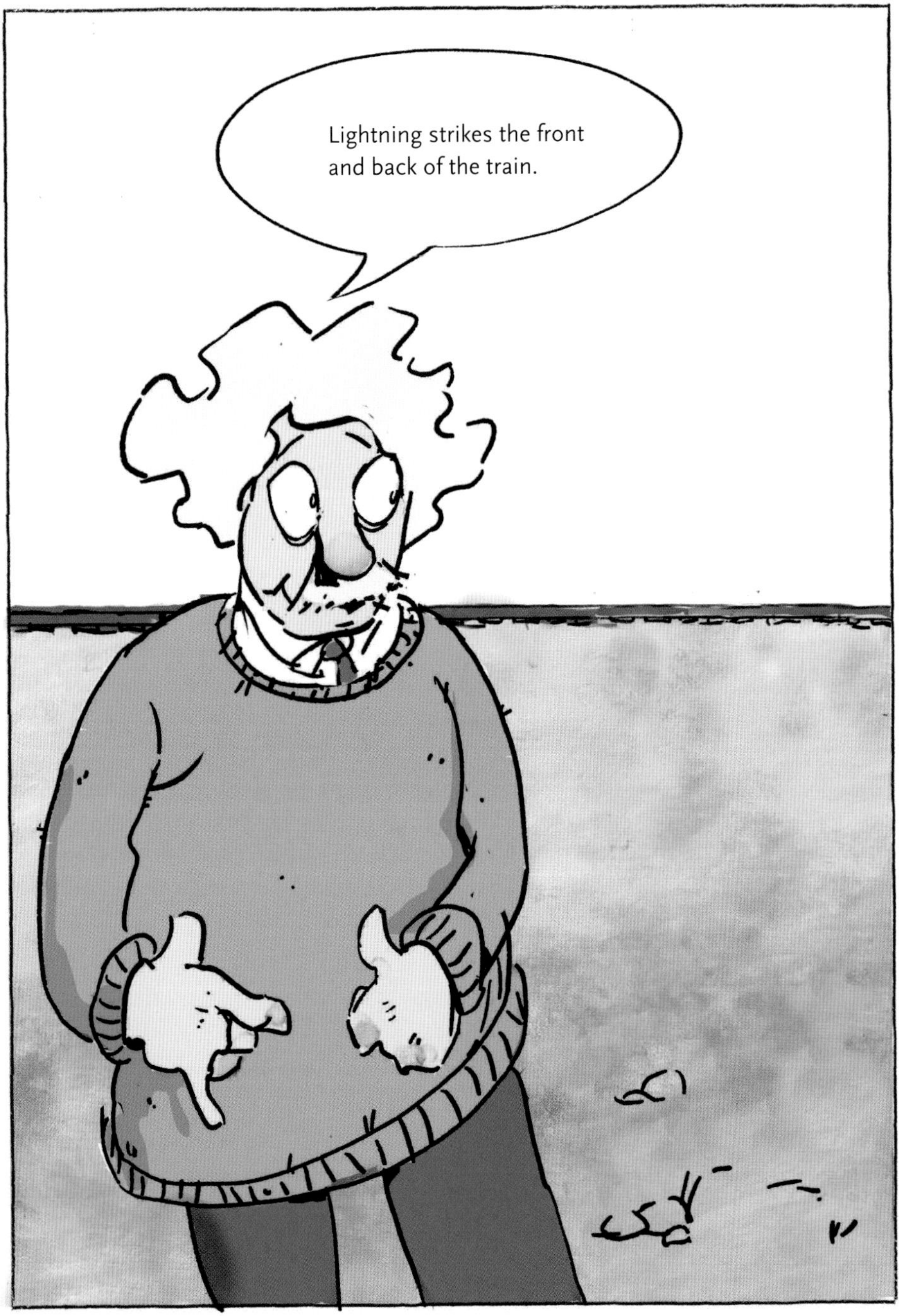
Lightning strikes the front and back of the train.

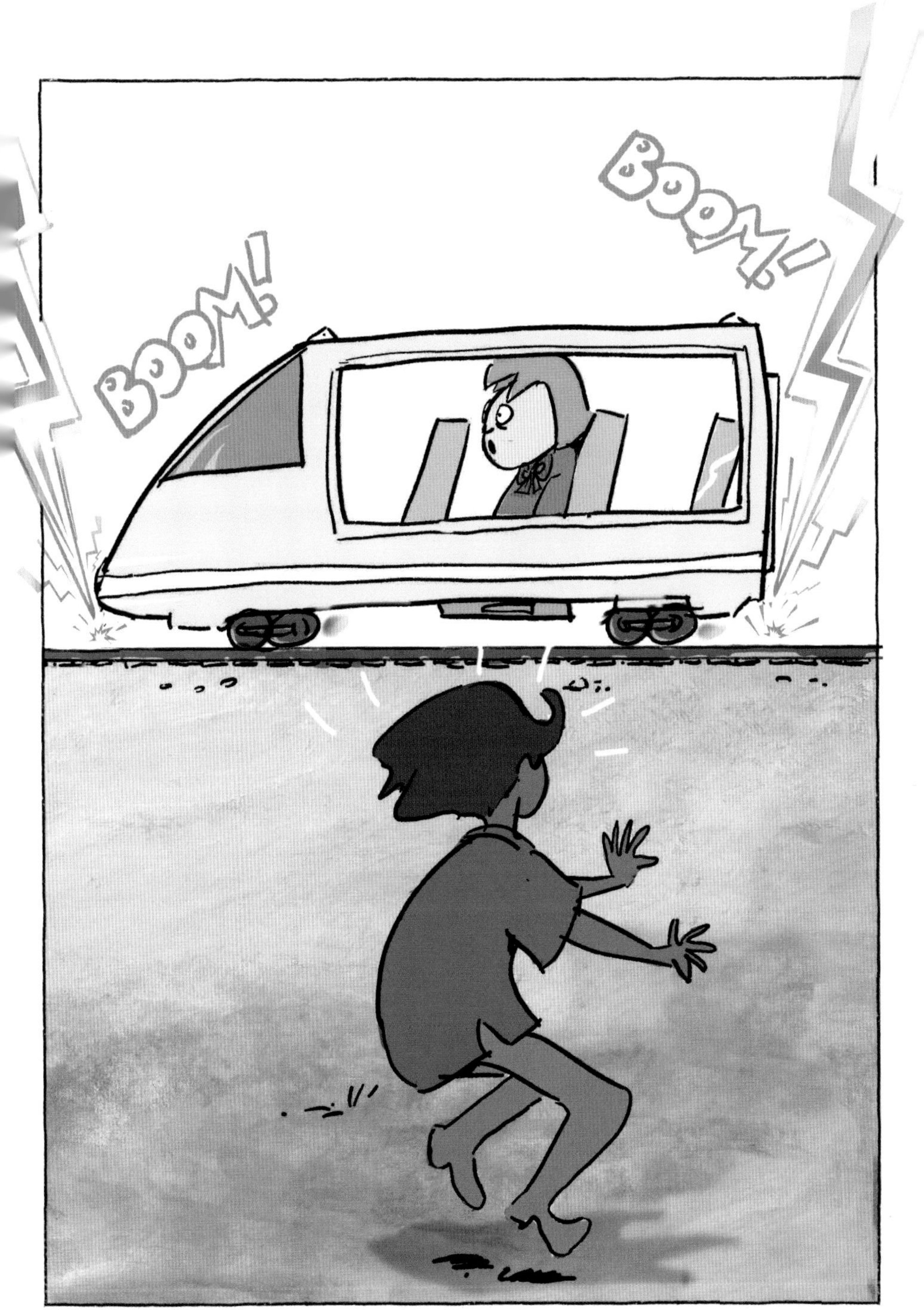
BOOM!
BOOM!

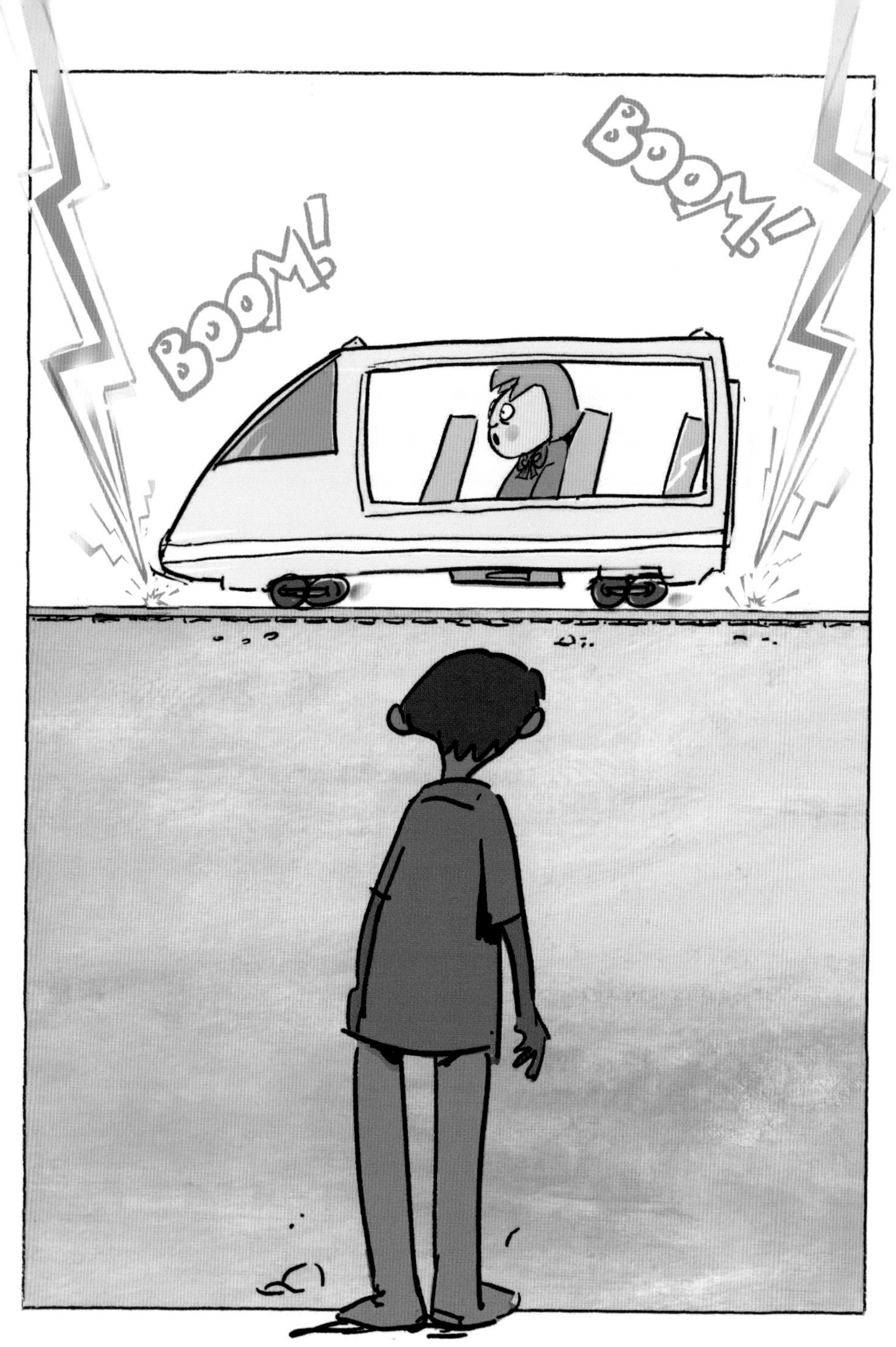
BOOM!
BOOM!

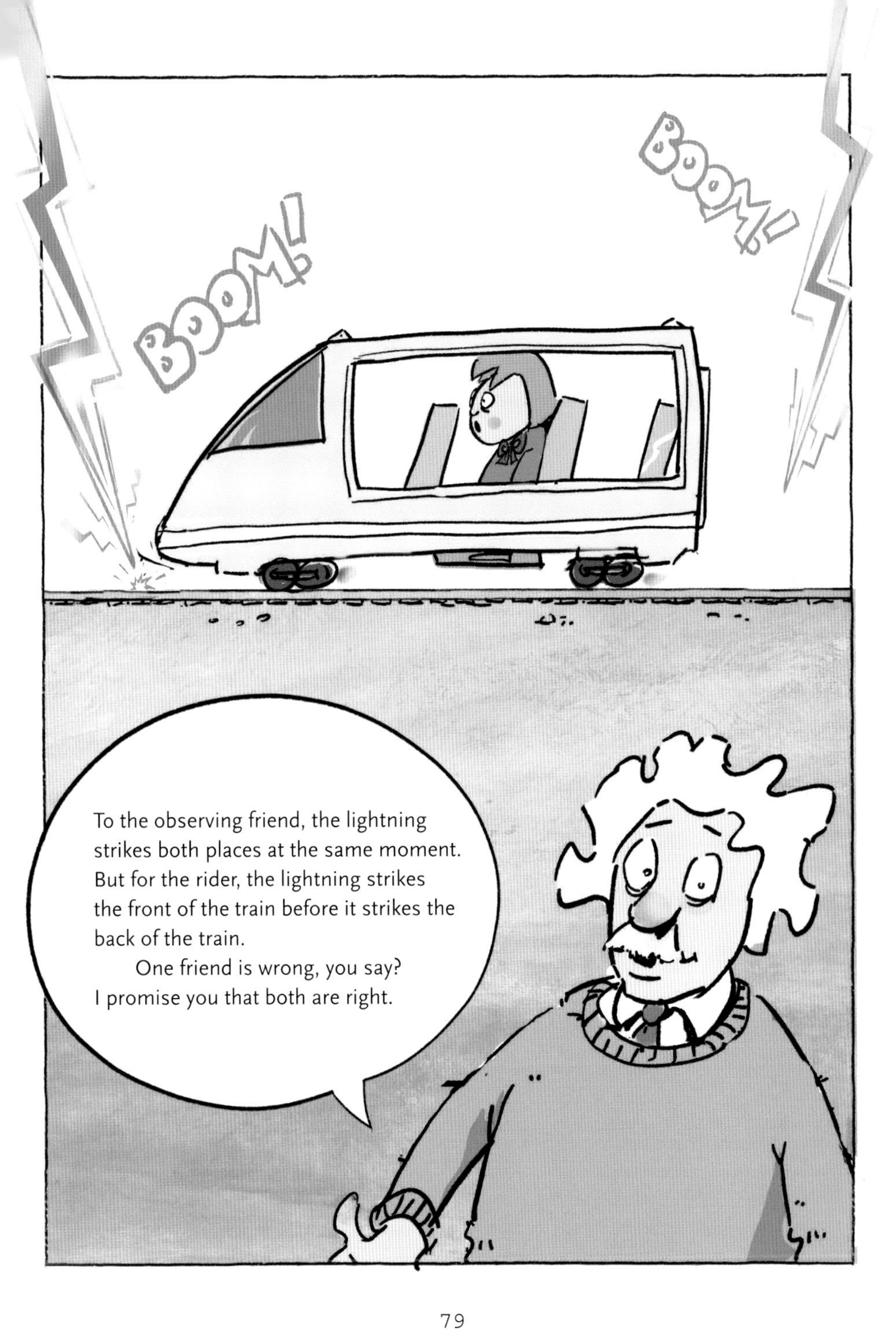
BOOM!
BOOM!
To the observing friend, the lightning strikes both places at the same moment. But for the rider, the lightning strikes the front of the train before it strikes the back of the train.
One friend is wrong, you say? I promise you that both are right.

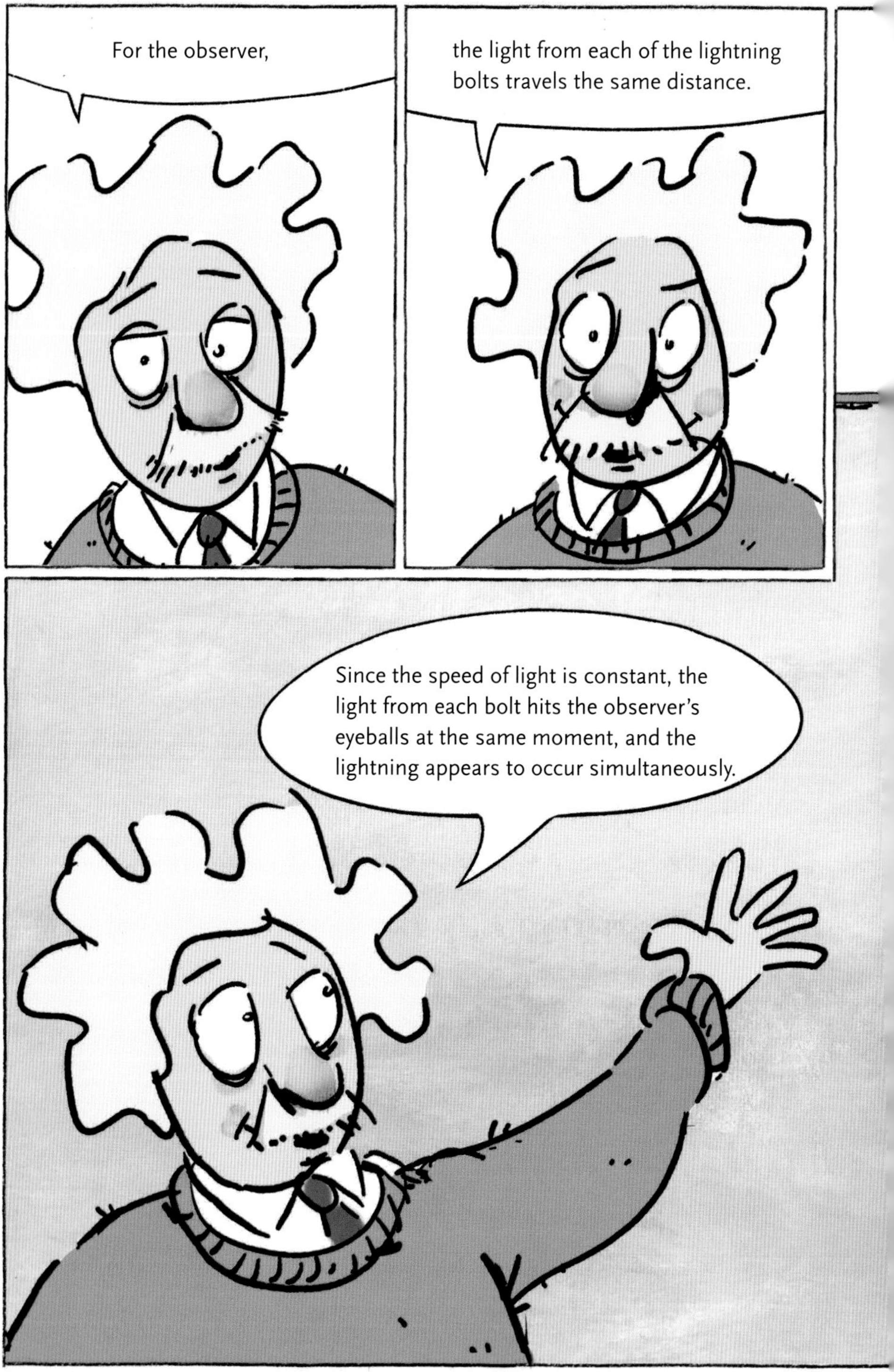
For the observer,
the light from each of the lightning bolts travels the same distance.
Since the speed of light is constant, the light from each bolt hits the observer's eyeballs at the same moment, and the lightning appears to occur simultaneously.

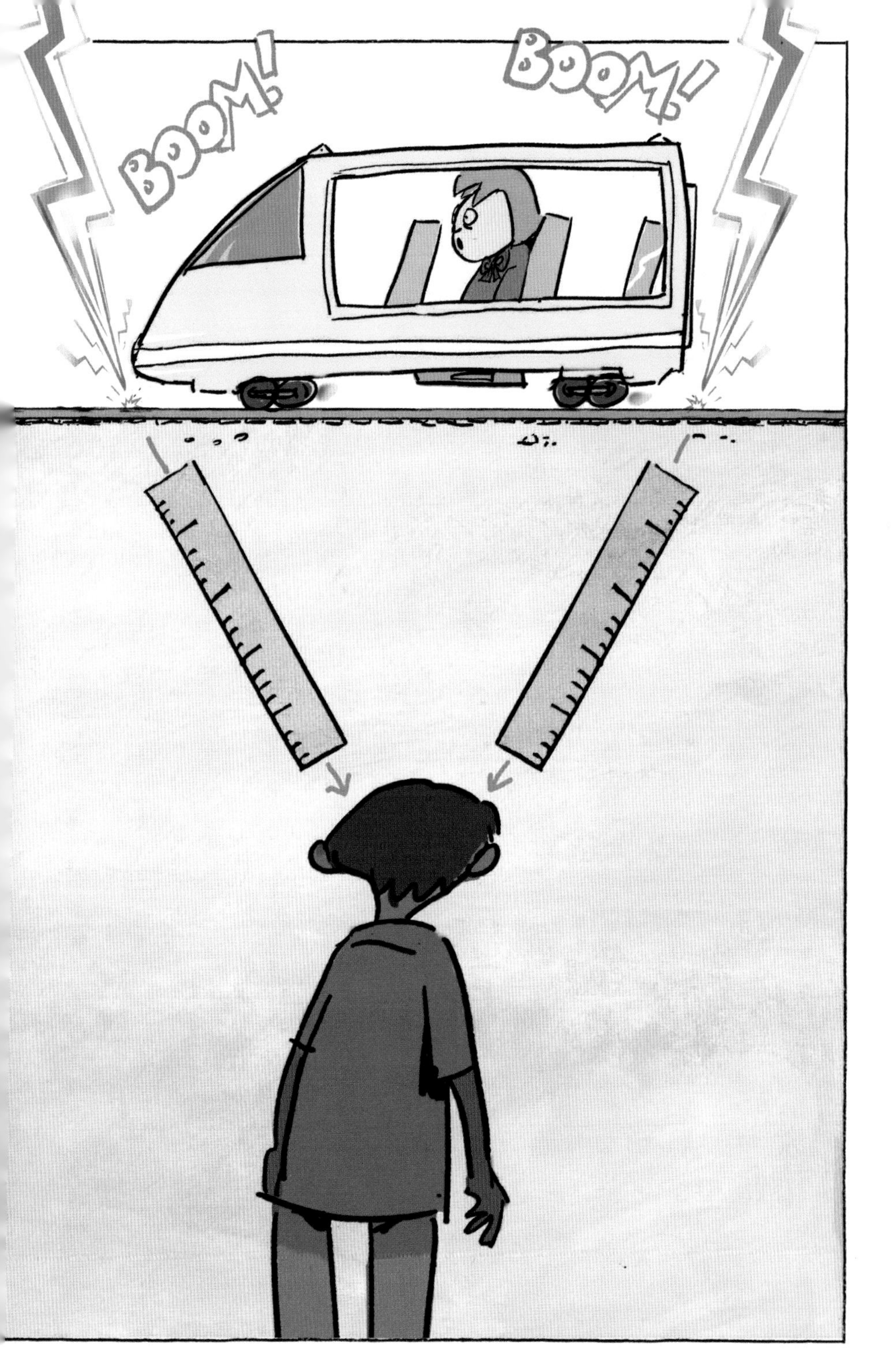
BOOM!
BOOM!

But the friend on the train sees something different. The moving train carries the rider closer to the lightning strike at the front of the train and away from the strike at the back of the train.

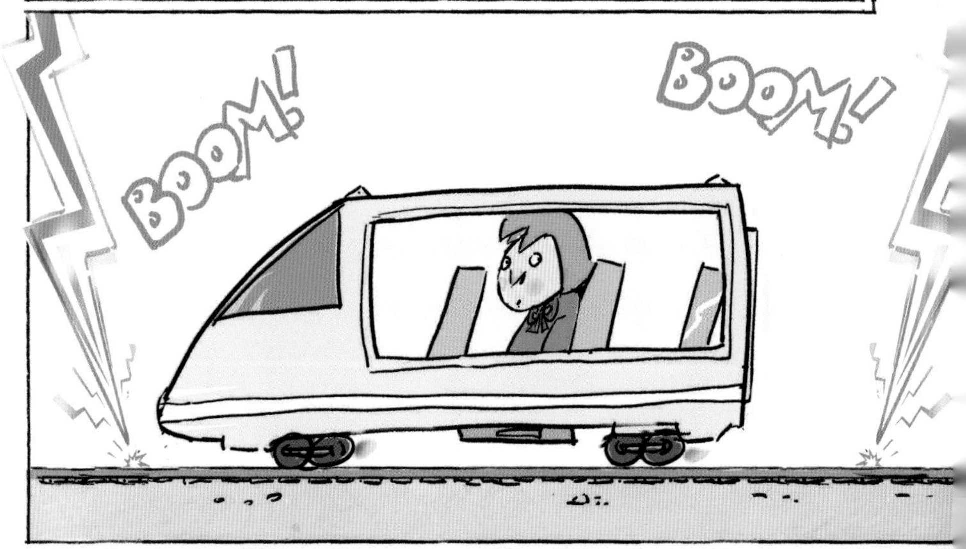
BOOM!
BOOM!

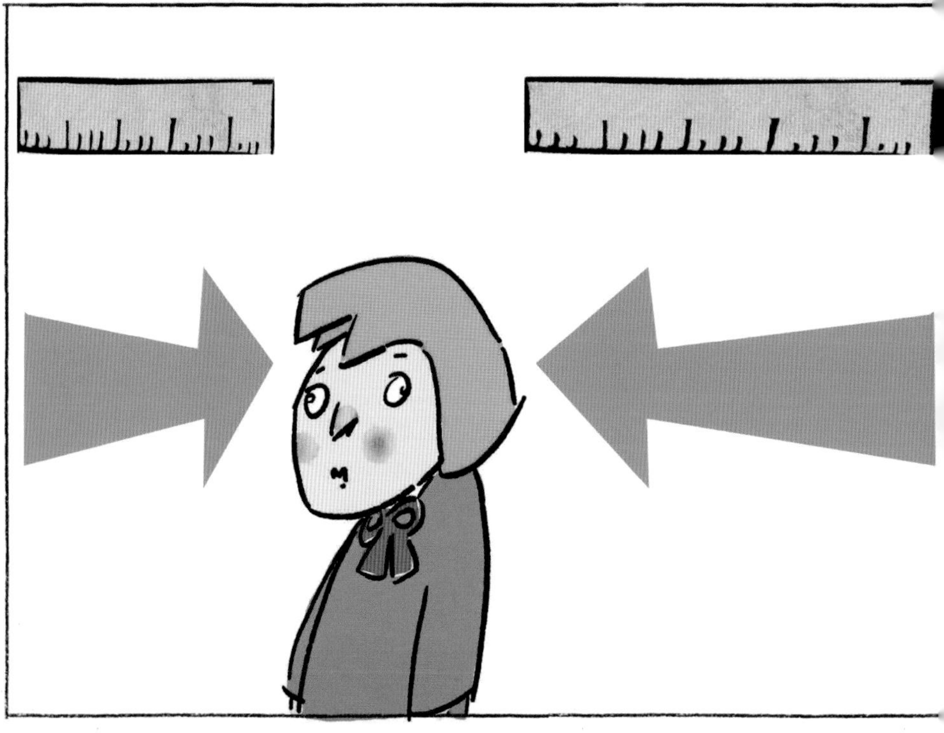

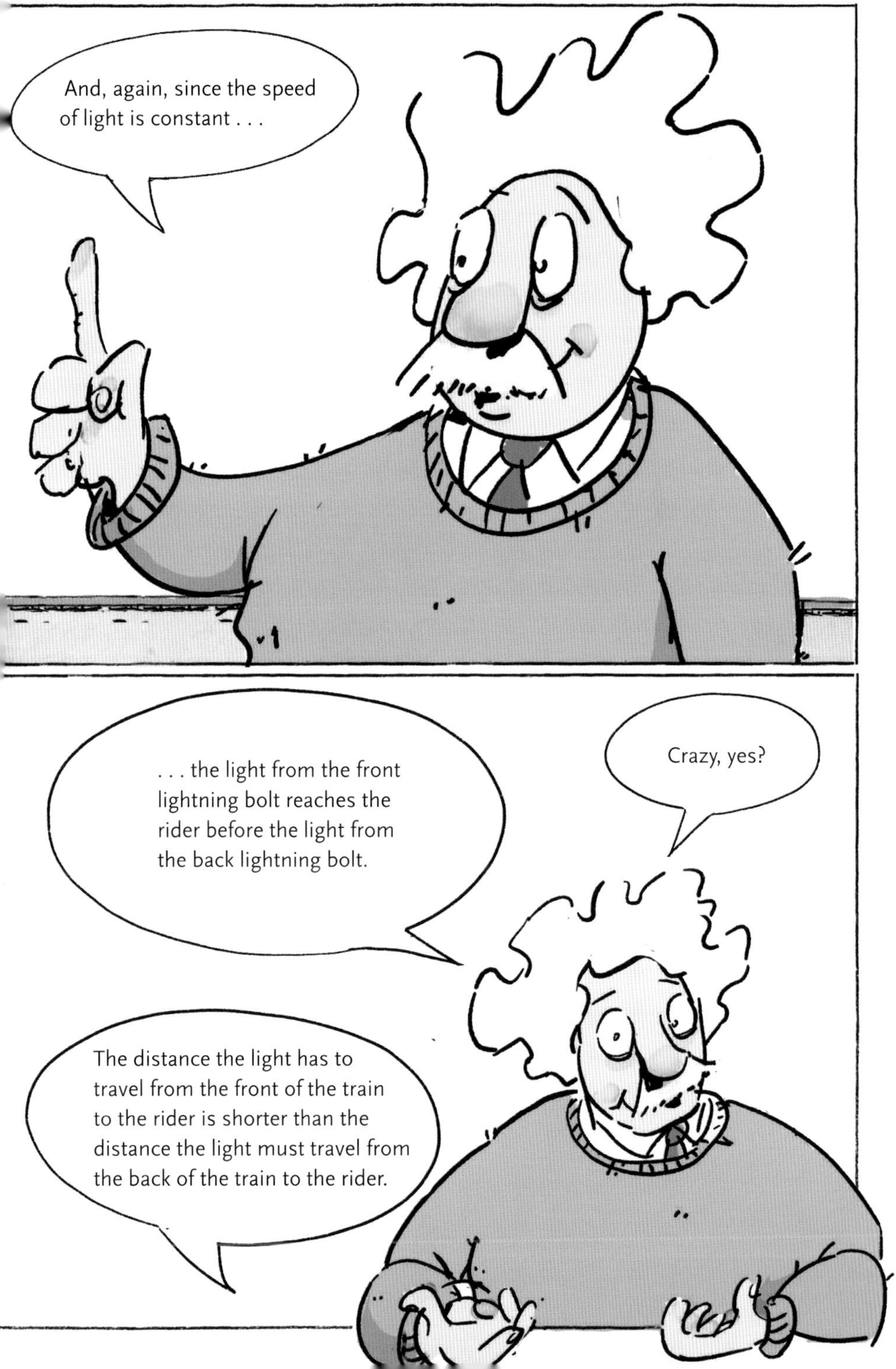
And, again, since the speed of light is constant . . .
. . . the light from the front lightning bolt reaches the rider before the light from the back lightning bolt.
Crazy, yes?
The distance the light has to travel from the front of the train to the rider is shorter than the distance the light must travel from the back of the train to the rider.

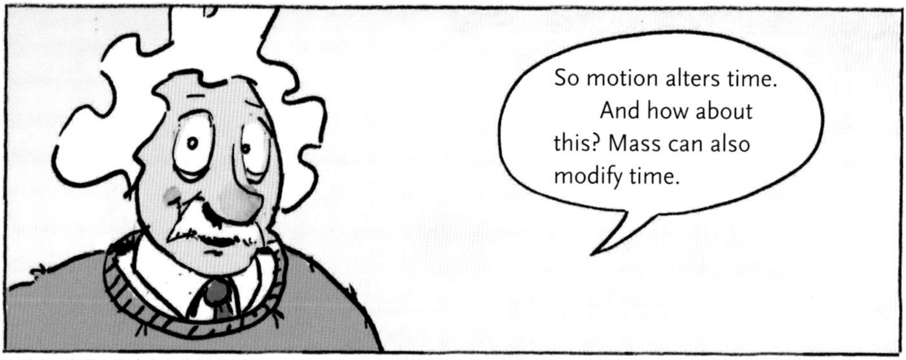
So motion alters time. And how about this? Mass can also modify time.

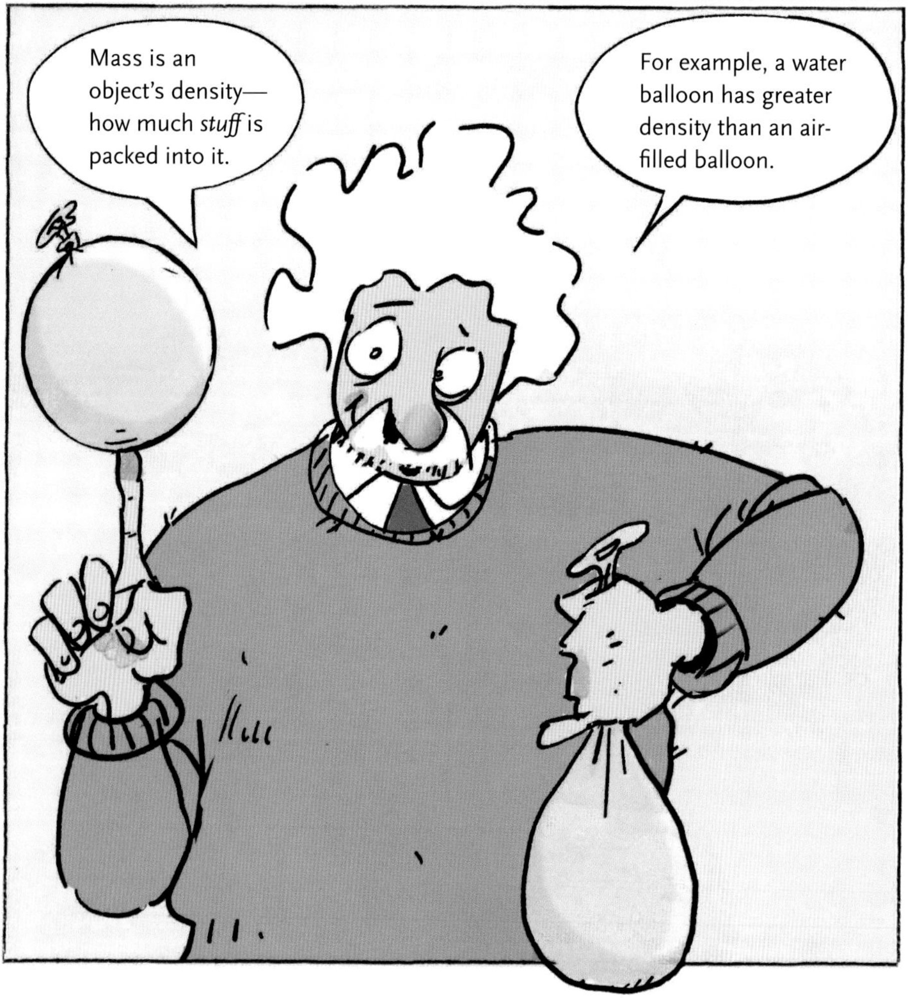
Mass is an object's density—how much *stuff* is packed into it.
For example, a water balloon has greater density than an air-filled balloon.

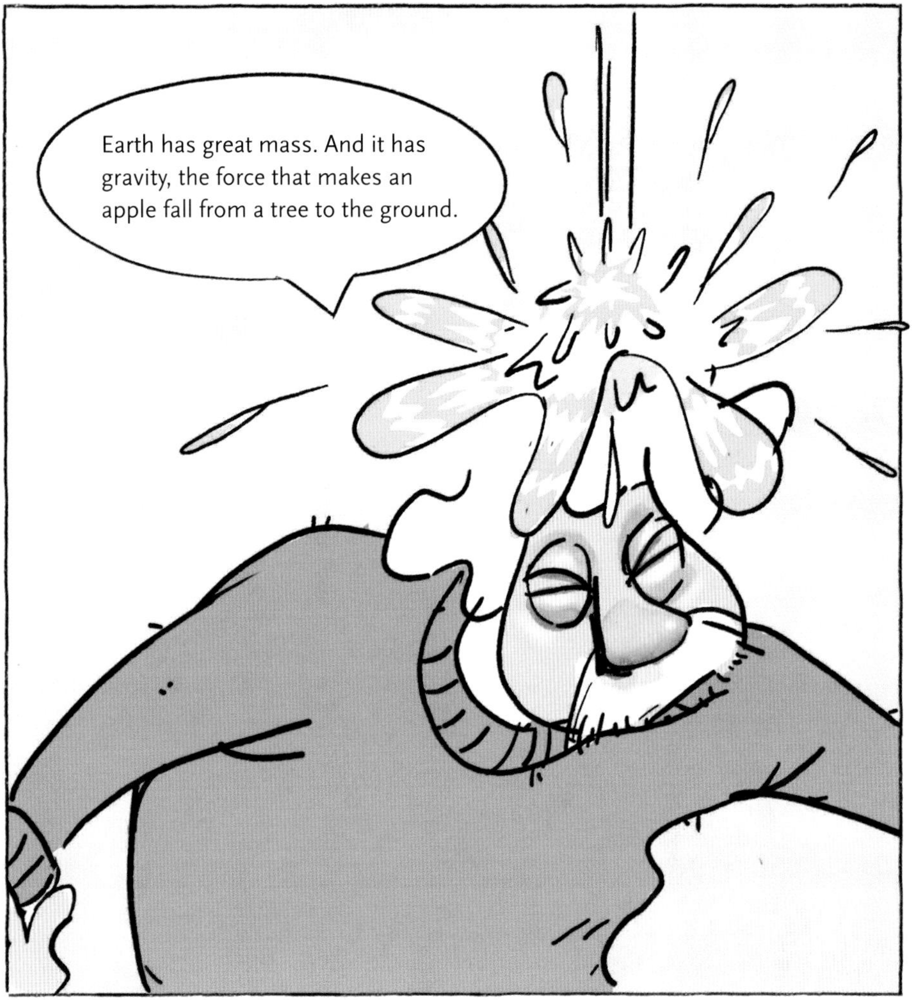
Earth has great mass. And it has gravity, the force that makes an apple fall from a tree to the ground.

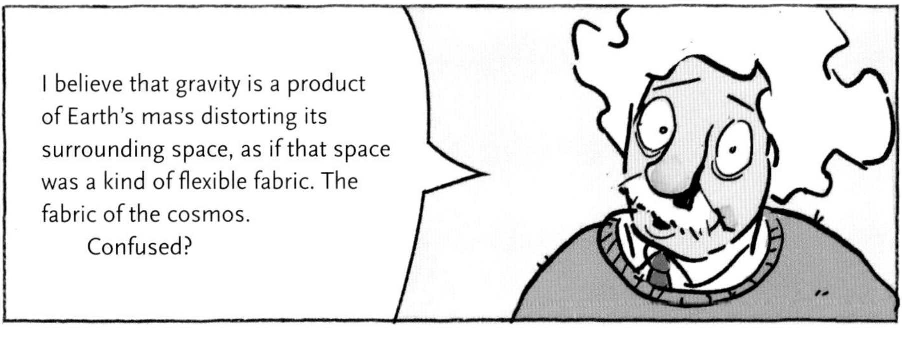
I believe that gravity is a product of Earth's mass distorting its surrounding space, as if that space was a kind of flexible fabric. The fabric of the cosmos.
Confused?

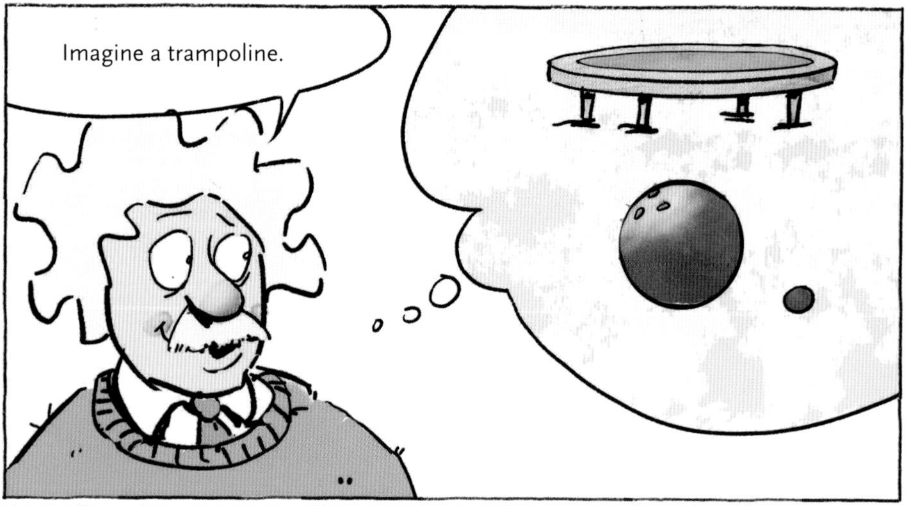
Imagine a trampoline.

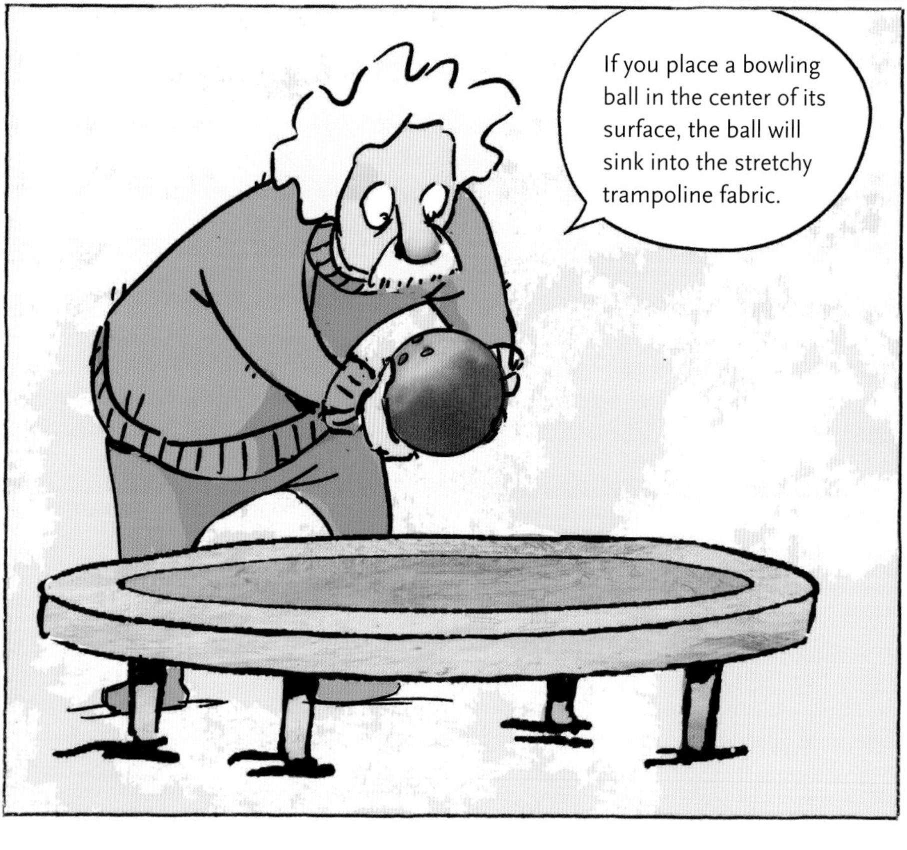
If you place a bowling ball in the center of its surface, the ball will sink into the stretchy trampoline fabric.

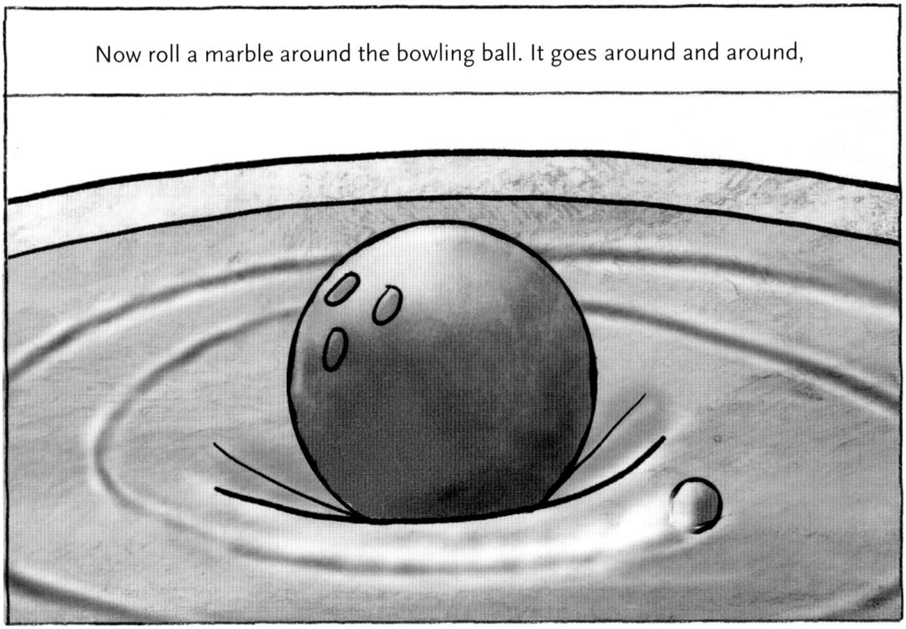
Now roll a marble around the bowling ball. It goes around and around,

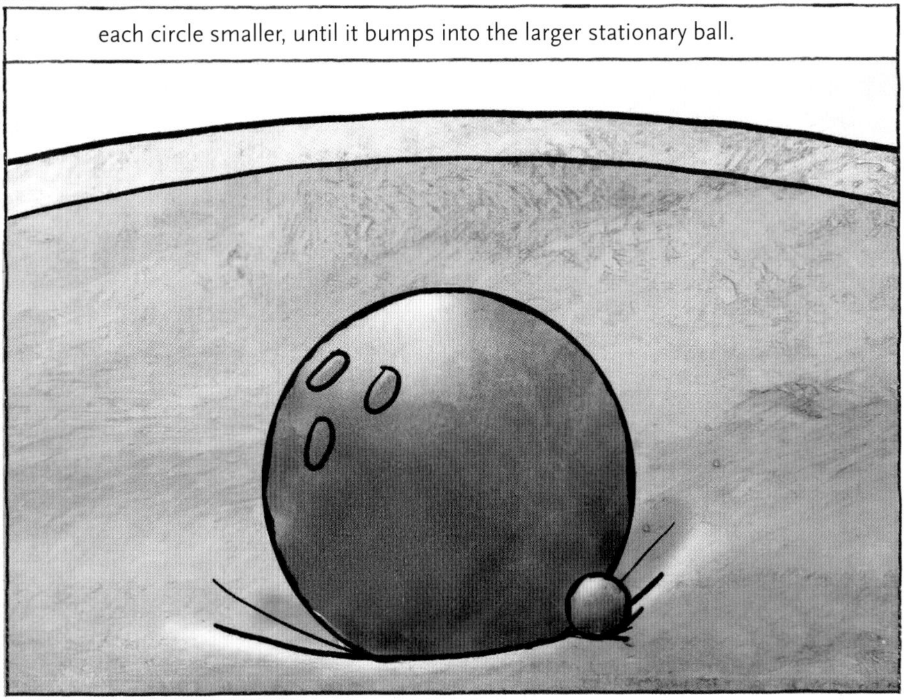
each circle smaller, until it bumps into the larger stationary ball.

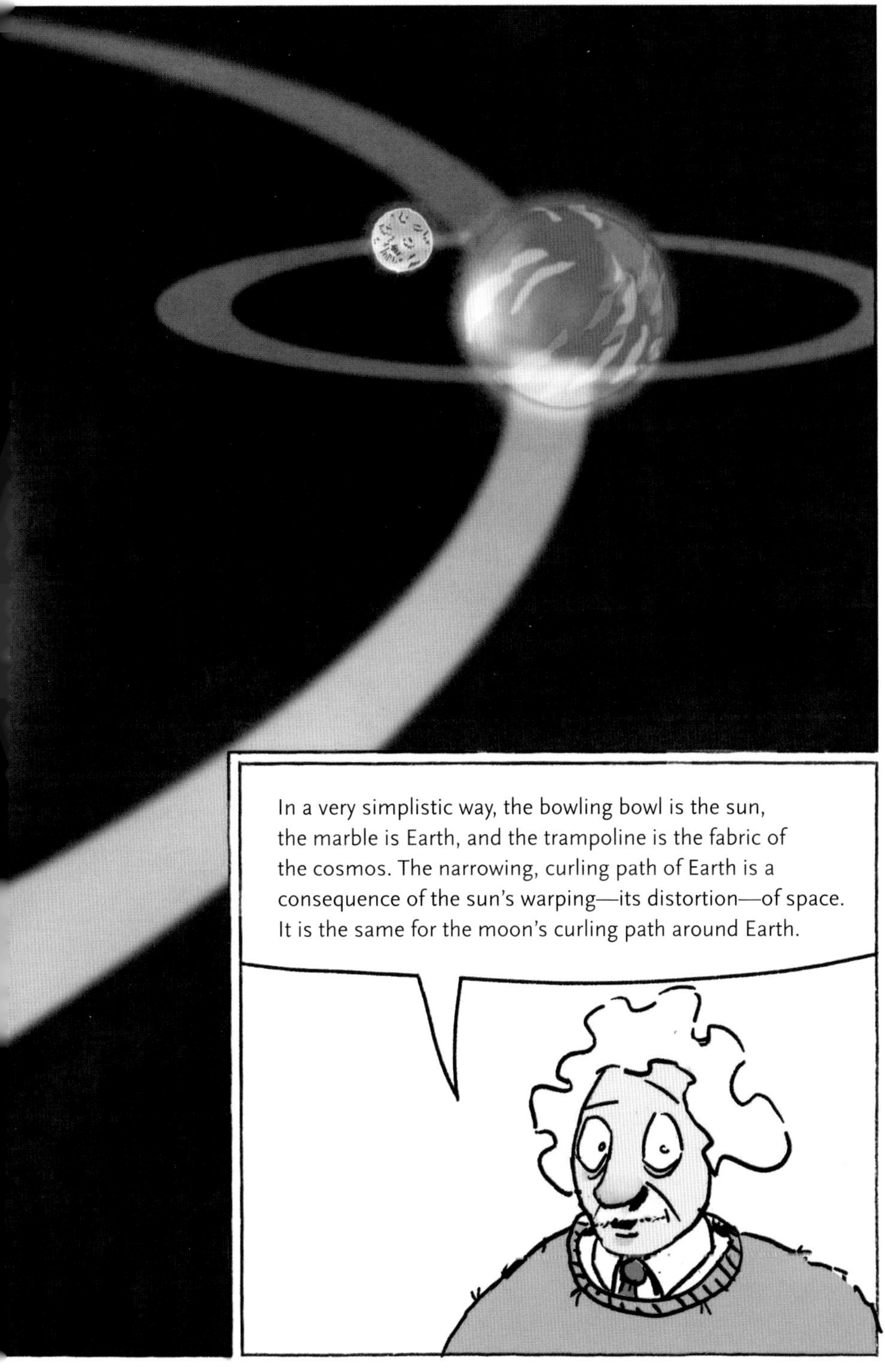
In a very simplistic way, the bowling bowl is the sun, the marble is Earth, and the trampoline is the fabric of the cosmos. The narrowing, curling path of Earth is a consequence of the sun's warping—its distortion—of space. It is the same for the moon's curling path around Earth.

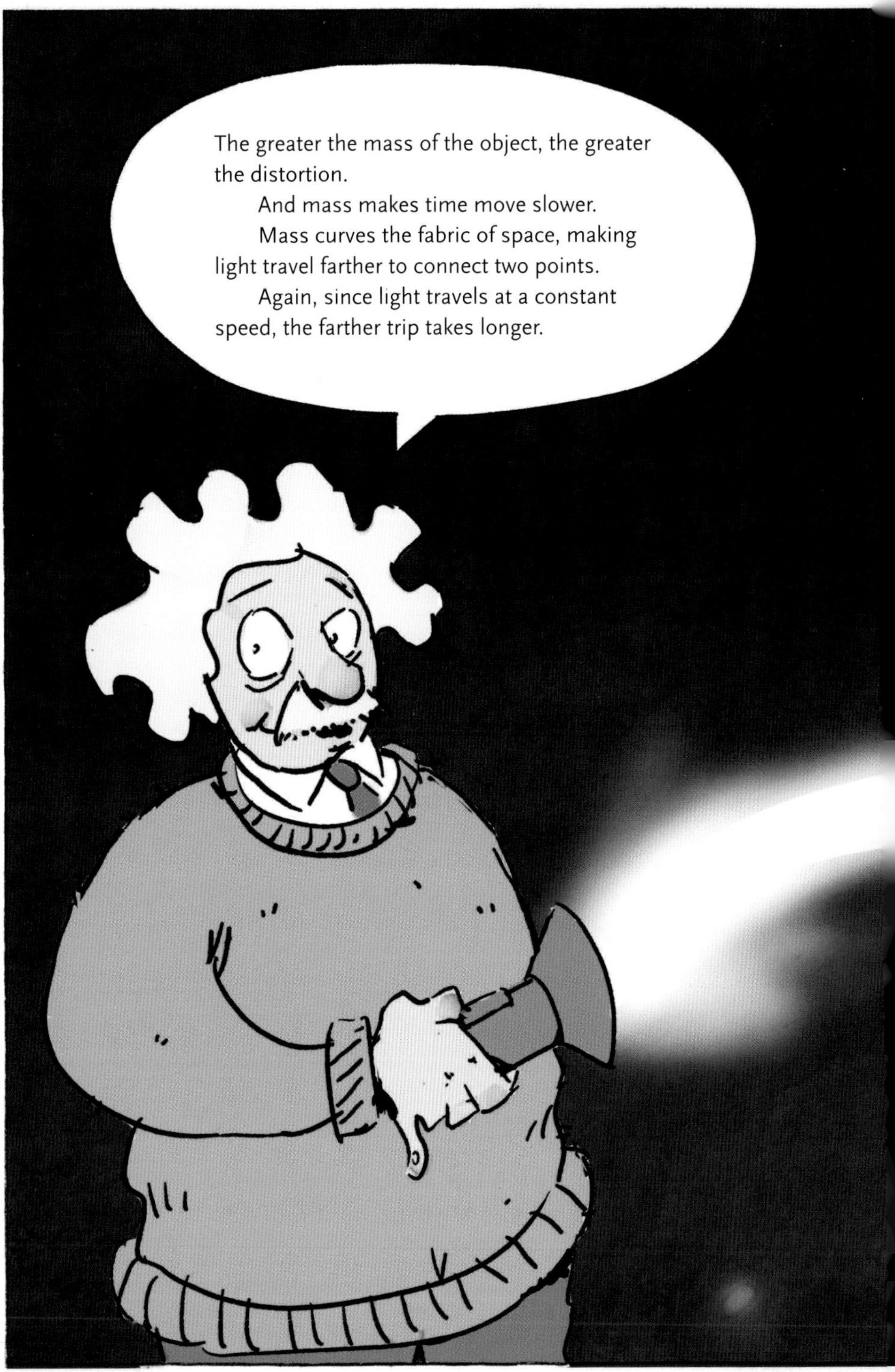
The greater the mass of the object, the greater the distortion.
And mass makes time move slower.
Mass curves the fabric of space, making light travel farther to connect two points.
Again, since light travels at a constant speed, the farther trip takes longer.

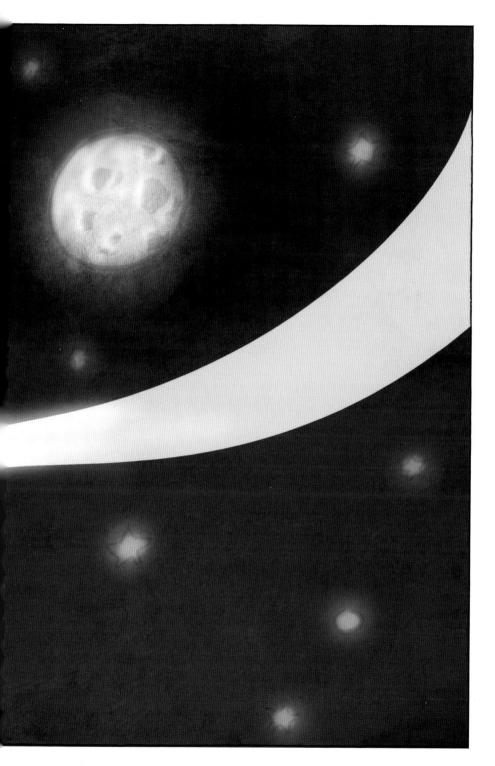

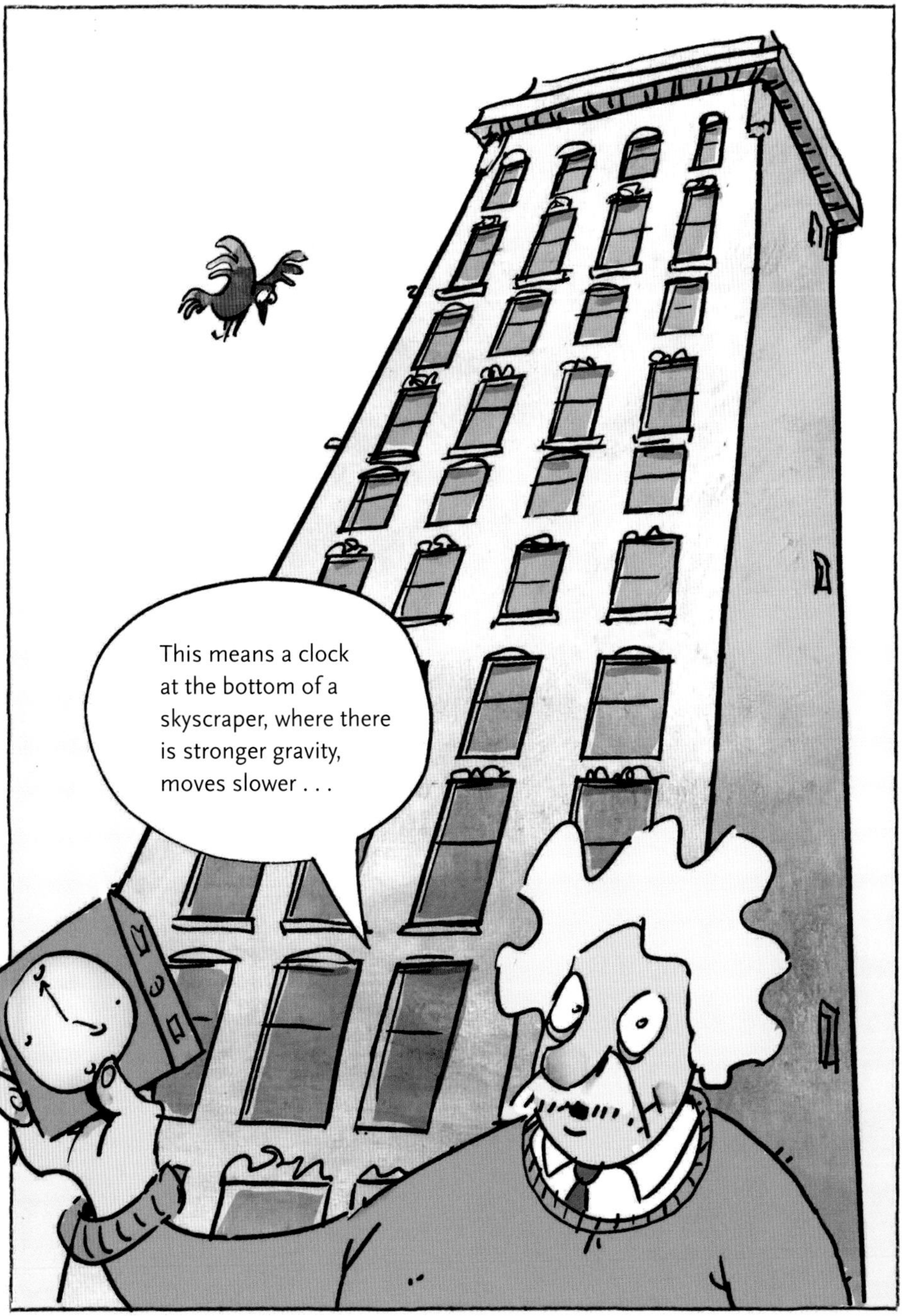
This means a clock at the bottom of a skyscraper, where there is stronger gravity, moves slower . . .

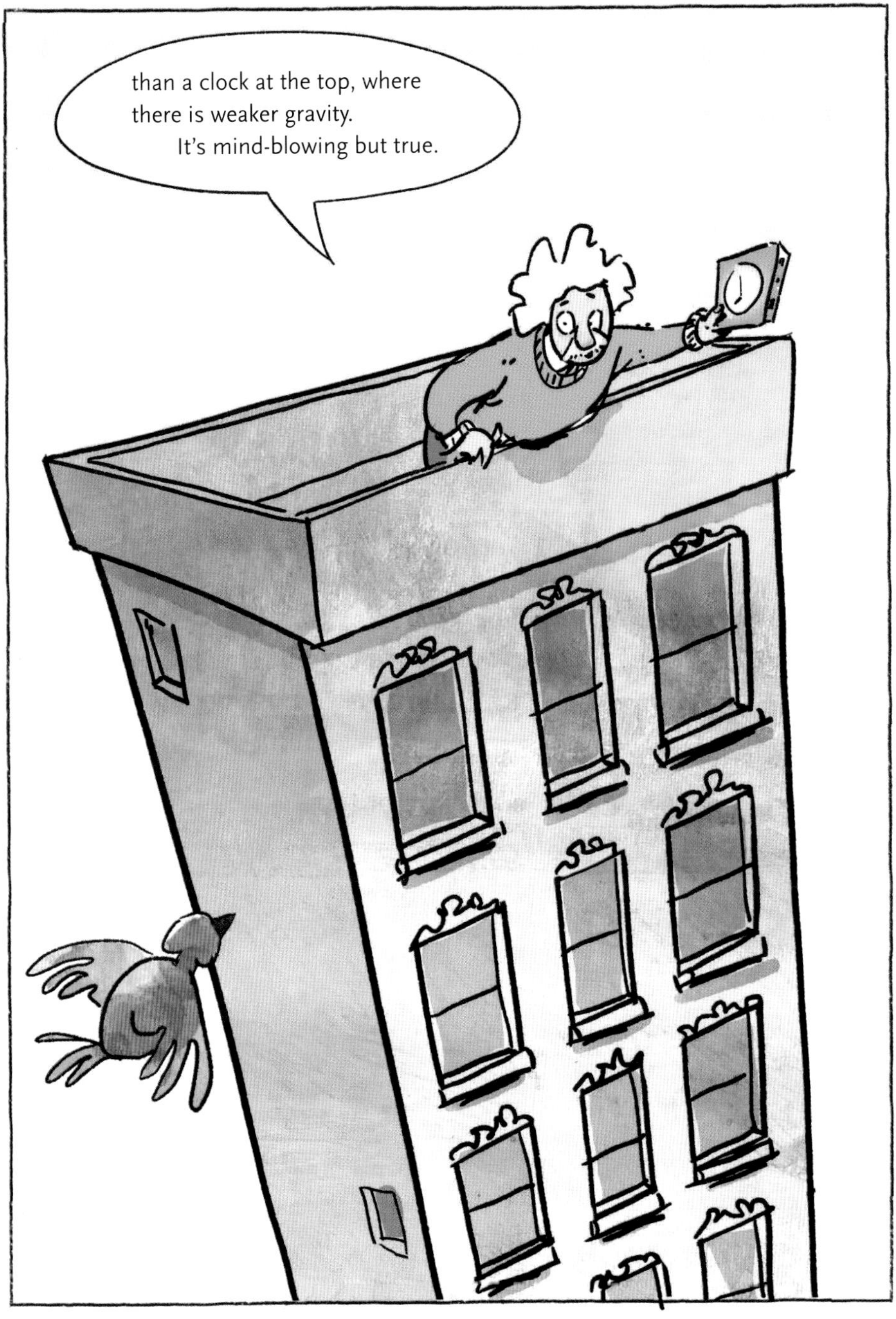
than a clock at the top, where there is weaker gravity. It's mind-blowing but true.

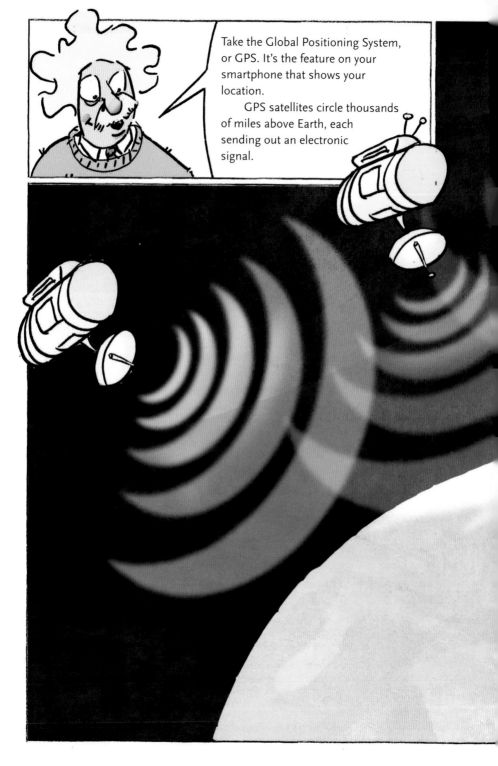

Take the Global Positioning System, or GPS. It's the feature on your smartphone that shows your location.

GPS satellites circle thousands of miles above Earth, each sending out an electronic signal.

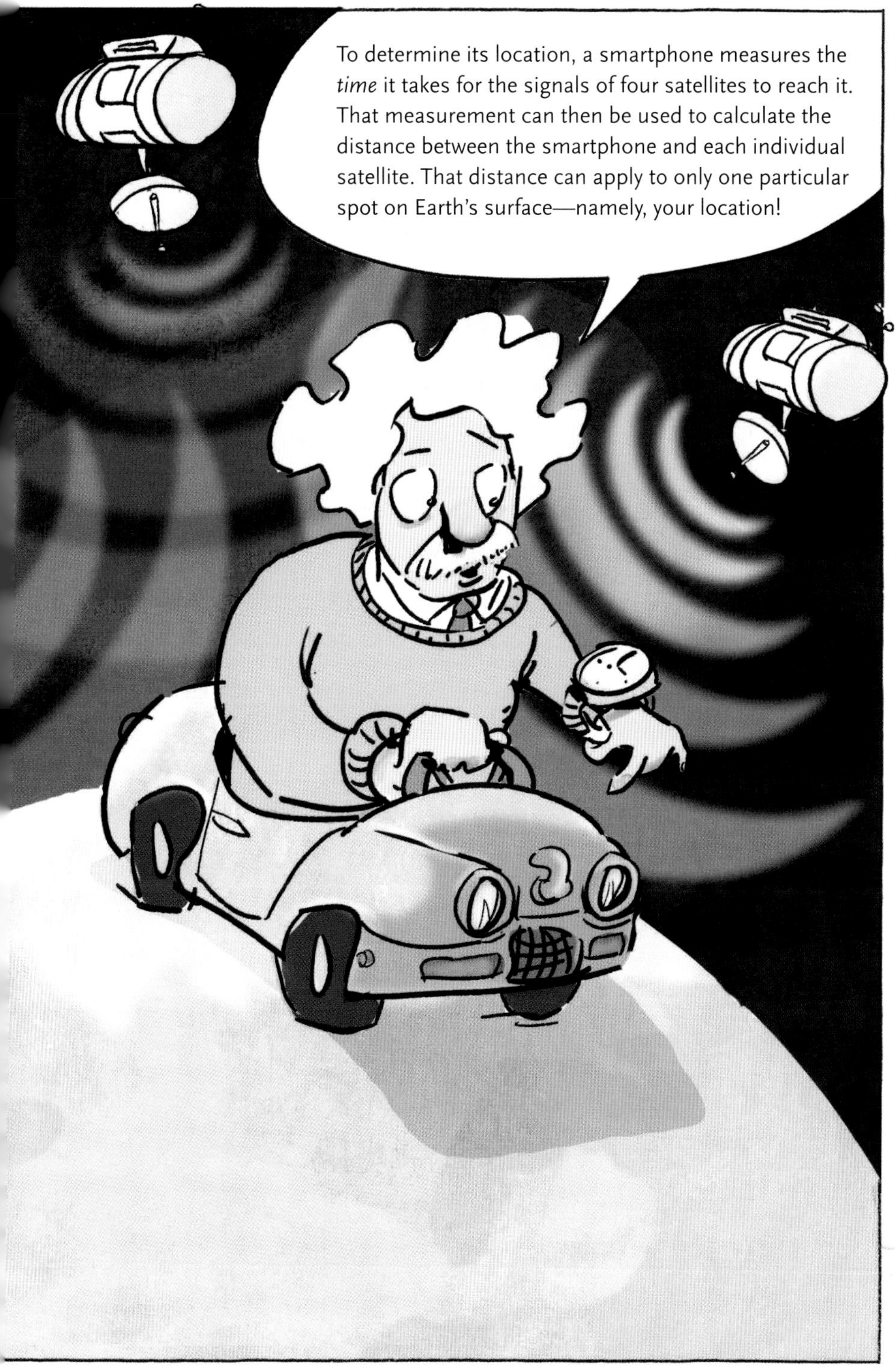
To determine its location, a smartphone measures the *time* it takes for the signals of four satellites to reach it. That measurement can then be used to calculate the distance between the smartphone and each individual satellite. That distance can apply to only one particular spot on Earth's surface—namely, your location!

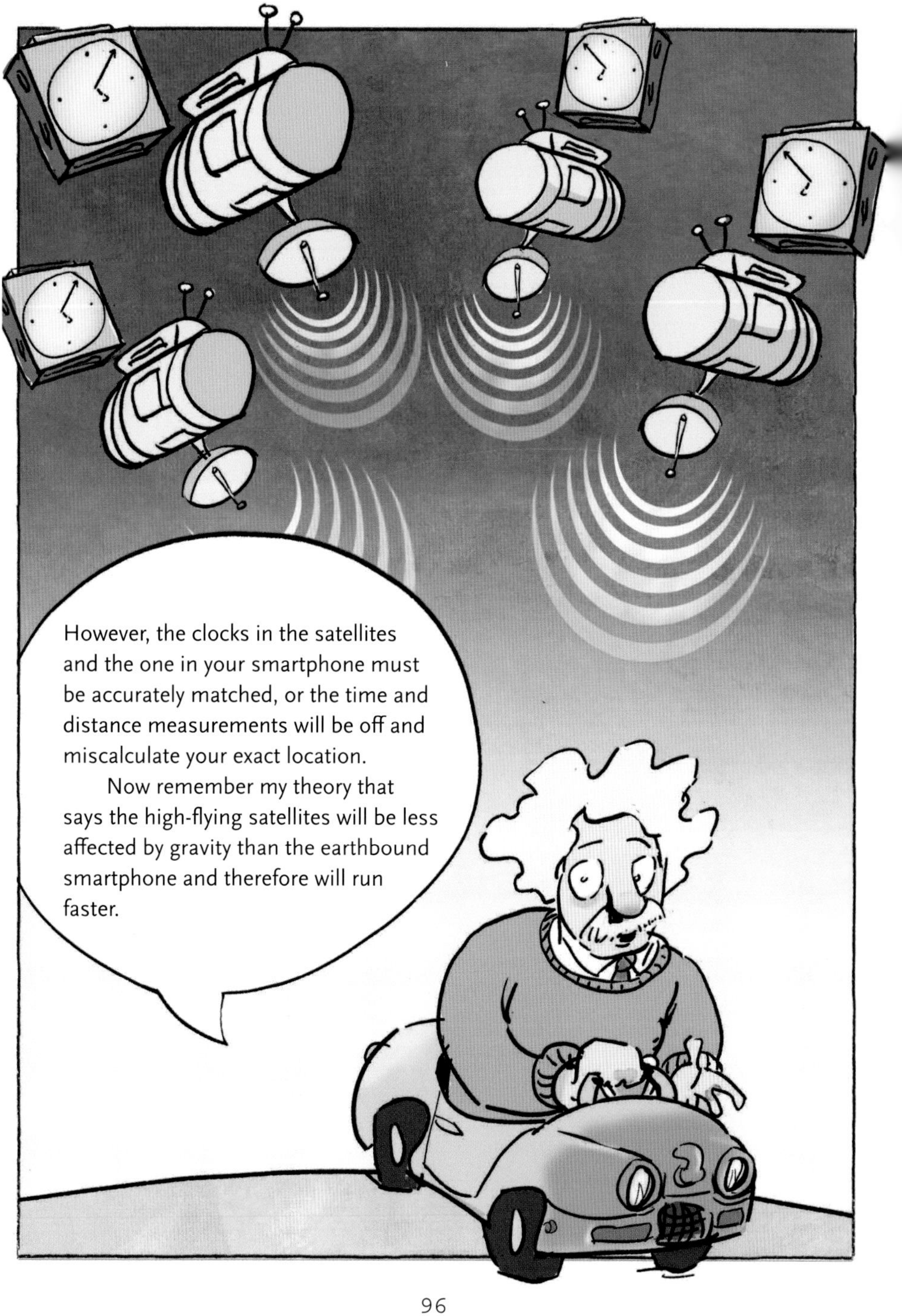
However, the clocks in the satellites and the one in your smartphone must be accurately matched, or the time and distance measurements will be off and miscalculate your exact location.
Now remember my theory that says the high-flying satellites will be less affected by gravity than the earthbound smartphone and therefore will run faster.

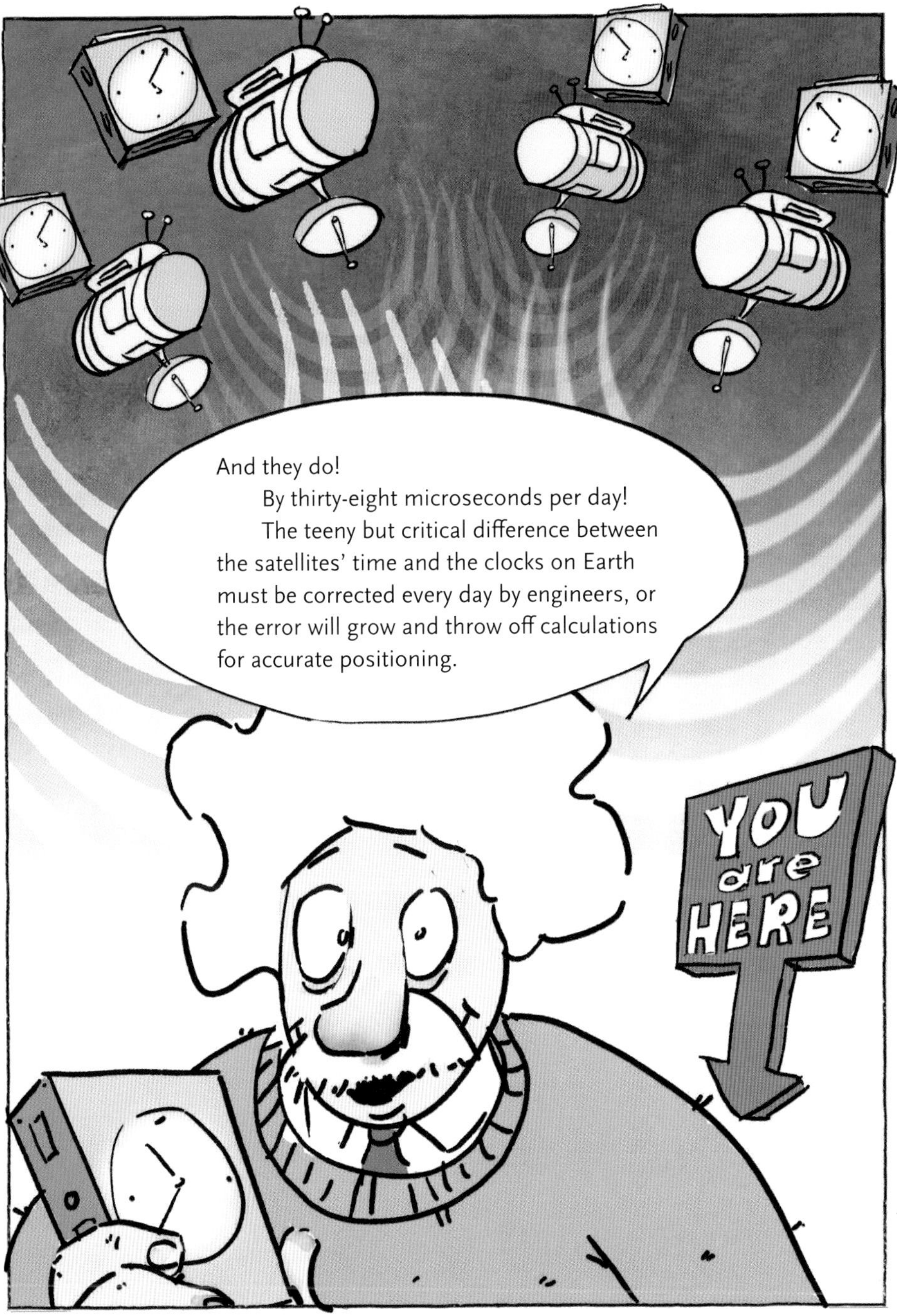
And they do!
By thirty-eight microseconds per day!
The teeny but critical difference between the satellites' time and the clocks on Earth must be corrected every day by engineers, or the error will grow and throw off calculations for accurate positioning.
YOU are HERE

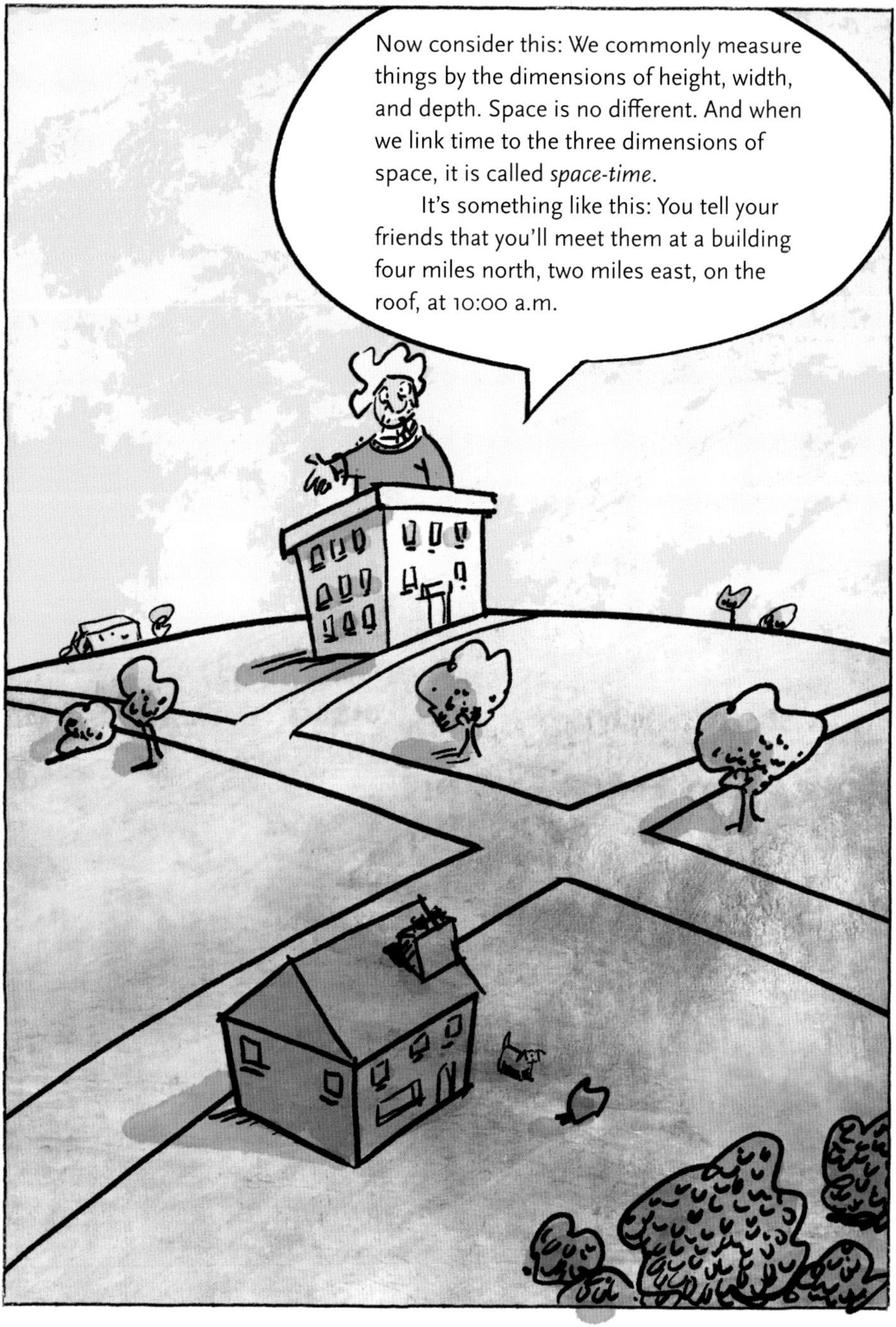
Now consider this: We commonly measure things by the dimensions of height, width, and depth. Space is no different. And when we link time to the three dimensions of space, it is called *space-time*.
It's something like this: You tell your friends that you'll meet them at a building four miles north, two miles east, on the roof, at 10:00 a.m.

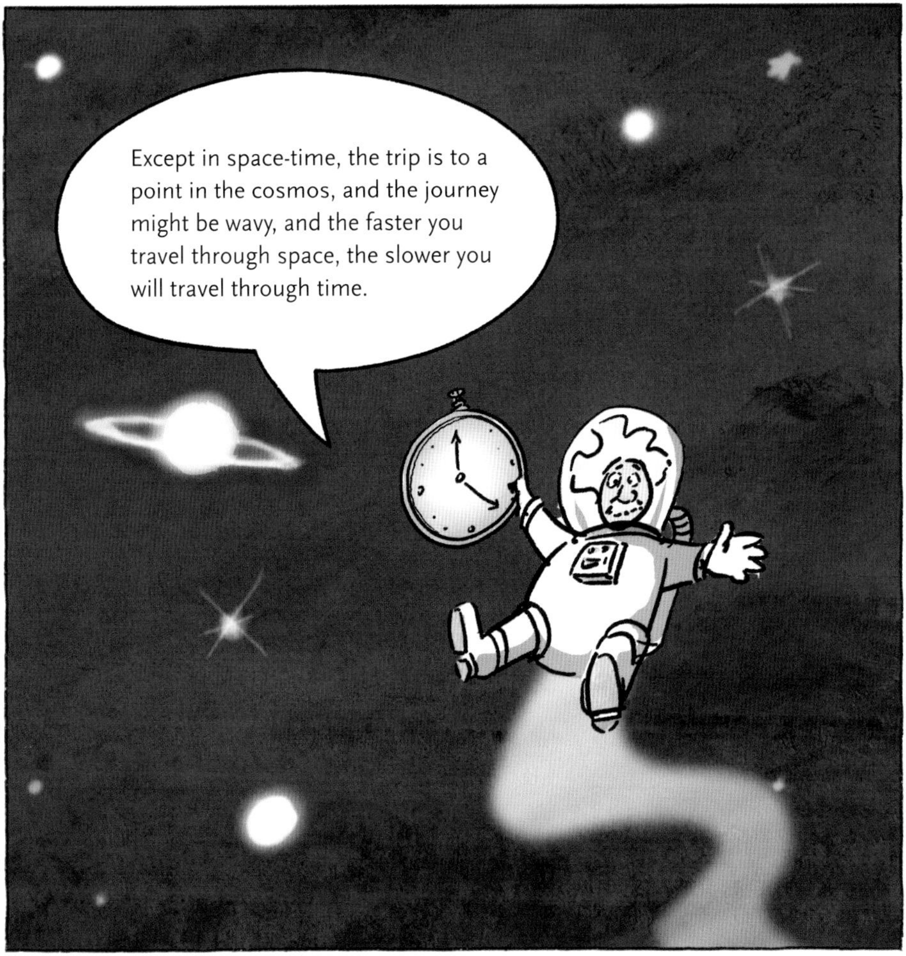
Except in space-time, the trip is to a point in the cosmos, and the journey might be wavy, and the faster you travel through space, the slower you will travel through time.

On the moon, a day is 56 microseconds shorter than it is on Earth. Because that tiny difference can have huge consequences over time, some scientists are calling for a special Moon Time Zone to be created for future moon dwellers.

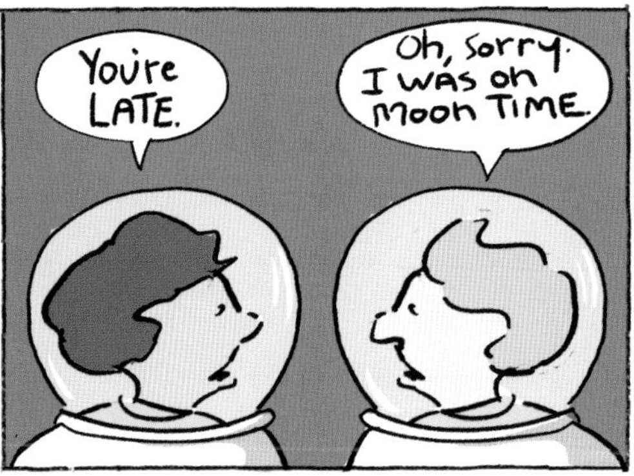
You're LATE.
Oh, sorry. I was on Moon TIME.

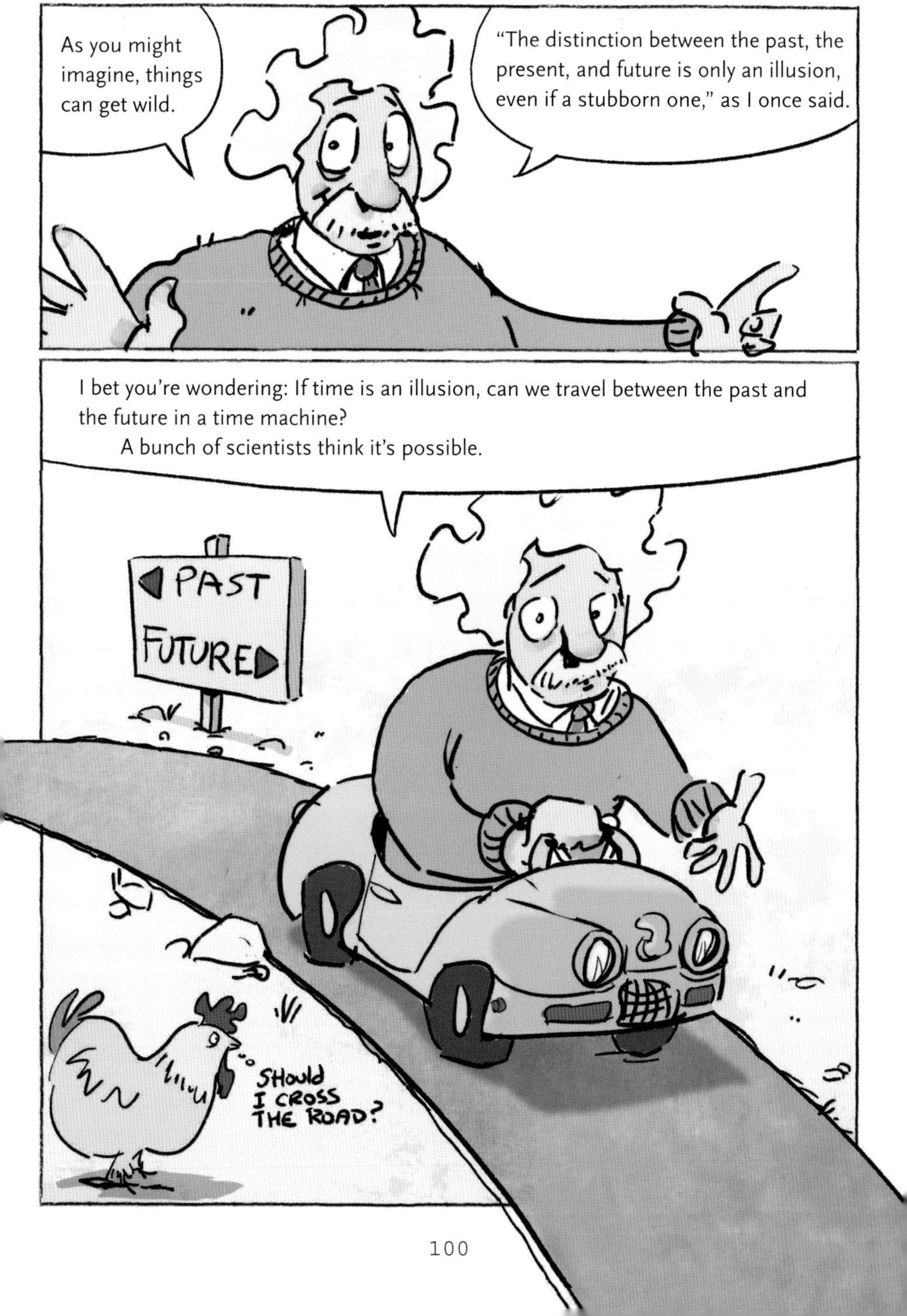
As you might imagine, things can get wild.
"The distinction between the past, the present, and future is only an illusion, even if a stubborn one," as I once said.
I bet you're wondering: If time is an illusion, can we travel between the past and the future in a time machine?
A bunch of scientists think it's possible.
PAST
FUTURE
SHOULD I CROSS THE ROAD?

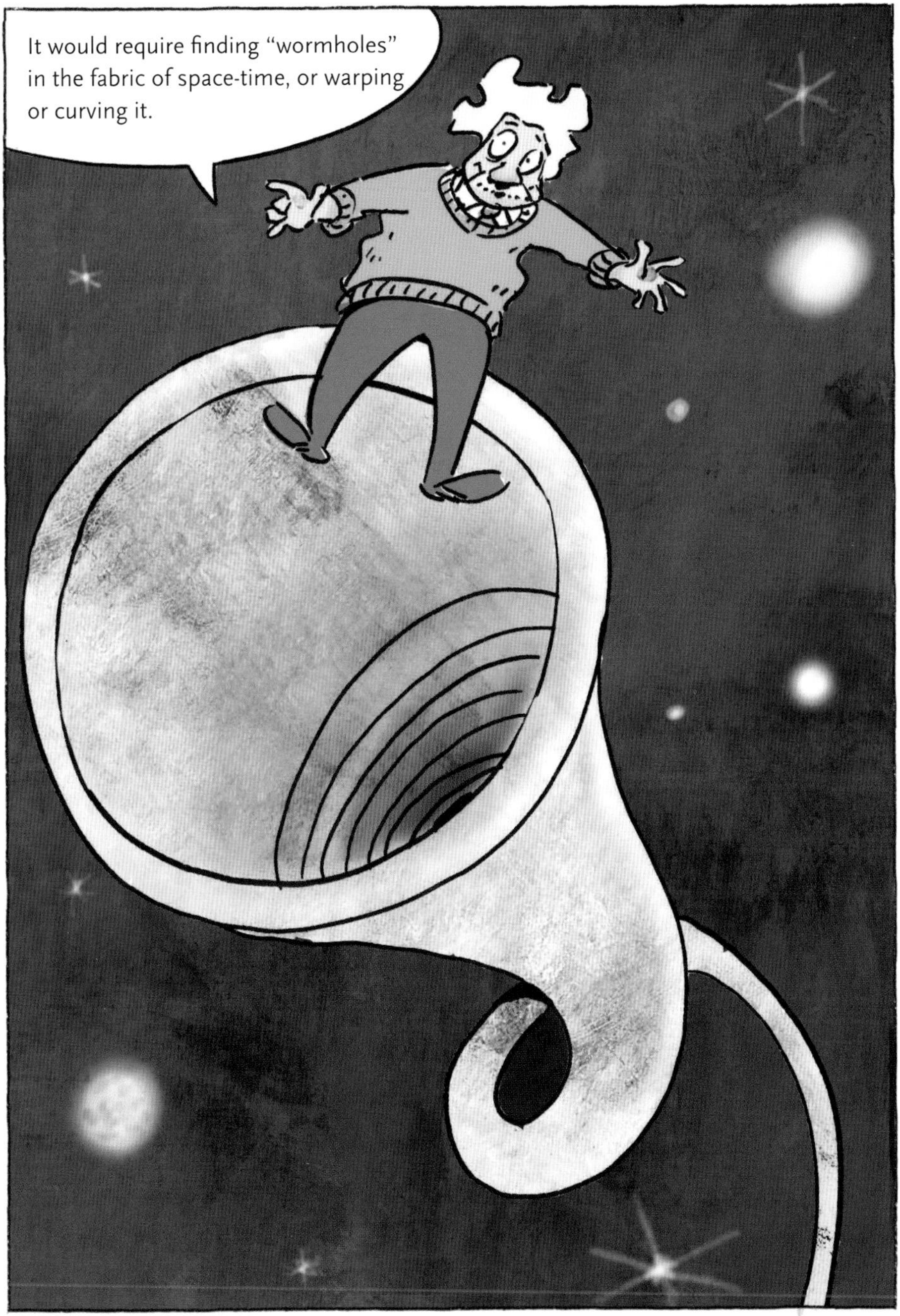
It would require finding "wormholes" in the fabric of space-time, or warping or curving it.

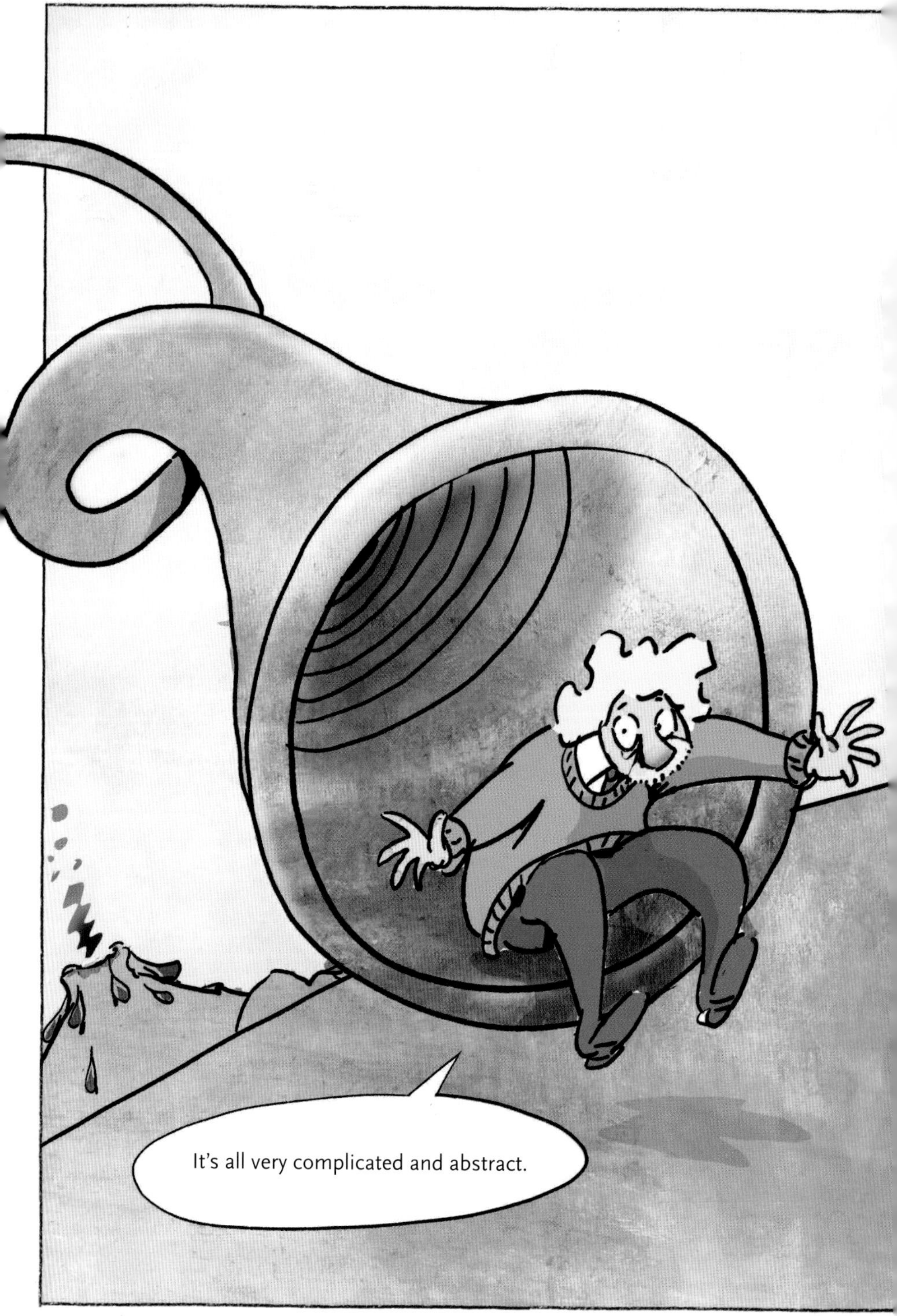
It's all very complicated and abstract.

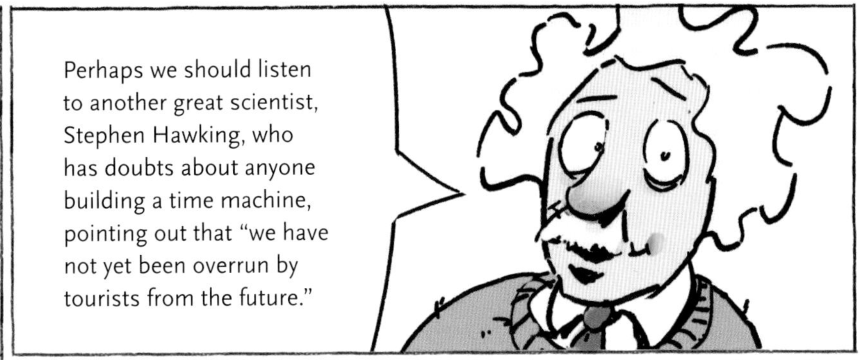
Perhaps we should listen to another great scientist, Stephen Hawking, who has doubts about anyone building a time machine, pointing out that “we have not yet been overrun by tourists from the future.”
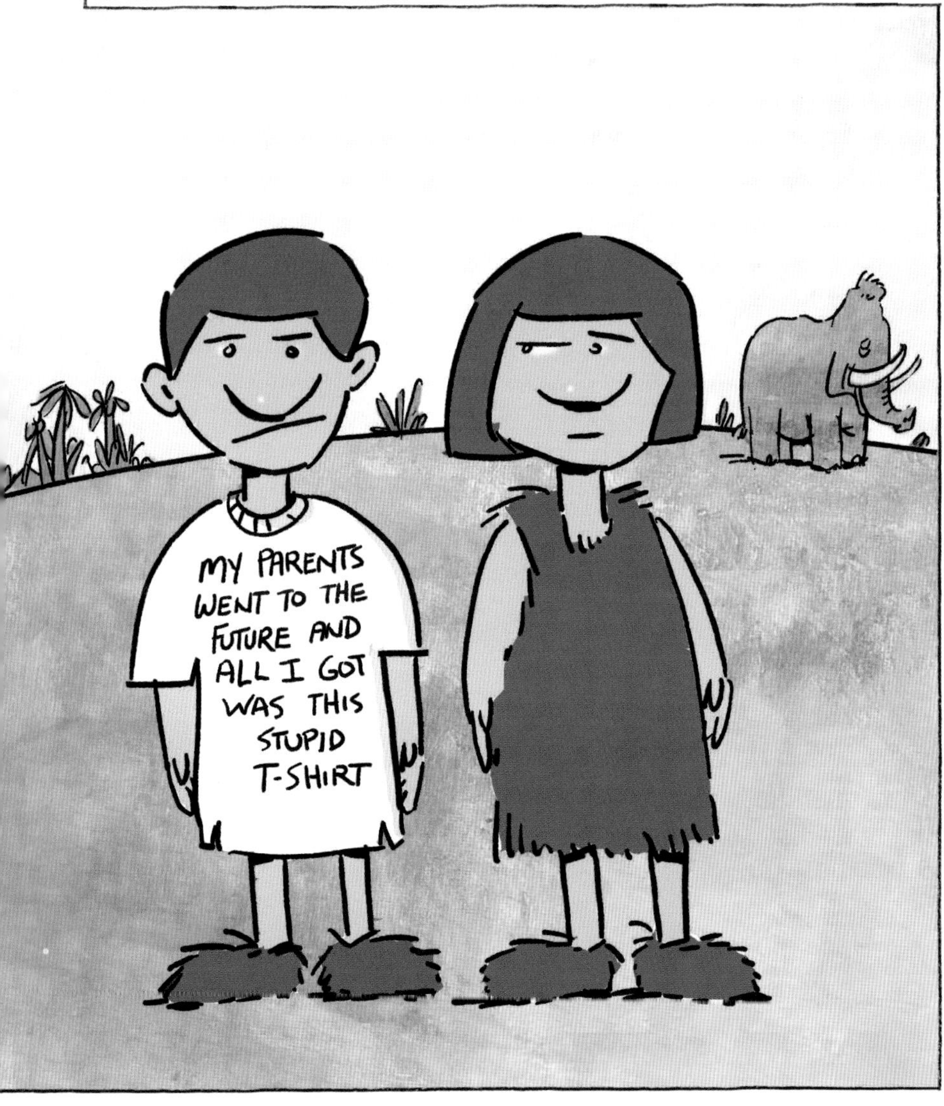
MY PARENTS WENT TO THE FUTURE AND ALL I GOT WAS THIS STUPID T-SHIRT

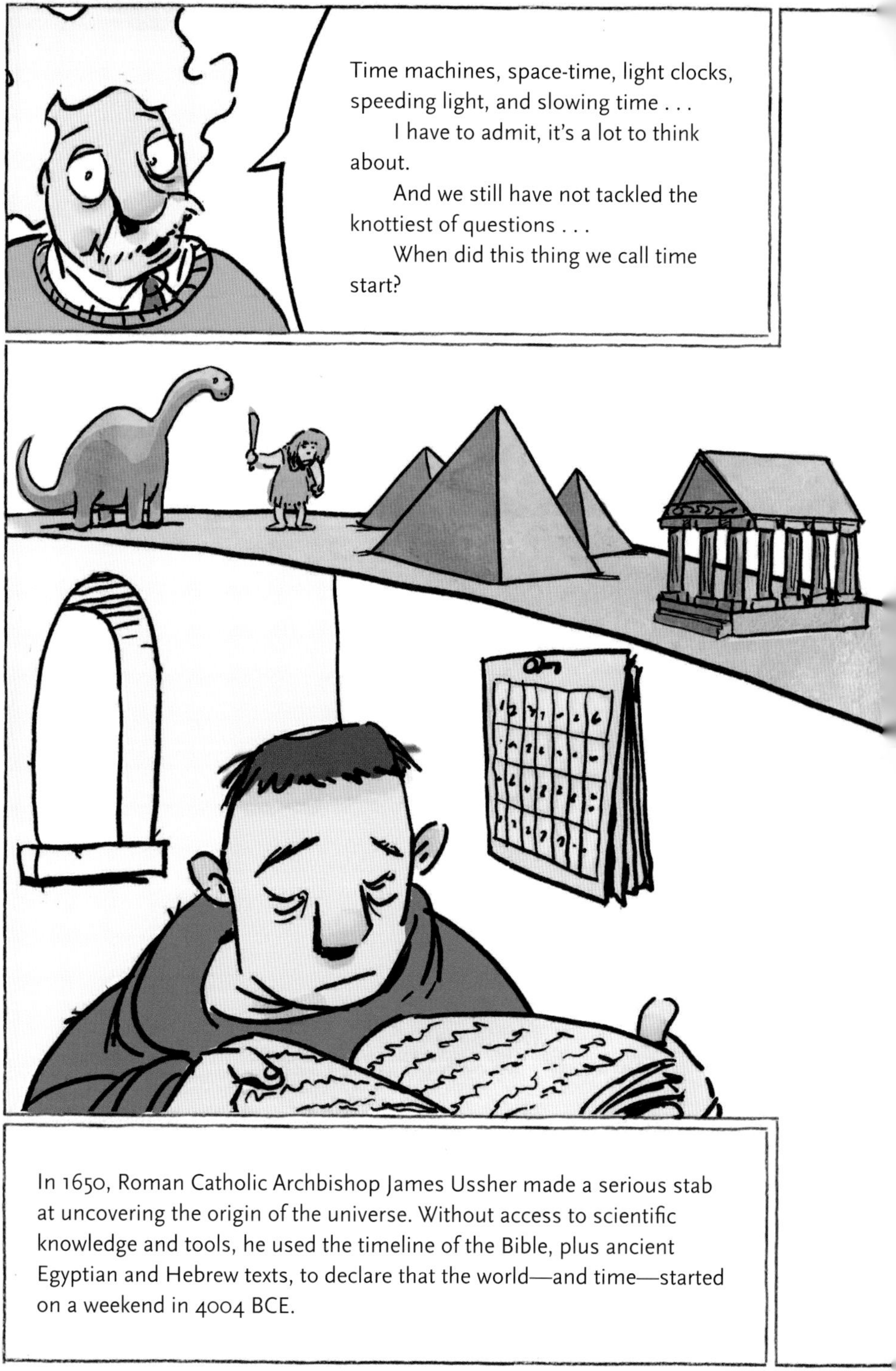
Time machines, space-time, light clocks, speeding light, and slowing time . . . I have to admit, it's a lot to think about. And we still have not tackled the knottiest of questions . . . When did this thing we call time start?
In 1650, Roman Catholic Archbishop James Ussher made a serious stab at uncovering the origin of the universe. Without access to scientific knowledge and tools, he used the timeline of the Bible, plus ancient Egyptian and Hebrew texts, to declare that the world—and time—started on a weekend in 4004 BCE.

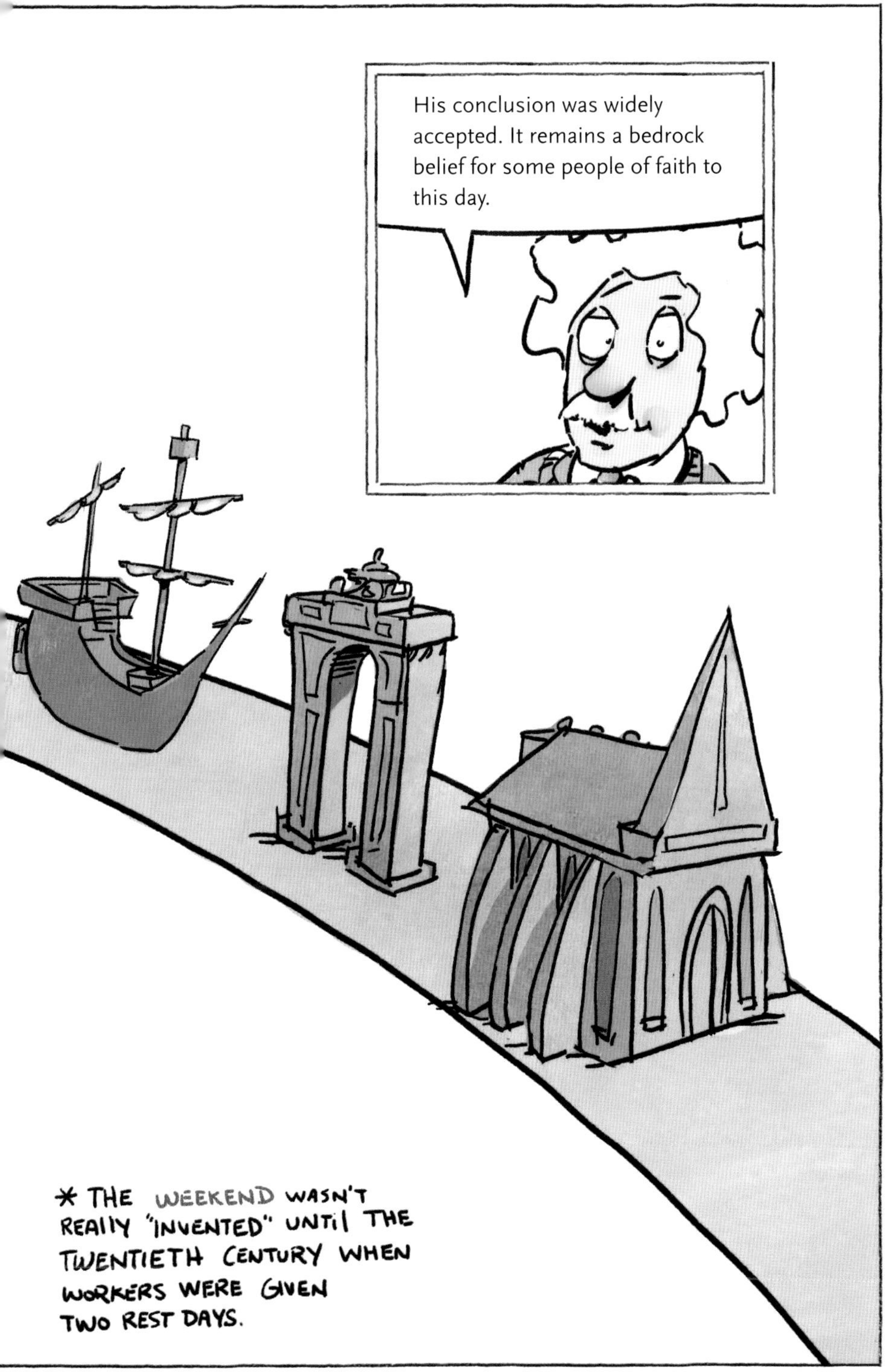
His conclusion was widely accepted. It remains a bedrock belief for some people of faith to this day.

* THE WEEKEND WASN'T REALLY "INVENTED" UNTIL THE TWENTIETH CENTURY WHEN WORKERS WERE GIVEN TWO REST DAYS.

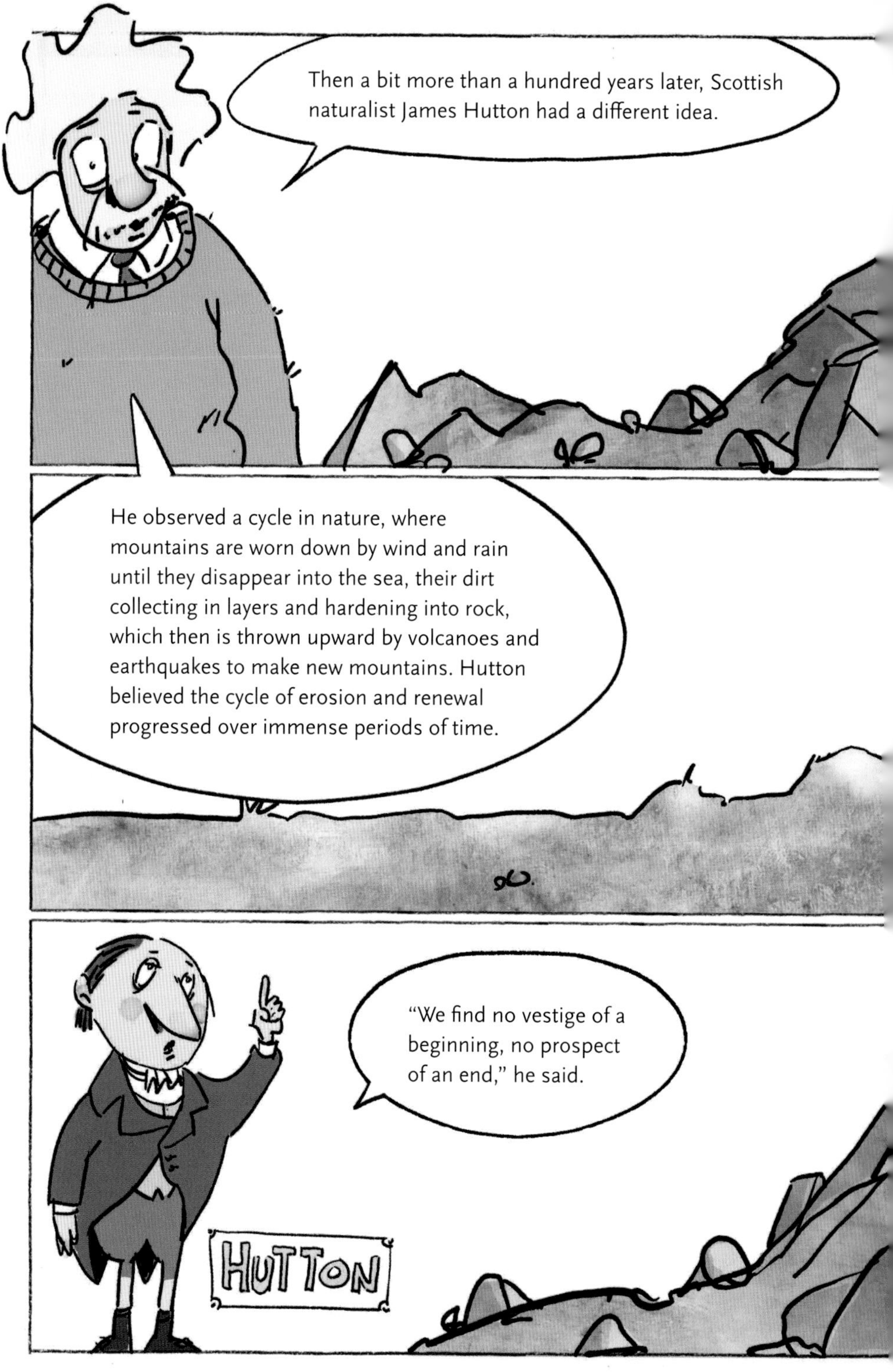
Then a bit more than a hundred years later, Scottish naturalist James Hutton had a different idea.
He observed a cycle in nature, where mountains are worn down by wind and rain until they disappear into the sea, their dirt collecting in layers and hardening into rock, which then is thrown upward by volcanoes and earthquakes to make new mountains. Hutton believed the cycle of erosion and renewal progressed over immense periods of time.
"We find no vestige of a beginning, no prospect of an end," he said.
HUTTON

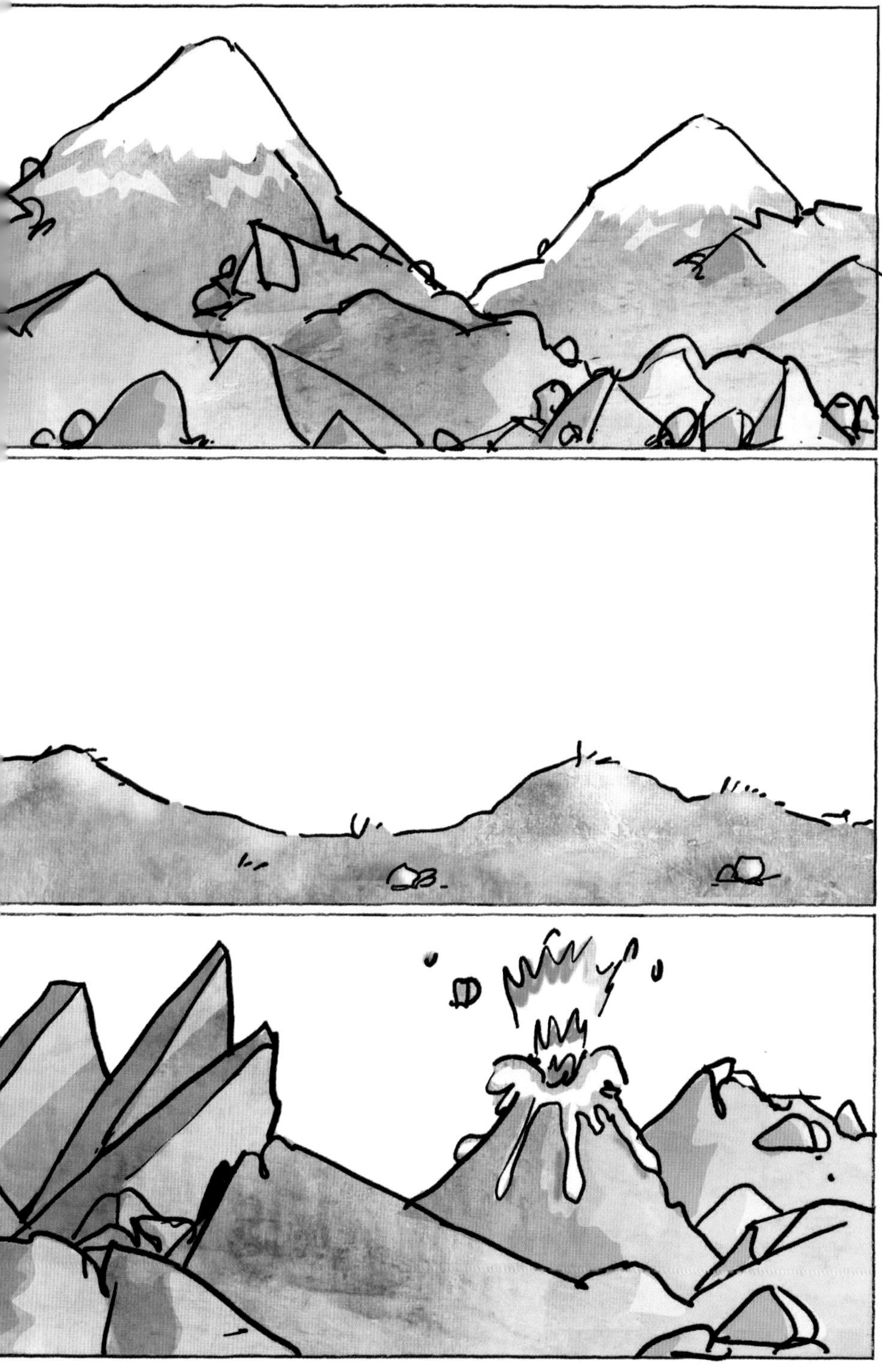

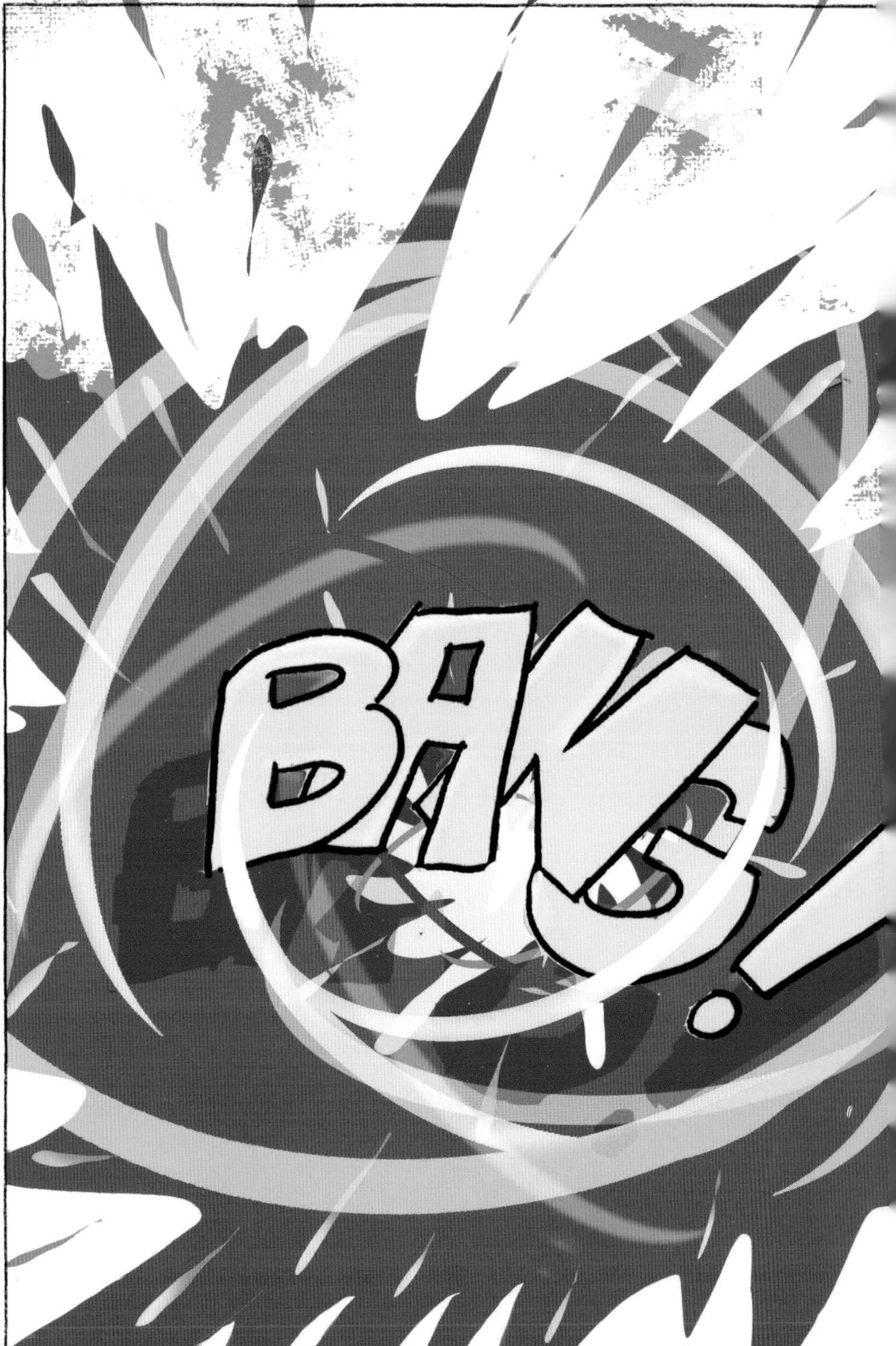
BANG!

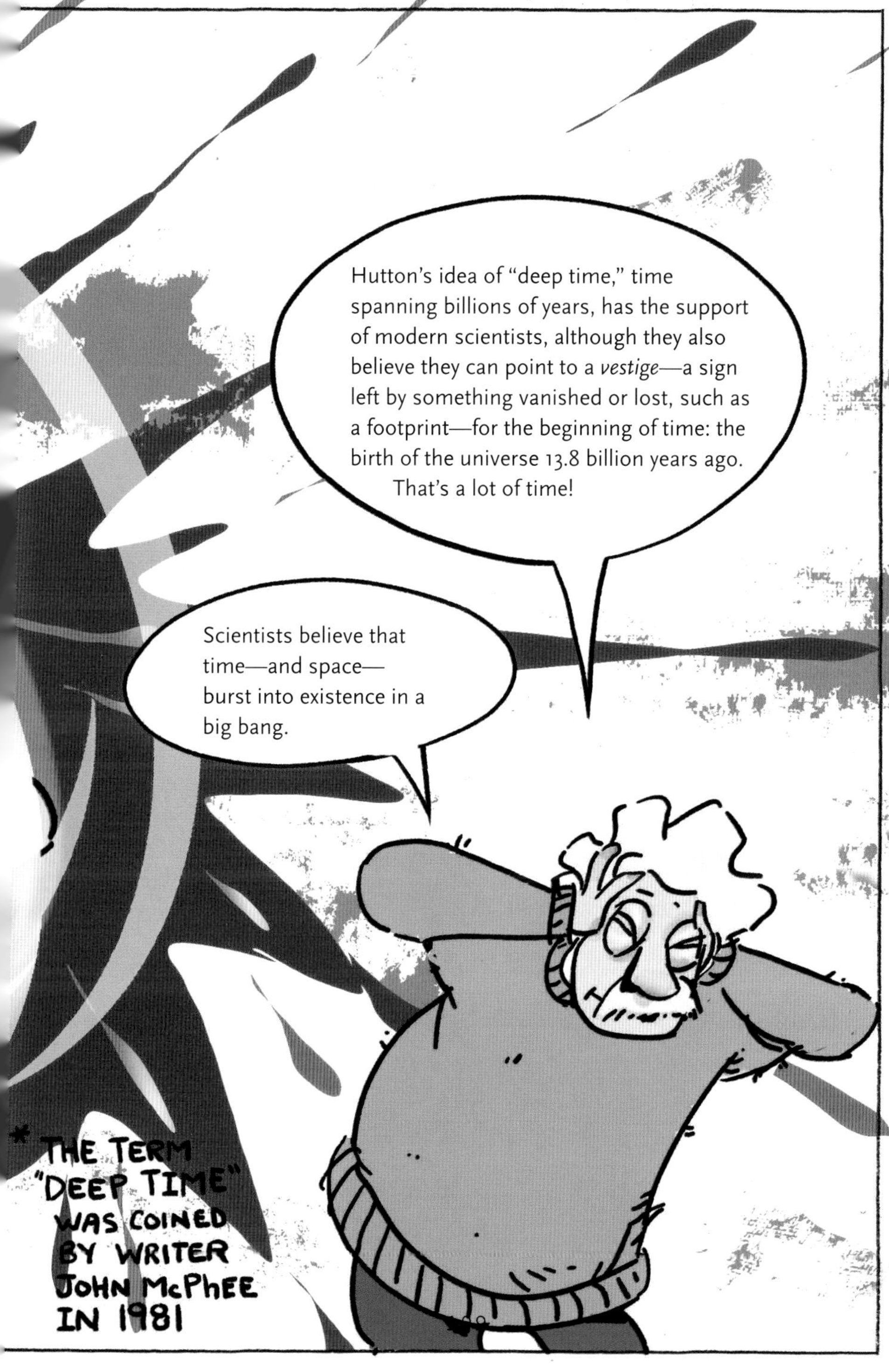
Hutton's idea of "deep time," time spanning billions of years, has the support of modern scientists, although they also believe they can point to a *vestige*—a sign left by something vanished or lost, such as a footprint—for the beginning of time: the birth of the universe 13.8 billion years ago. That's a lot of time!
Scientists believe that time—and space—burst into existence in a big bang.
* THE TERM "DEEP TIME" WAS COINED BY WRITER JOHN McPHEE IN 1981

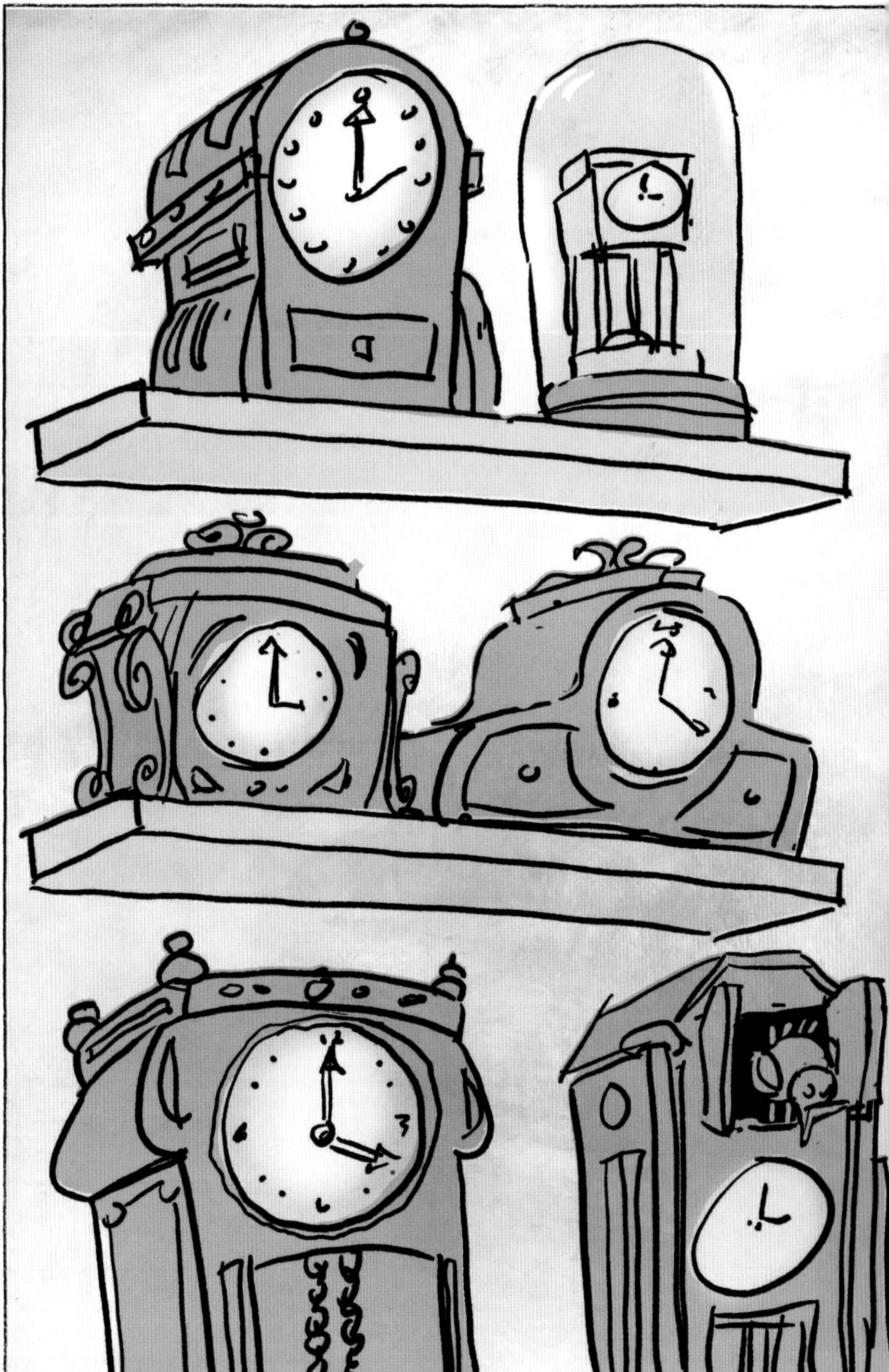

And will time end?

Oh, a lot of very smart people have ideas, but to be honest, no one really knows.

If you find time puzzling, you are not alone.

Nearly two thousand years ago, a learned man named Augustine of Hippo said, “What is time? Who can explain this easily and briefly? . . . We surely know what we mean when we speak of it. We also know what is meant when we hear someone else talking about it. What, then, is time? Provided that no one asks me, I know. If I want to explain it to an inquirer, I do not know.”

Interesting, yes? You have plenty of time to think about it and have your own Big Ideas.

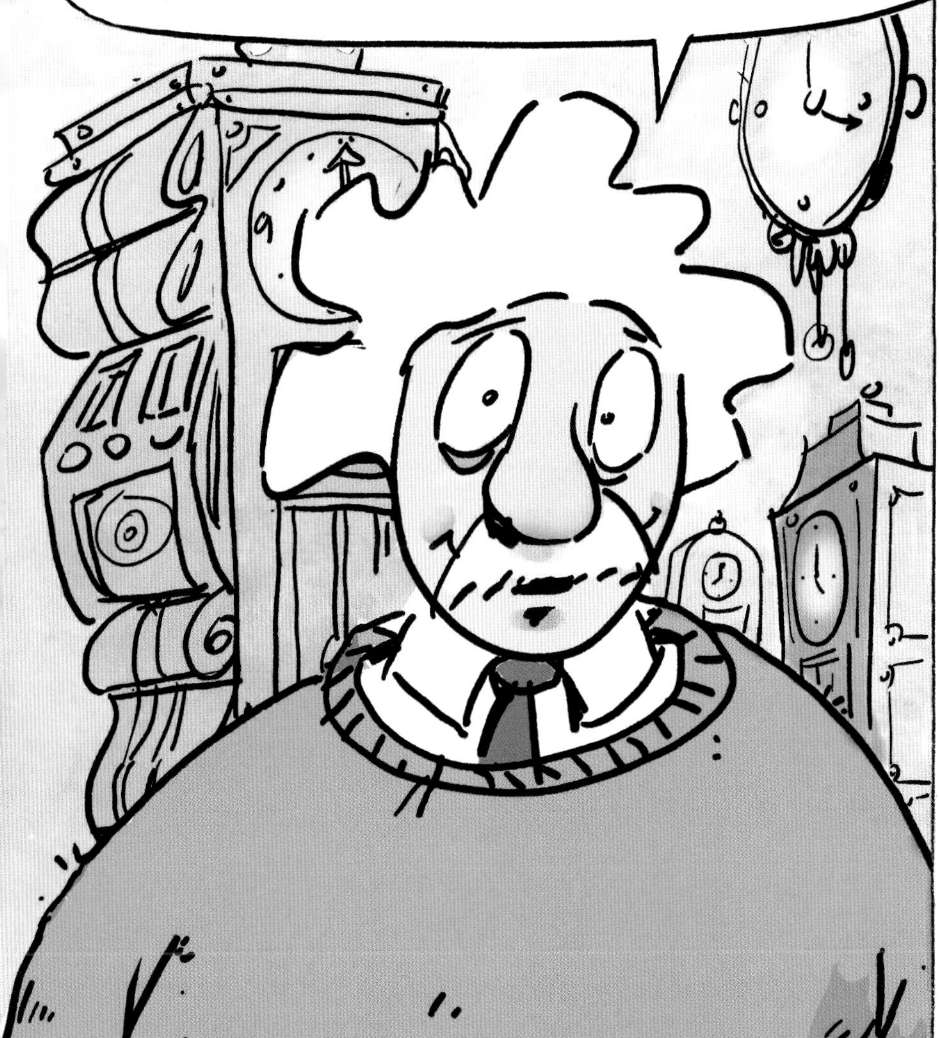

SELECT TIMELINE

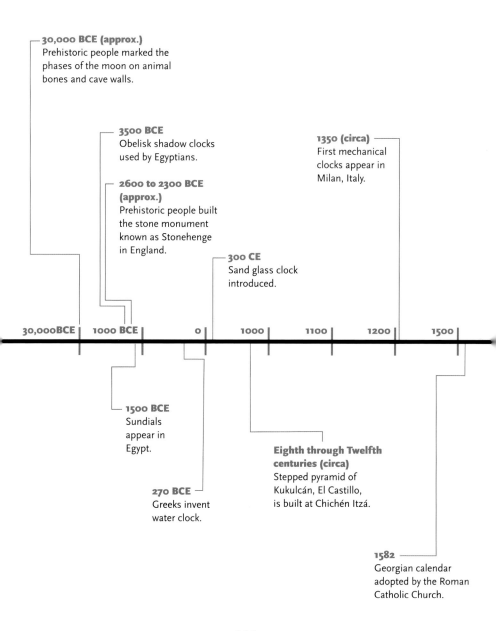

30,000 BCE (approx.)
Prehistoric people marked the phases of the moon on animal bones and cave walls.

3500 BCE
Obelisk shadow clocks used by Egyptians.

2600 to 2300 BCE (approx.)
Prehistoric people built the stone monument known as Stonehenge in England.

1350 (circa)
First mechanical clocks appear in Milan, Italy.

300 CE
Sand glass clock introduced.

30,000BCE | 1000 BCE | 0 | 1000 | 1100 | 1200 | 1500

1500 BCE
Sundials appear in Egypt.

Eighth through Twelfth centuries (circa)
Stepped pyramid of Kukulcán, El Castillo, is built at Chichén Itzá.

270 BCE
Greeks invent water clock.

1582
Georgian calendar adopted by the Roman Catholic Church.

1609
Galileo improves the telescope and makes astronomical discoveries.

1650
Roman Catholic Archbishop James Ussher uses the Bible's timeline to calculate the world's creation as 4004 BCE.

1675 (circa)
Pendulums and mainsprings greatly improve accuracy of mechanical clocks.

1687
Isaac Newton publishes the Mathematical Principles of Natural Philosophy, part of which proposes his Law of Universal Gravity.

1905
Albert Einstein's annus mirabilis (miracle year). Within one year, he published a series of papers including *The Theory of Special Relativity*.

1921
Albert Einstein wins Nobel Prize.

1926
Local watchmakers propose adding an illuminated wristwatch to the Statue of Liberty.

1927
Bell Telephone Laboratories creates a quartz clock.

1949
Harold Lyons develops an atomic clock.

1978–1993
Satellites are placed in space to create the Global Positioning System.

| 1600 | 1700 | 1800 | 1900 | 1950 | 1970 | 1990 |

1721
George Graham achieves accuracy of pendulum clock to within one second a day.

1736
John Harrison's marine clock was successfully tested by the British Navy.

1788
James Hutton first describes "deep time" (though the term is coined 200 years later).

1884
Prime meridian and international date line established.

1971
The Hafele–Keating experiment demonstrates that a clock in motion runs slower than a clock not in motion.

1981
The term "deep time" is coined by writer John McPhee.

2024
NASA proposes creating a new lunar time zone, Coordinated Lunar Time (LTC), to ensure the success of future multinational missions to the moon. Moon time passes 56 microseconds faster each Earth day.

WHO WAS
ALBERT EINSTEIN?

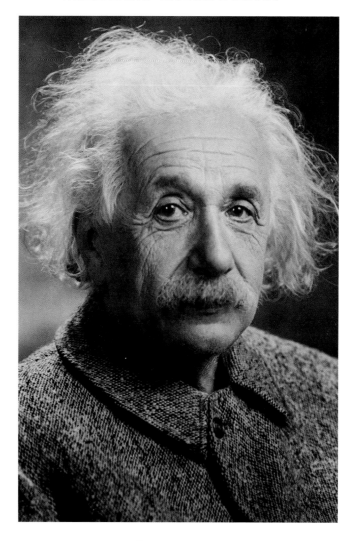

Albert Einstein, 1947

Albert Einstein's reputation as one of the greatest scientific thinkers of all time is firmly intact more than a half century after his death. His famous equation—$E=MC^2$—and his theories of time and space are keystones of modern science.

Born in Germany in 1879 to Jewish parents, young Einstein was a remarkable and precocious math whiz. In other school subjects, those in which he was disinterested or that demanded rote learning, he had only middling success. At sixteen, he attempted to enter college before finishing high school but failed the university entrance exam.

He eventually entered college and, after graduating, took a job as a government patent examiner, a person who evaluated new inventions. In moments away from work and home responsibilities, Einstein pondered novel and extraordinary ideas. In 1905, he published *On the Electrodynamics of Moving Bodies*, his thoughts concerning the nature of light, $E=MC^2$, the joining of matter and energy, and possibly the most famous equation ever conceived; as well as *Relativity: The Special and the General Theory*, outlining the nature of light, time, and space. They were astonishing accomplishments, and 1905 is often referred to as Einstein's "annus mirabilis" or miracle year. In 1921, he won the Nobel Prize in physics for *Electrodynamics*.

By 1933, Einstein was a famous scientist. Yet his fame did not insulate him from the antisemitic hatred of the Nazis, who were then ruling Germany. Seeing that his Jewish roots put him danger, Einstein immigrated to the United States.

In 1939, he wrote to Franklin D. Roosevelt, alerting the president of a Nazi plan to build an atomic bomb; Einstein proposed the need for more American nuclear research. Nearly disregarded, the letter eventually inspired the Manhattan Project and the production of an American atomic bomb. But Einstein played no role in its construction and was banned from the project as a security risk because of his socialist politics and pacifism.

Einstein never stopped pursuing big and astonishing ideas, but cutting-edge physics, such as quantum mechanics, moved on without him.

Albert Einstein died in New Jersey in 1955. The doctor who performed the autopsy to determine the cause of death—heart failure—made off with Einstein's brain and kept it in a jar for more than forty years. Its fate is described in Michael Paterniti's enchanting book, *Driving Mr. Albert: A Trip Across America with Einstein's Brain*.

NOTES

Page 34—"Absolute, true . . . from its own nature [it] flows": Whitrow, p. 100.

Page 35—". . . this present moment is common to all things that are now in being": Whitrow, p. 101.

Page 94—"The distinction between the past, the present, and future is only an illusion": Davies, p. 70.

Page 97—"We have not yet been overrun by tourists from the future": Hawking, p. 206.

Page 100—"We find no vestige of a beginning, no prospect of an end": *James Hutton: The Founder of Modern Geology*.

Page 105—"What is time? Who can explain this easily and briefly?": Clegg, p. 39.

SELECT BIBLIOGRAPHY

Articles

"A Revolution in Timekeeping." National Institute of Standards and Technology, U.S. Government. See nist.gov/pml/time-and-frequency-division/popular-links/walk-through -time/walk-through-time-revolution.

"A Walk Through Time—Ancient Calendars." National Institute of Standards and Technology, U.S. Government. See www.nist.gov/pml/time-and-frequency-division /popular-links/walk-through-time/walk-through-time-ancient-calendars.

"Bang, Bounce or Something Else?" Simons Foundation, April 22, 2020. See www. simonsfoundation.org/2020/04/22/bang-bounce-or-something-else.

Beacock, Ian. "A Brief History of (Modern) Time." *Atlantic*, December 22, 2015. See www.theatlantic.com/technology/archive/2015/12/the-creation-of-modern-time/421419.

Betts, Jonathan D. "Clepsydra: Timekeeping Device." *Encyclopedia Britannica*. See www. britannica.com/technology/clepsydra.

Bilbos, Konstantin. "How Does an Atomic Clock Work?" Time and Date. See www. timeanddate.com/time/how-do-atomic-clocks-work.html.

Birchall, Ben. "A Brief History of Telling Time." *The Conversation*, May 15, 2016. See theconversation.com/a-brief-history-of-telling-time-55408.

Bouchard, R. Philip. "Word Connections: Sun, Moon, and Stars." Medium.com, March 21, 2017. See medium.com/the-philipendium/word-connections-sun-moon-stars -946d9d0e5a13.

"Constant Speed." *Einstein* exhibition, American Museum of Natural History. See www. amnh.org/exhibitions/einstein/light/constant-speed.

Costa, David. "24-Hour Clock: Time Convention." Encyclopedia *Britannica*. See www. britannica.com/topic/24-hour-clock.

Cottier, Cody. "Why Is January 1 the Beginning of a New Year?" *Discover*, December 30, 2020. See www.discovermagazine.com/the-sciences/why-is-january-1-the-beginning-of-a -new-year.

Delber, Caroline. "Sad! This Is When the Universe Will Truly End." *Popular Mechanics*, August 24, 2020. See www.popularmechanics.com/space/deep-space/a33612633/when-will-the-universe-end.

Dickerson, Kelly, and Natalie Musumeci. "Here's Why Astronauts Age Slower Than the Rest of Us Here on Earth." *Business Insider*, January 1, 2023. See www.businessinsider.com/do-astronauts-age-slower-than-people-on-earth-2015-8?op=1.

Doggett, L. E. "Calendars." Eclipse: NASA. See eclipse.gsfc.nasa.gov/SEhelp/calendars.html.

"Early Clocks." National Institute of Standards and Technology (NIST). See nist.gov/pml/time-and-frequency-division/popular-links/walk-through-time/walk-through-time-early-clocks.

"The Early Years." *Einstein* exhibition, American Museum of Natural History. See www.amnh.org/exhibitions/einstein/life-and-times/the-early-years.

"Equinox." *National Geographic*. See education.nationalgeographic.org/resource/equinox.

Falk, Dan. "Arrows of Time." *Quanta*. See www.quantamagazine.org/what-is-time-a-history-of-physics-biology-clocks-and-culture-20200504.

Farrier, David, and Aeon. "How the Concept of Deep Time Is Changing." *Atlantic*, October 31, 2016. See www.theatlantic.com/science/archive/2016/10/aeon-deep-time/505922.

"Gregorian Calendar." *Encyclopedia Britannica*. See www.britannica.com/topic/Gregorian-calendar.

Greshko, Michael. "Origins of the Universe, Explained." *National Geographic*, January 18, 2017. See www.nationalgeographic.com/science/article/origins-of-the-universe.

Harvey, Ailsa, and Vicky Stein. "Is Time Travel Possible?" Space.com November 24, 2022. See www.space.com/21675-time-travel.html.

Hawking, Stephen. "The Beginning of Time." See www.hawking.org.uk/in-words/lectures/the-beginning-of-time.

Heineman, Kristin. "Why Are There Seven Days in a Week?" *Discover Magazine*, January 15, 2020. See www.discovermagazine.com/planet-earth/why-are-there-seven-days-in-a-week.

Helmenstine, Anne Marie. "What Is time? A Simple Explanation." ThoughtCo.com, November 26, 2019. See www.thoughtco.com/what-is-time-4156799.

"History of the Calendar." Historyworld.net. See historyworld.net/wrldhis/plaintexthistories.asp?historyid=ac06.

"How Does GPS Work?" Space Place: NASA. See spaceplace.nasa.gov/gps-pizza/en.

"How We Divide Time." Royal Museums Greenwich (UK). See www.rmg.co.uk/stories/topics/why-12-months-year-seven-days-week-or-60-minutes-hour.

"It's All Relative." *Einstein* exhibition, American Museum of Natural History. See www.amnh.org/exhibitions/einstein/time/its-all-relative.

Jaffe, Andrew. "The Illusion of Time." *Nature*, April 16, 2018. See nature.com/articles/d41586-018-04558-7

"James Hutton" (biography). Scottish Science Hall of Fame. See digital.nls.uk/scientists/biographies/james-hutton.

"James Hutton: The Founder of Modern Geology." Earth Inside and Out collection, American Museum of Natural History. See www.amnh.org/learn-teach/curriculum-collections/earth-inside-and-out/james-hutton.

Kamrin, Janice. "Telling Time in Ancient Egypt." Heilbrunn Timeline of Art History, Metropolitan Museum of Art, February 2017. See www.metmuseum.org/toah/hd/tell/hd_tell.htm.

Kennel, Joanne. "How Gravity Changes Time: The Effect Known as Gravitational Time Dilation." *Science Explorer*, November 16, 2015. See thescienceexplorer.com/universe/how-gravity-changes-time-effect-known-gravitational-time-dilation.

Lombardi, Michael A. "Why Is a Minute Divided into 60 Seconds, an Hour into 60 Minutes, Yet There Are Only 24 Hours in a Day?" *Scientific American*, March 5, 2007. See www.scientificamerican.com/article/experts-time-division-days-hours-minutes.

"Lunar Calendar and How Moon Phases Work." Human Origin Project. See humanoriginproject.com/the-lunar-calendar-and-how-moon-phases-work.

Mann, Adam. "What Is Space-Time?" Livescience.com, May 20, 2021. See www.livescience.com/space-time.html.

Matson, John. "How Time Flies: Ultraprecise Clock Rates Vary with Tiny Differences in Speed and Elevation." *Scientific American*, September 23, 2010. See www.scientificamerican.com/article/time-dilatioc.

"A Matter of Time." *Einstein* exhibition, American Museum of Natural History. See www.amnh.org/exhibitions/einstein/time/a-matter-of-time.

"Maya and the Sun." Living Maya Time, Smithsonian National Museum of the American Indian. See maya.nmai.si.edu/sites/default/files/transcripts/the_maya_and_the_sun.pdf.

May, Andrew. "What Is Time Dilation?" Livescience.com, November 17, 2021. See www.livescience.com/what-is-time-dilation#section-time-dilation-defined.

"The Mayas: The Equinox and the Solstice." YucatánToday.com. See yucatantoday.com/en/mayas-equinox-and-solstice.

Morrison, Jim. "The Blasphemous Geologist Who Rocked Our Understanding of Earth's Age." *Smithsonian Magazine*, August 29, 2016. See www.smithsonianmag.com/history/father-modern-geology-youve-never-heard-180960203.

Mueller, Jennifer. "How to Determine Longitude." Wiki How, January 6, 2023. See www.wikihow.com/Determine-Longitude.

Mulvihill, Mary. "How an Archbishop Calculated the Creation." *Irish Times*, September 25, 2003. See www.irishtimes.com/news/how-an-archbishop-calculated-the-creation-1.378556.

"NASA's Guide to Near-light-speed Travel." Goddard Media Studios: NASA, August 14, 2020. See svs.gsfc.nasa.gov/13653.

"New Year Festival." *Encyclopedia Britannica*. See www.britannica.com/topic/New-Year-festival.

Nicholson, Kate. "Winter Solstice at Stonehenge: The Ancient Tradition Explained." MSN.com, December 21, 2022. See www.msn.com/en-us/health/wellness/winter-solstice-at-stonehenge-the-ancient-tradition-explained/ar-AA15wIUc.

O'Callaghan, Jonathan. "How Does Time Work?" Space.com, August 26, 2022. See www.space.com/time-how-it-works.

Odenwald, Sten. "The Struggle to Find the Origins of Time." *Astronomy*, May 24, 2022. See astronomy.com/magazine/news/2022/05/the-struggle-to-find-the-origins-of-time.

"Oldest Lunar Calendars." Solar System Exploration Research Virtual Institute: NASA. See sservi.nasa.gov/articles/oldest-lunar-calendars.

Panek, Richard. "The Year of Albert Einstein." *Smithsonian Magazine*, June 2005. See www.smithsonianmag.com/science-nature/the-year-of-albert-einstein-75841381.

"Prime Meridian." *National Geographic*. See education.nationalgeographic.org/resource/prime-meridian.

"Resetting the Theory of Time." NPR.com, May 17, 2013. See www.npr.org/2013/05/17/184775924/resetting-the-theory-of-time.

"Revolution: Time." *Einstein* exhibition, American Museum of Natural History. See www.amnh.org/exhibitions/einstein/time/revolution-time.

Schneider, Susan. "Spacetime Emergence, Panpsychism and the Nature of Consciousness." *Scientific American*, August 6, 2018. See blogs.scientificamerican.com/observations/spacetime-emergence-panpsychism-and-the-nature-of-consciousness.

Shubinski, Raymond. "A Brief History of Time: What Is It and How Do We Define It?" *Astronomy*, January 6, 2022. See astronomy.com/magazine/news/2022/01/a-brief-history-of-time-what-is-it-and-how-do-we-define-it.

Siegal, Ethan. "Did Time Have a Beginning?" *Forbes*, June 7, 2019. See www.forbes.com/sites/startswithabang/2019/06/07/does-time-have-a-beginning/?sh=8a61c4a513b1.

Smolin, Lee. "Spacetime Is Not Necessarily Continuous." *Scientific American*, October 24, 2014. See www.scientificamerican.com/article/spacetime-is-not-necessarily-continuous.

Sollinger, Marc. "The Invention of Time." WGBH News, February 15, 2016. See www.wgbh.org/news/2016/02/15/innovation/invention-time.

"Summer Solstice." History.com. See www.history.com/topics/natural-disasters-and-environment/history-of-summer-solstice.

"Summer Solstice Traditions from Around the World." *National Geographic,* June 20, 2019. See www.nationalgeographic.com/culture/article/summer-soltice-history-around-world.

Sutter, Paul. "What If the Universe Had No Beginning?" Livescience.com, October 11, 2021. See www.livescience.com/universe-had-no-beginning-time.

"Time." *Einstein* exhibition, American Museum of Natural History. See www.amnh.org/exhibitions/einstein/time.

"Time Machines." *Einstein* exhibition, American Museum of Natural History. See www.amnh.org/exhibitions/einstein/time/time-machines.

"Time Travel." *Einstein* exhibition, American Museum of Natural History. See www.amnh.org/exhibitions/einstein/time/time-travel.

"Understanding Gravity—Warps and Ripples in Space and Time." Space & Time collection, Australian Academy of Science. See www.science.org.au/curious/space-time/gravity.

Waldrop, Mitch. "Einstein's Relativity Explained in 4 Simple Steps." *National Geographic*,

May 16, 2017. See www.nationalgeographic.com/science/article/einstein-relativity-thought-experiment-train-lightning-genius.

Wall, Mike. "The Big Bang: What Really Happened at Our Universe's Birth?" Space.com, February 21, 2022. See www.space.com/13347-big-bang-origins-universe-birth.html.

"What Is an Atomic Clock?" Moon to Mars: NASA, June 19, 2019. See www.nasa.gov/feature/jpl/what-is-an-atomic-clock.

"Why Are There 24 Hours in a Day and 60 Minutes in an Hour?" ScienceABC.com, February 8, 2023. See www.scienceabc.com/eyeopeners/why-are-there-24-hours-in-a-day-and-60-minutes-in-an-hour.html.

"Why Do We Have Special Names for Full Moons?" Royal Museums Greenwich (UK). See www.rmg.co.uk/stories/topics/what-are-names-full-moons-throughout-year.

Books

Augustine. *Confessions of St Augustine*. August 7, 2023. See gutenberg.org/files/3296/3296-h/3296-h.htm.

Clegg, Brian. *How to Build a Time Machine: The Real Science of Time Travel*. New York: St. Martins, 2011.

Coveney, Peter, and Roger Highfield. *The Arrow of Time: A Voyage Through Science to Solve Time's Greatest Mystery*. New York: Fawcett Columbine, 1990.

Davies, Paul. *About Time: Einstein's Unfinished Revolution*. New York: Simon & Schuster, 1995.

Hawking, Stephen. *The Illustrated A Brief History of Time*. New York: Bantam Books, 1996.

Paterniti, Michael. *Driving Mr. Albert: A Trip Across America with Einstein's Brain*. New York: Dial Press, 2001.

Whitrow, G. J. *The Nature of Time*. New York: Holt, Rinehart and Winston, 1972.

Videos

Ash, Arvin. "General Relativity Explained Simply and Visually." See www.youtube.com/watch?v=tzQC3uYL67U.

———. "4D Spacetime and Relativity Explained Simply and Visually." See www.youtube.com/watch?v=ZfR1Jc6Zglo.

Greene, Brian. "The Nature of Space and Time." Center for Inquiry, January 22, 2020. See www.youtube.com/watch?v=M22MEShcyx8.

———. "Space, Time, and Einstein." World Science Festival, July 30, 2020. See www.youtube.com/watch?v=CKJuC5CUMgU.

"Neil deGrasse Tyson Explains Time Dilation." StarTalk, February 8, 2022. See www.youtube.com/watch?v=1BCkSYQoNRQ.

"Time Dilation—Einstein's Theory of Relativity Explained!" Science ABC, April 13, 2018. See www.youtube.com/watch?v=yuD34tEpRFw.

"What Exactly Is Spacetime? Explained in Ridiculously Simple Words." Science ABC, October 4, 2021. See www.youtube.com/watch?v=3khY_bwf5FY.

"Why Does Time Slow Down as You Approach the Speed of Light?" David/Owlcation, June 29, 2022. See owlcation.com/stem/Why-Does-Time-Slow-Down-As-You-Approach-the-Speed-of-Light.

ACKNOWLEDGMENTS

I'd like to thank Professor Luis Álvarez-Guamé of Stony Brook University in New York for his thoughts, advice, and encouragement.

AUTHOR'S NOTE

Time has been one of the most perplexing, confounding, and challenging subjects I've tackled in thirty years. The story of *marking* time—slicing it into years, months, days, hours, minutes, and seconds—is straightforward, but exploring the very *idea* of time, well, that is something entirely different.

It turns out time is a knot of space, mass, and speed, and a Gordian one at that. The nature of time's passage; the question of simultaneity; the notion of a fabric of time able to be folded, bent, and torn—all test our understanding of the very essence of reality. Is it merely a consequence of one's point of view? Other questions tumble forth: Is time timeless? Does it have a beginning? Does it have an end?

I closed the book with a snippet from Saint Augustine's *Confession*, where he wrestled with the confounding nature of time. The more complete version follows.

> What is time? Who can explain this easily and briefly? Who can comprehend this even in thought so as to articulate the answer in words? Yet what do we speak of, in our familiar everyday conversation, more than of time? We surely know what we mean when we speak of it. We also know what is meant when we hear someone else talking about it. What then is time? Provided that no one asks me, I know. If I want to explain it to an inquirer, I do not know. But I confidently affirm myself to know that if nothing passes away, there is no past time, and if nothing arrives, there is no future time, and if nothing existed there would be no present time. Take the two tenses, past and future. How can they "be" when the past is not now present and the future is not yet present? Yet if the present were always present, it would not pass into the past: it would not be time but eternity. If then, in order to be time at all, the present is so made that it passes into the past, how can we say that this present also "is"? The cause of its being is that it will cease to be. So indeed we cannot truly say that time exists except in the sense that it tends toward non-existence.

INDEX

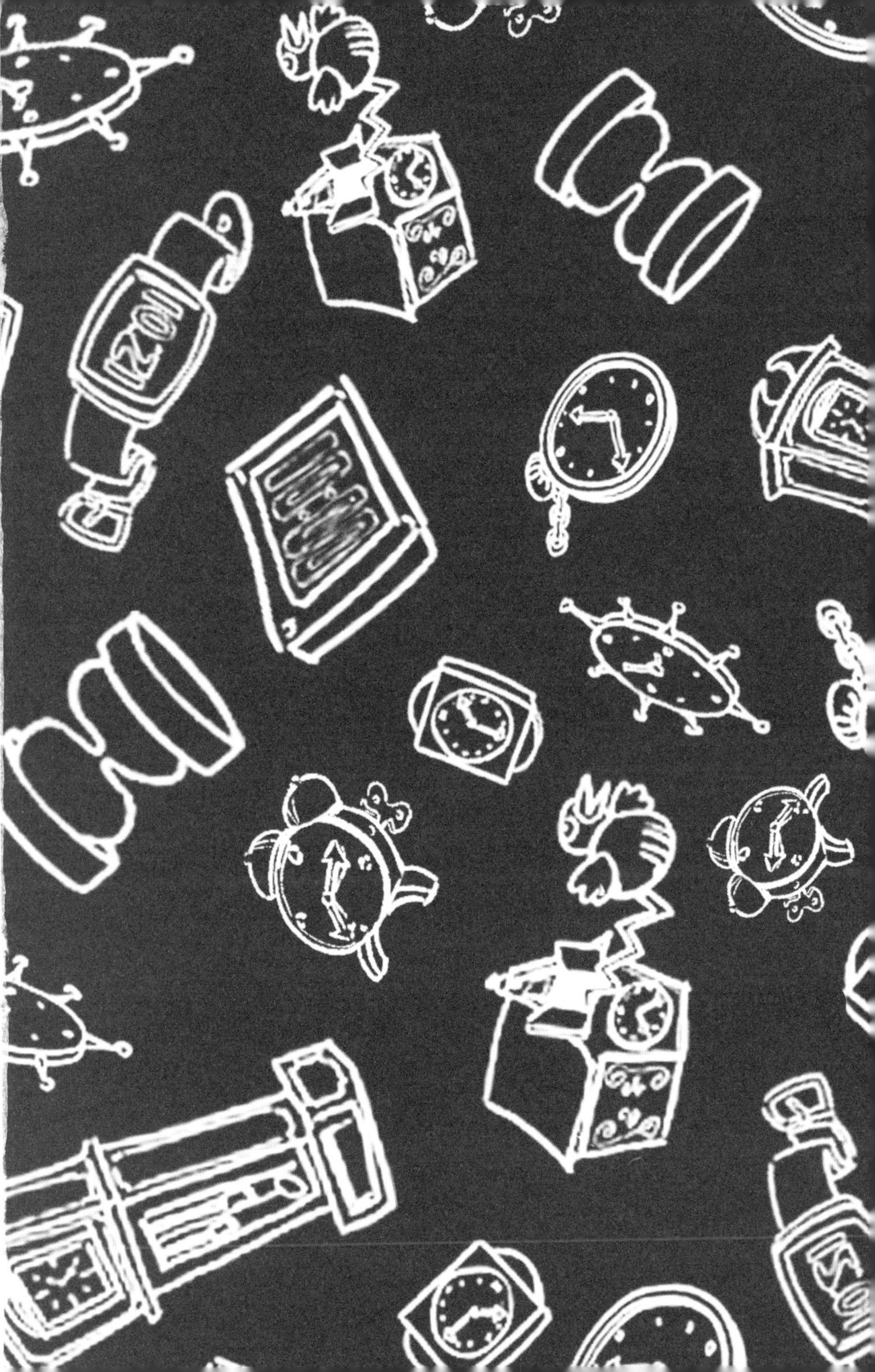

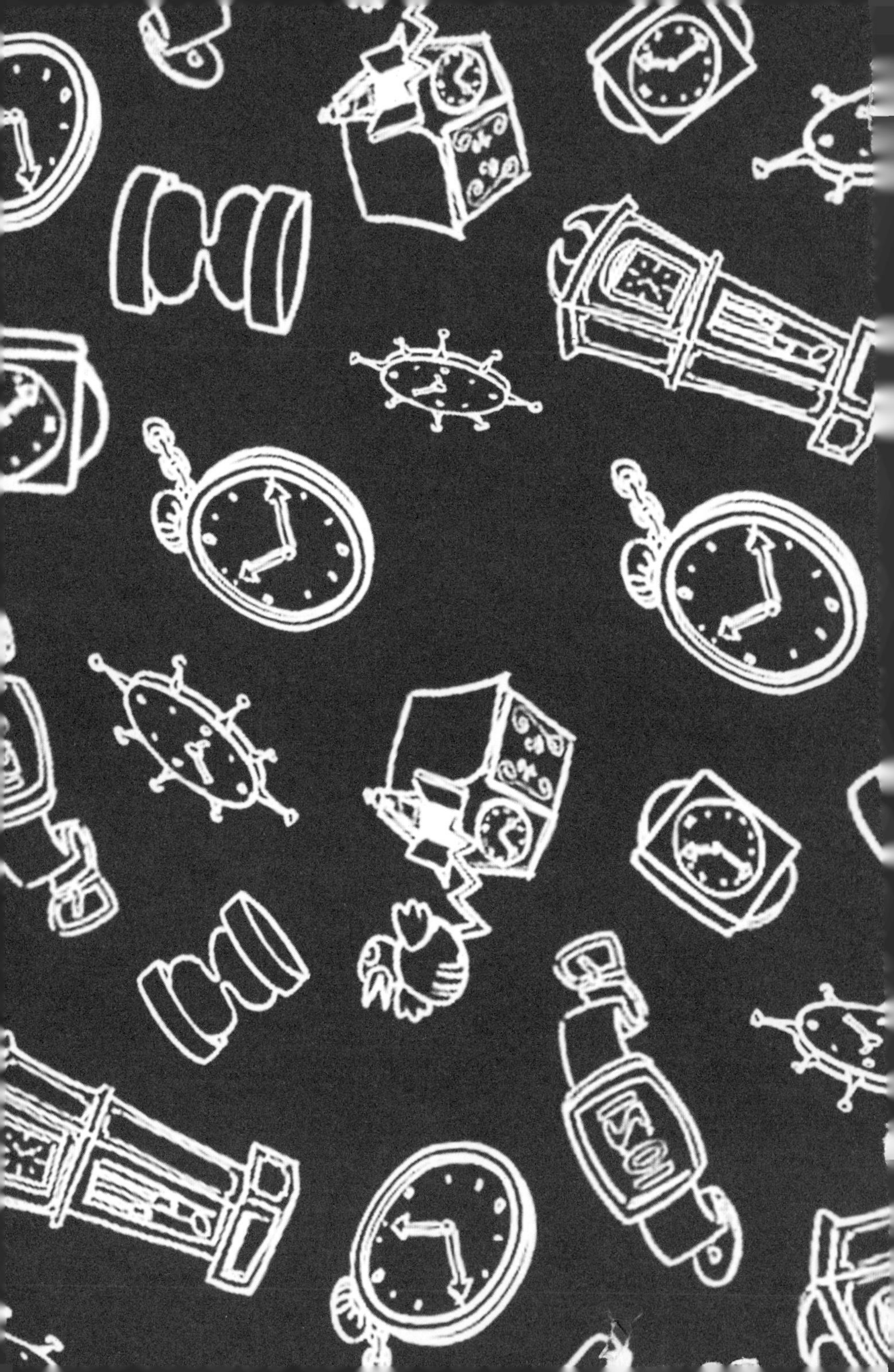